DANIEL WILLIAMS HARMON

A Journal of Voyages and Travels

in the interior of

North America

between the 47th and 58th degree of
North latitude, extending from Montreal
nearly to the Pacific Ocean, a distance of
about 5000 miles, including an account
of the Principal occurences during a residence of nearly nineteen years in different
parts of that country

To which are added

A Concise Description of the face of the Country,
Its Inhabitants, their manners,
customs, laws, etc.

BY

Daniel W. Harmon
a Partner in the Northwest Company

ILLUSTRATED

MCMXXII
ALLERTON BOOK CO.
New York

INTRODUCTION

LIFE on the plains was hard; yet it was a life with a lure, a life on which only old age or declining health made men turn their backs. To the lover of exploration, like Mackenzie, a limitless field was open; others, such as the two Alexander Henrys, uncle and nephew, turned to study the manners and customs of the Indians. The "Voyages and Travels" of Daniel Williams Harmon have a double interest; an unwearied traveller, he was also a shrewd observer and student of language.

Harmon was a Vermont lad, who entered the service of the Northwest Company in 1800, and was sent west. For the next nineteen years he did not come east of Fort William; not till May, 1819, did he turn his back on the west, and return to his native State, where in the next year his journals were edited and published by the Rev. Daniel Haskel.

Harmon had been brought up in a New England home, and the drunkenness and vice of the wild life were at first repugnant to him. Frequent loneliness increased a natural tendency to introspection, and in 1813 a severe inward struggle ended in his conversion (p. 195). The reverend editor, who frankly states in his preface that he rewrote the whole work, and that its style "is not properly my own, nor that of Mr. Harmon, but something between both," has often been accused of having amplified, and even inserted, the frequent moralisings, which contrast oddly with other passages of the work, such as that in which Harmon records his reasons for taking an Indian concubine (p. 118). But the lessons learned at the knee of a New England mother are slow to be uprooted, and though the words are obviously those of the editor, I see no reason to doubt that the sentiments are those of the traveller.

At this time the competition of the N. W. Co., the X. Y. Co., and the H. B. Co. drove their agents to all lengths to get furs, and drunkenness among the Indians was at its worst. Here are two extracts from the diary of Alexander Henry the younger, a contemporary of Harmon.

"Sunday, Jan. 1, 1801, I gave my men some high wine, flour and sugar; the Indians purchased liquor, and by sunrise every soul of them was raving drunk—even the children.

"April 30, 1804. Indians having asked for liquor, and having promised to decamp and hunt well all summer, I gave them some. Grande Gueule stabbed Capot Rouge, Le-

Boeuf stabbed his young wife in the arm. Little Shell almost beat his mother's brains out with a club, and there was terrible fighting among them. I sowed garden seeds."

Yet if the red man became a fiend under the influence of drink, when sober he was a kindly host, and an unwearied guide and trapper. The half-breeds, too, though they drove Harmon to say that he would rather have fifty drunken Indians about than five Canadians (p. 73), were nevertheless such hardy *voyageurs* that the American J. J. Astor said of them that one Canadian was worth three Americans for river service. Moreover, after the N. W. Co. became in 1821 merged in the H. B. C. a stricter control was exercised.

Concubinage between white and red was universal, and was looked on by the Indian maidens as rather an honour; so that Mr. Haskel tells us that when the men returned to civilisation "these women and children . . . have become so numerous as to be a burden to the concern; and a rule has been established that no person in the service of the Company shall hereafter take a woman from among the natives to reside with him, as a sufficient number of a mixed blood can be found who are already connected with the Company."

Yet this evil can be exaggerated. The

white man was usually faithful to his squaw, and on his departure either made suitable provision for her and for her children, or even brought her back with him to civilisation. This was the case with Harmon, who married his Cree bride in due form, and begat fourteen children, some of the descendants of whom are living in Canada to-day.

W. L. GRANT.

PREFACE,

BY THE EDITOR.

HAVING prepared the following work for the press, I have a few things to say respecting it, and the part in regard to it, which I have performed.

The authour of these Voyages and Travels, had no thought, while in the N. W. Country, of making publick his Journal. It was commenced and continued, partly for his own amusement, and partly to gratify his friends, who, he thought, would be pleased to be informed, with some particularity, on his return, how his time had been employed, during his absence. When he returned to civilized society, he found that curiosity was awake, in regard to the state of the country which he had visited; and the repeated questions, relating to this subject, which he was called upon to answer, together with the suggestions of some persons, in whose judgment he placed much confidence, that such a publication might be useful, first determined him to commit the following work to the press.

Had he carried into the wilderness a greater
stock of general information, and expected,
on his return, to appear in this manner before
the publick, his inquiries would undoubtedly
have been more extensive, and the result of
them would be more satisfactory, to men of
science. Had literary men been in the habit
of traversing the regions which he has visited,
he would have left it to them, to give an
account of them to the publick. Having remained nineteen years in the interiour of
North America, without visiting, during that
time, the civilized part of the world, and
having, many times, changed the place of his
residence, while there, he has had an opportunity for taking a wide survey of the country, and of its inhabitants; and if the information which he has collected, be not equal
to his opportunities, it is such as no other
existing publication will fully afford.

McKenzie's Voyages give some account of
a considerable part of the country which is
here described. His residence in it, however,
was much shorter than that of the authour
of this work, and his personal acquaintance
with the different parts of it, was much more
limited. It is not intended, by this remark
to detract from the reputation, which that
respectable traveller and his work, have de-
servedly gained. By his toilsome and dangerous voyage to the North Sea, and by
leading the way, through the Rocky Mountains, to the Pacific Ocean, he has richly

merited the commendation which he has received. By comparing the following work with that of McKenzie, it will appear, that, though the geographical details are less minute, the country surveyed, if we except the voyage to the North Sea, which is wholly out of the sphere of this publication, is considerably more extensive; and the information, in regard to the inhabitants, is much more particular. Considerable additions are here made, to the existing stock of geographical information, particularly as it respects the country beyond the Rocky Mountains. The basis of the map, here given to the publick, is that of Sir Alexander McKenzie, drawn by Arrowsmith. That map has received many corrections, and to it many important additions have been made, by the authour of this work; so that it is presumed now to be the most correct map of the interiour of North America, which has ever been published.

Literary men have recently taken much interest in comparing the different Indian languages, spoken on this continent, with each other, and with other languages, particularly with those anciently spoken on the other continent. A very considerable vocabulary of the one which is spoken, with a little variation of dialect, through the long tract of country, from a little back of Montreal to the Rocky Mountains, and one less extensive of the principal language spoken

beyond it, are here given. Sir Alexander
McKenzie has given a vocabulary of the first,
which will be found, on comparison, to be
somewhat different from that, which is contained in this work. Two reasons may be
assigned for this. In the country about the
Athabasca Lake, where McKenzie principally
resided, the Cree or Knisteneux language is,
in some measure, a mixed dialect; and it is
far less pure, than that which is spoken by
the inhabitants of the plains. The words,
also, are spelled by McKenzie, much according to the French sound of the letters, which
is frequently calculated to mislead an English
reader. Thus, the name of God, or the Good
Spirit, which McKenzie spells Ki-jai-Manitou,
is here spelled Kitch-e-mon-e-too. The above
remark will account, in a great measure, for
this difference; and for that which will be
found, in the spelling of many other words.
This is the native language of the wife of
Mr. Harmon, (for so I may now call her,
as they have been regularly married) and
great pains have been taken to make this
vocabulary correct, by marking the nice
distinctions in the sound of the words, as
derived from her repeated pronunciation of
them. With this language he is, also, well
acquainted, since it has been daily spoken
in his family, and by himself, for many
years.

The education of the authour of this work
was not classical; and had it been more ex-

tensive than it was, a residence for more than half of his life, since he has arrived to years of understanding, in a country where the English language is rarely spoken, would have poorly qualified him to give to this publication, a suitable English dress.

The editor undertook the business of preparing this work for the press, with some reluctance, arising from the shortness of the time that could be allowed him for the performance of it, and the numerous avocations of the gospel ministry, which would leave but a part of that time at his own command. For undertaking it at all, in such circumstances, his only apology is, that, in the opinion of the authour, there was no other person, conveniently situated for personal intercourse with him, who would be willing to undertake it, whose circumstances would be more favourable. It is by the particular request of the authour, and not because I suppose that I have performed the office of an editor, in a manner creditable to myself, that I have consented to connect my name with this publication.

The following work was furnished to my hand, fully written out; and though I have written it wholly over, I should have been much better able to satisfy myself, with respect to its style, if I could as fully have possessed the materials, in the form of notes and sketches, or by verbal recitals. Every man's own mind is the mould of his language; and he who has attempted to vary that of another, if he be at all accustomed to writing, must have found the task more difficult than original composition. The style of this work is not properly my own, nor that of Mr. Harmon, but something between both.

There is one subject, on which I wish especially to address a few remarks, through the medium of this preface, to the christian publick, and to all who feel any regard for the welfare of the Indian tribes, whose condition is unfolded in this work. As Mr. Harmon has returned to the interiour of North America, and, therefore, the observations which follow, will not be submitted to his inspection, before they are made publick, the editor alone must be made accountable for them.

In surveying the widely extended trade of the North West Company, we perceive evidence of an energy and perseverance, highly creditable to the members of it, as men of business. They have explored the western wilds, and planted their establishments over a tract of country, some thousands of miles in extent. They have made the savages of the wilderness tributary to the comforts of civilized society; and in many instances, they have exhibited a surprising fortitude, in exposing themselves to hardship and to danger.

The souls of the Indians are of more value than their furs; and to raise this people in

the scale of intellectual existence, to surround them with the comforts of civilization,
to rescue them from the gloom of superstition, to mould their hearts to christian
kindness, and to cheer their dying hour with
a well founded hope of immortal glory and
blessedness, constitutes an aggregate of good
sufficient to call forth exertion for their relief.
The time is rapidly coming, when christian
benevolence will emulate the activity and perseverance, which have long been displayed in
commercial enterprizes; when no country will
remain unexplored by the heralds of the
cross, where immortal souls are shrouded
in the darkness of heathenism, and are perishing for lack of vision. The wandering and
benighted sons of our own forests, shall not
be overlooked. They are not a race abandoned by God, to inevitable destruction;
though the idea has, strangely, gotten possession of some minds. In proportion to
the efforts which have been made, perhaps
no missions to the heathen have been
crowned with greater success, than those to
the American Aborigines. To this fact, the
fruit of the labours of Elliott, of the May-
hews, of Brainerd, of the Moravians, and,
especially of the recent establishment among
the Cherokees, will bear abundant witness.

The Indian tribes, whose condition is unfolded in this work, have claims upon christian compassion; and some facts, which the
authour has disclosed to me, have led me to

suppose, that a missionary establishment might be made, with reference to their instruction, with a fair prospect of success, and with less expense, than ordinarily attends such operations.

In the numerous establishments of the North West Company, there are from twelve to fifteen hundred women and children, who are wholly, or in part, of Indian extraction. Women have, from time to time, been taken from among the Natives, to reside in the forts, by the men in the service of the Company; and families have been reared, which have generally been left in the country, when these men have retired to the civilized parts of the world. These women and children, with a humanity which deserves commendation, are not turned over to the savages; but they are fed, if not clothed, by the Company. They have become so numerous, as to be a burden to the concern; and a rule has been established, that no person, in the service of the Company, shall hereafter take a woman from among the Natives to reside with him, as a sufficient number, of a mixed blood, can be found, who are already connected with the Company. There are, also, in the N. W. country, many superannuated Canadians, who have spent the flower of their days in the service of the Company, who have families that they are unwilling to leave; and having nothing to attract them to the civilized world, they continue under the protection of the Company, and are supplied by them, with the necessaries of life.

A plan has been in contemplation, to provide for the future maintenance of these people, and for the relief of the Company from an increasing burden, which is, to establish a settlement on the Rainy Lake River, where the soil is excellent, to which the people, above mentioned, may resort. To enable them to make a beginning, in the cultivation of the land, and in the erection of mills, &c., the Company propose to give them fifteen or twenty thousand dollars, and to appoint one of the Partners to superintend the affairs of the settlement, for three years, or for a longer time, if it shall be necessary.

It appears highly probable, that a settlement might thus be formed, which, in a few years, would secure to those who should belong to it, the comforts of life, as the fruit of their own industry; and should they prosper, so far as to raise a supply beyond their own necessities, it might, with mutual advantage, be disposed of to the Company.

The Partners and Clerks of the North West Company, who are in the Indian country, as well as some of those who reside in Canada, and elsewhere, have subscribed several thousand dollars, toward the establishment of a school, either at the Rainy Lake, or at Fort William, for the instruction of the children, connected with their establishments.

Some of these children are the offspring of
parents, who survey their comparative deg-
radation, with the deep interest of a strong
natural affection, who are able to bear the
expense of their education, and who would
cheerfully contribute, in this way, to raise
them to increased respectability, comfort and
usefulness. Should this school be established,
such persons would be required to support
their children, who should belong to it; while
the children of the poor, would be taught
gratuitously.

These facts have opened to my mind a
prospect, to which I wish to direct the eye
of christian benevolence. I would ask, with
deep interest, some one of the institutions,
whose object is the diffusion of civilization
and christianity among the Indian tribes,
whether a missionary establishment might
not be formed, in concert with the North
West Company, which would, with much
less trouble and even expense to them, accomplish the object which the Company
have in view, than any establishment which
they could independently make; and which
would, at the same time, have a most aus-
picious bearing upon the religious interests
of the tribes of the N. W. Country.

A school for the instruction of children in
the arts of life, and in the rudiments of
science, as well as in the principles of the
christian religion, forms the basis of the most
efficient missionary exertions among the In-

dians. The school among the Cherokees, is a most interesting object to christian benevolence; and as the fruit of it, the light of science, and the still brighter light of the Sun of Righteousness, is shedding a cheering radiance over many minds, that would otherwise have been shrouded in intellectual and moral darkness. The school has received the unqualified approbation of men of all descriptions who have visited it, among whom are many persons of the most distinguished character and rank in civil life. If such a school were established, at a convenient place in the N. W. Country, it would be as the Day Spring from on High to a region, now overspread by an intellectual and moral midnight.

Men, occupied as the gentlemen of the North West Company are, in the overwhelming cares of a vast commercial concern, would find it difficult to bestow all that attention on a school for the instruction of the children and youth, now in their establishments, whom they might think it proper to educate, which would be necessary to secure its proper management. Could this care be entirely taken off their hands, by men of known and approved characters, acting under a responsibility to some respectable society; by men who would feel all the interests which christian benevolence can create in the welfare of the children and youth committed to their care, it does ap-

pear to me, that they would gladly co-oper-
ate with them.

As the North West Company from motives
of interest, as well as from more noble con-
siderations, would contribute something to
the support of such an establishment, should
it meet their approbation, the expense of it
would, of course, be less to the society that
should embark in the undertaking, than is
commonly incurred, in establishments of this
sort.

The children and youth above mentioned,
might be instructed in the arts of civilized
life, in science and in christianity, with much
greater ease than the children of the Natives,
even if they could as easily be obtained;
and when instructed, they would be equally
promising, as the instruments of spreading
civilization and the religion of the gospel,
among the Indian tribes. They have always
been habituated to a life, in a great measure
settled; and they would, therefore, endure
confinement, better than children who have
lived among the wandering savages. They
are partially civilized, by an intercourse with
those, who have carried into the wilderness
many of the feelings and habits of civilized
society. They would not be liable to be
withdrawn, at an improper time, from the
place of their education, by the whims and
caprice of unstable parents. At the same
time, being familiarly acquainted with the
manners and customs and feelings of the

savages, by a frequent intercourse with them, being able to speak their languages, and having some of the Indian blood circulating in their veins, they would, when properly instructed, be as well qualified to gain access to the Natives, and to have influence over them, as if they had originally been taken, directly from their families.

As this establishment could probably be made, with the greatest convenience, within the British dominions, it might, perhaps, be undertaken with the surest prospect of success, by some society in Great Britain. The Society in Scotland for Propagating Christian Knowledge has, heretofore, contributed to the support of missionaries among the American Indians; and might, perhaps, be willing to engage in this undertaking. The Society in Massachusetts for Propagating the Gospel among the Indians of North America has, in some instances, if I mistake not, acted in concert with the Society in Scotland, above mentioned; and might, perhaps, conveniently do it in this instance. Every association, however, who may become acquainted with the facts here disclosed, will be able themselves, to judge most correctly, of their own resources, and of their own duty.—At Fort William, on Lake Superior, a very considerable number of the partners of the North West Company assemble annually, about the middle of June, at which meeting, many important arrangements are made, respecting the

business of the Company. At such a meeting
an agent from some benevolent association,
might ascertain their feelings, in regard to
such an establishment as I have proposed.

The Aborigines of America, are capable of
being exalted in the scale of existence, and
of arriving, even at eminence, in the arts and
sciences. The native oratory of some of
them, is proverbial in civilized countries,
and has caused them to be enrolled among
the sons of genius. Many of them afford
proof, that they possess acute and comprehensive minds; and as a people, their mental
capacity is certainly respectable. Nor, perhaps, can a people be found on the earth
who are not raised above them by superior
cultivation and means of improvement, who
possess greater elevation of feeling, and who
appear more majestick in ruins. Their virtues and their vices too, are not those of
ignoble minds. Let their condition be improved by the arts of civilized life, their
minds be enlightened by science, and their
hearts be softened by the genial influence of
Christianity, and they will assume a respectable rank among the nations. Could we hear
some of their superior geniuses unfold to
their countrymen the wonderful scheme of
redeeming mercy, with the brilliancy and
pathos, which have characterised some of
their speeches, on the interests of their tribes,
—with a brilliancy, rendered more splendid
by cultivation, and a pathos, made doubly

tender by the softening influence of the gospel, who would not listen to them with admiration and with pleasure? Might we not hope that, by the blessing of God, they would be made the honoured and happy instruments, of turning many of their countrymen, from the errour of their ways to the wisdom of the just. Could numbers of them be brought to concert plans for the extension of the gospel, in the North Western wilds, with the skill, and to execute them with the fortitude and perseverance, which they display in warring upon each other, the happiest results might be expected.

Whether the suggestions here made deserve consideration or not, I cheerfully submit to the wisdom and benevolence of those, for whom they were especially intended. Such has been my own view of the importance of the subject here presented, that I should have charged myself with a culpable neglect, if I had failed to improve this opportunity, to hold it up to the attention of the christian publick.

DANIEL HASKEL.

Burlington, Vt., August 2, 1820.

CONTENTS

CONTENTS

JOURNAL.

Tuesday, 29. LA CHINE. Yesterday, I left
Montreal, for this place, in company with
several other Clerks; and am on my way to
the interiour, or Indian countries, there to
remain, if my life should be spared, for seven
years, at least. For this space of time I am
under an engagement to serve as a clerk to
the North West Company, otherwise denominated McTavish, Frobisher & Co. The goods
intended for the interiour or upper countries,
are here put on board of canoes. These
canoes which are constructed of the bark of
the birch tree, will carry a burden of three
and an half or four tons each; and are severally manned by eight or nine Canadians,
who are said to manage them with greater
dexterity, than any other people.

Wednesday, 30. POINT CLAIRE. Rainy evening. For the first time in my life, I am to
pass the night in a tent. In the former part
of the day, I was employed in marking bales
of goods, which are to be sent to the Grand
Portage or General Rendezvous. About 12

o'clock, I embarked on board of one of the
canoes, destined for the above mentioned
place. The whole squadron, which consists
of thirty canoes, is divided into three brigades. One or two Guides or Pilots are at-
tached to each brigade. Their business is,
to point out the best course up and down
the streams and through the lakes, and to
take charge of the canoes and property on
board. They attend to the repairs of the
canoes, which are frequently broken, and
have the same command over the men, at-
tached to their respective brigades, as the
commander of a vessel has, over the men on
board. The Voyagers, as the men are called,
have many of the customs of sailors; and
among them the following. By all those on
board, who have never passed certain places,
they expect to be treated with something to
drink; and should a person refuse to comply
with their requisitions, he would be sure of
being plunged into the water, which they
profanely call, baptizing him. To avoid such
a disaster, I gave the people of my canoe a
few bottles of spirits and porter, by drinking
which, they became very merry, and exhibited the reverse of their appearance a few
days since, when, with heavy hearts and
weeping eyes, they parted from their relations. Shortly after we had pitched our
tents, an Irish gentleman, whose house was
near the margin of the water, politely invited me to take tea with him.

Friday, May 2. *Chute au Blondeau.* We have a strong head wind. But, since yesterday morning, we have come nearly sixty miles, and have passed two Rapids. At these places, most of the property was taken out of the canoes, and carried across the Portages, on the backs of the people. The young men, who have never been in the Indian countries, now began to regret that they had enlisted into this service, which requires them, as they say, to carry burdens like horses, when, by remaining in their own country, they might have laboured like men.

Sunday, 4. The wind has been so high, during the whole of the day, that we could not go upon the water. I have therefore passed the time in reading, and in the society of a fellow-clerk.

Monday, 5. We are now about one hundred and twenty miles from Montreal. This afternoon, our people killed a deer, with their setting poles, as he was crossing the river.

Tuesday, 6. *The Three Kettles.* In the former part of the day, we passed a beautiful water-fall, where the Riviere au Rideau, or Curtain River, falls into this, which is the Ottawa River. The former is ten or twelve rods wide, and the water falls perpendicularly, about forty feet, presenting at a little distance, an appearance at once pleasing and grand. We are now about one hundred and fifty miles from Montreal; the land on each side of the river is very level, and the soil appears to be good. William McGilvray, Esq. passed us this evening, in a light canoe, bound like ourselves, to the Grand Portage.

Thursday, 8. *Au Chat*. We now, for the first time, see Indian huts or tents.

Friday, 9. We arrived this morning, at this place, where the North West Company have a small establishment; and I have passed the afternoon, in shooting pigeons.

Saturday, 10. *Grand Calumet*. This Portage is nearly two miles long; and over it, the people carry both the canoes and their loading. Here stands a house, built by those who came here to traffick with the Indians; but which has been abandoned for several years, as the Indians, who formerly hunted in this vicinity, are now gone farther north, where Beaver, &c. are found in greater plenty. Behind this house, I found a small bark canoe, in which I embarked alone, for the purpose of shooting ducks. Having proceeded some distance from the shore, the canoe overset, and I fell, with my gun, into the water. Having my great coat on, it was with no small difficulty that I reached the shore; and I was happy to escape, with the loss of only my gun.

Sunday, 11. We are encamped on an Island opposite to Fort Coulonge. Soon after we arrived here, the person who has the establishment in charge, came to invite a fellow-clerk, who travels in the same canoe with me, and myself, to sup with him, to which I readily agreed; but my companion chose to remain with the canoes. I was treated with all the politeness of which a Canadian is master, which is not a little; for in this, as well as in many other respects, the Canadians resemble their ancestors, the French.

Monday, 12. We are encamped on a large sand bank. I have had a little conversation with my fellow-traveller, respecting his conduct the last evening, while I was absent. When I departed for the Fort, I gave him the keys of our travelling box and basket, that he might have the means of making a supper; and on my return, I was not a little surprised at finding not only him, but several of the common labourers, much intoxicated. I reprimanded Mr. P. with considerable severity, to-day, and told him, that if I should ever again find him in the like shameful condition, I should be under the disagreeable necessity of informing our employers of his conduct, as soon as we should reach Head-quarters. He promised that he would not again be guilty of such conduct; but I should place more reliance on his promise, had not his mother been a *squaw*. There seems to be in the blood of an Indian, a kind of predisposition to intemperance.— We barter with the natives, receiving sugar for biscuit, of which, as well as of pork, beef and spirits, they appear to be uncommonly fond.

Tuesday, 13. We are encamped on a rocky
bank, where it is impossible to find a smooth
place, sufficiently large to pitch a tent; we
are therefore obliged to make our bed between two large rocks, and sleep in the open
air. On the north side of the river are mountains, which appear almost destitute of timber, of any kind.

Wednesday, 14. We shall again sleep where
we did last night, as the people have been
employed, during the whole of the day, in repairing the canoes, which had become leaky.

Thursday, 15. *Roche Capitaine Portage.*
This Portage is so named from a large rock,
that rises to a considerable height above
the water, in the middle of the rapid. During the day, we have come up several difficult
ones, where many persons have been drowned,
either in coming up or going down. For
every such unfortunate person, whether his
corpse is found or not, a cross is erected by
his companions, agreeably to a custom of
the Roman Catholics; and at this place, I
see no less than fourteen. This is a melancholy sight. It leads me to reflect on the
folly and temerity of man, which cause him
to press on in the path, that has conducted
so many of his fellow creatures, prematurely
to the grave. Thus in hope of gaining a
little money, which can minister but imper-
fectly to our comfort, and that, during a
short season, we expose ourselves to death.

Friday, 16. Came up a rapid where, a

few years since, two canoes, in going down, were broken, and several men were drowned; therefore, we see more crosses erected.

Saturday, 17. Roderick McKenzie, Esq. agent for the North West Company, passed us, who, with those that accompany him, is on his way to the Grand Portage.

Sunday, 18. *The Lazy Portage.* This day we left the Ottawa River on our right hand, and came up a small river, that falls into it. About noon, we passed a cave, in the side of a high hill. This cave, I am told, is spacious; but we were in too great haste, to permit my examining it. This I was the more inclined to do, as I am told that the natives relate many remarkable stories respecting it; and among others, that a large animal remains in it, which they call a Man-eater, and which devours all those, who have the presumption to approach the entrance, of his solitary dwelling.

Monday, 19. *The Pines.* Came up several bad rapids; but have been so fortunate, thus far, as to meet with no disaster. The banks on each side of the river, for a considerable distance, are a perfect natural wall, formed of smooth stones; and are about one hundred feet high.

Tuesday, 20. *La Vase,* or *Miry-place.* During the whole of this day, we have been crossing ponds, and small lakes.

Wednesday, 21. After coming over a number of short portages, and crossing several ponds, and descending a small river, at the source of which is a height of land, we have at length arrived at a place, called the Meadows, which constitutes the north end of Lake Nipisangue, or, as it is commonly written, Nippising. Here we find several Indians, who appear to be in poor circumstances. We, however, obtain from them a little sugar, and a few wooden dishes and spoons, for which we give them provisions.

Thursday, 22. Sailed a part of the day, on the above mentioned lake; but, towards noon, the wind was so high, that we were obliged to encamp on a small island, which is almost destitute of wood.

Friday, 23. *The Lost Child.* This place took its name from the following circumstance. Several years since, the natives, being encamped here, lost a child, for whom they made diligent search, but in vain. They imagined, however, that they heard his lamentations in the bowels of the earth; whereupon they commenced digging, but to no purpose; the reason of which they conceived to be, that the Devil, or Bad Spirit, as he is called by the Indians, was continually carrying him from one place to another, in the earth. Many large holes have actually been dug in the earth, as our people have shown me.

In the morning we left Lake Nipisangue, and have ever since been descending the French River, which is a considerable stream.

In the latter part of the day, we passed a narrow place in the French River, to which, a number of years since, many of the most abandoned and savage Natives were accustomed to resort every spring, and where they built a kind of Fort, or stone wall, which is still to be seen. Behind this, these villains secreted themselves; and, when the voyagers were passing by, discharged volleys of shot into their canoes, and of course, as the distance was small, killed many of them. They would then rush from their hiding place, and fall upon and butcher the remainder, and go off with the plunder, which they had thus seized, into a distant part of the country. But the better sort of their countrymen, would not join them in such barbarous and unprovoked hostilities. At length the good Indians, who were well disposed towards the white people from Canada, pronounced these murderers a nuisance to society, and made war upon them, until the greater part of them were destroyed. The few that survived, retired into a distant part of the country, and nothing has since been heard, respecting them. The friendly Indians, for their exertions in extirpating their unworthy relations, were handsomely rewarded by the North West Company.

The Canadian Voyagers, when they leave one stream to go up or down another, have a custom of pulling off their hats, and making the sign of the cross, upon which one in

each canoe, or at least, in each brigade, repeats a short prayer. The same ceremonies
are observed by them, whenever they pass a
place, where any one has been interred, and
a cross has been erected. Those, therefore,
who are in the habit of voyaging this way,
are obliged to say their prayers more frequently perhaps, than when at home; for
at almost every rapid which we have passed,
since we left Montreal, we have seen a number of crosses erected; and at one, I counted
no less than thirty! It is truly melancholy,
and discouraging, seriously to reflect on the
great number of my fellow creatures, who
have been brought to an untimely end, by
voyaging this way, as I know not but I shall
myself, also, be doomed to the same watery
grave. With such dismal spectacles, however,
almost continually before our eyes, we press
forward, with all the ardour and rashness
of youth, in the same dangerous path, stimu-
lated by the hopes of gratifying the eye, and
of securing a little gold.

Saturday, 24. *Lake Huron.* We find on
the shore of this lake, low Cranberries, in
great abundance.

Sunday, 25. The wind has been so high,
that it has prevented us from sailing, the
greater part of the day. We are encamped
on an island, of which there are many in this
lake. On one of them, it is reported, that
the Natives killed a snake, which measured
thirty-six feet in length. The length and

size of this astonishing serpent, they had engraved on a large smooth rock, which saw, as we passed by. But we have often seen other engravings, on the rocks, along the rivers and lakes, of many different kinds of animals, some of which, I am told, are not now to be found, in this part of the world, and probably never existed.

Wednesday, 28. *Island of St. Joseph.* To this place the British troops came and built a fortification, when the Americans took possession of Michilimackinack. There are stationed here one Captain, one Lieutenant, one Ensign, and thirty nine privates. The fort is built on a beautiful rise of ground, which is joined to the main island by a narrow neck of land. As it is not long since a settlement was made here, they have only four dwelling houses and two stores, on the other parts of the peninsula; and the inhabitants appear like exiles. The North West Company have a house and store here. In the latter, they construct canoes, for sending into the interiour, and down to Montreal. Vessels, of about sixty tons burden, come here from Detroit and Mackana and Soult St. Maries. The whole island is computed to be about twenty miles in circumference; the soil is good; it is distant, nearly nine hundred miles from Montreal, and forty-five from Mackana, and is in Lat. 47° North. Spirits are sold here for six dollars a gallon; and other things, in the same proportion.

Thursday, 29. Duncan McGilvray, Esq. one of the agents for the North West Company, arrived in the morning, at St. Josephs, from Mackana; and soon after, we embarked on board of our canoes, to come to this small Island. As the weather is calm, my fellow-traveller and I intend sleeping in our canoe; but the labourers will pass the night on shore.

Friday 30. *Soult St. Maries.* Here the North West Company have another establishment on the north side of the Rapid; and on the opposite shore, there are a few Americans, Scotch and Canadians, who carry on a small traffic with the Natives, and also till the ground a little. The soil about Lake Huron, which we have just passed, appears to be good, and the face of the country is low and level.—Here the North West Company have built locks, in order to take up loaded canoes, that they may not be under the necessity of carrying them by land, to the head of the Rapid; for the current is too strong to be stemmed by any craft. The Company are likewise building a saw mill, at the foot of the Rapid, to furnish boards, &c. for the Grand Portage, &c. Here is the outlet of Lake Superiour, by which its waters pass into Lake Huron. On each of these lakes, the North West Company have a vessel. One goes to the Grand Portage, and the other to Detroit, &c.

Saturday, 31. We shall sleep where we

did the last night. Several of us have visited the people, who live on the other side of the rapid, where we saw a dance of the Natives, who are Sauteux or Chippeways.

Sunday, June 1. *Point au Pin*, or *Pine Point*, in Lake Superiour. We here find the vessel that sails from this to the Grand Portage. I went on board, and the Captain informed me, that she would carry about ninety five tons, and that she makes four or five trips every season. I left the Soult St. Maries, in company with three hundred men, who are in thirty five canoes.

Monday, 2. *Point aux Arable*, or *Maple Point*. We now form four Brigades, in which there are six clerks.

Tuesday, 3. A high wind during the whole day. In the morning, we attempted to sail, but soon found we could not, without shipping a great deal of water; we therefore soon landed again, and are encamped, within one hundred rods of the place where we tarried the last night.

Wednesday, 4. As it has rained and snowed all day, accompanied by a high wind, we have not been able to leave our encampment of the last night. Mons. St. Germain, who has the charge of a small Fort, belonging to the North West Company, not far from this, visited us, and brought with him a few necessaries.

Thursday, 5. Although the swells in the Lake are very high, we have made good progress, during the whole day. We are encamped near a large rock, on which the Natives, as they pass this way, leave an arrow or two, or some other article of little value to appease the Devil, or Muchamunatoo, as they call him, and prevent him from doing them harm.

Sunday, 8. In the course of the day, we have passed several islands, which, as well as the main land, appear to be covered with little else besides moss, with here and there a shrubby spruce.

Monday, 9. In the morning we passed another Fort, belonging to the North West Company.

Tuesday, 10. We are obliged to anchor our canoes by a small island, instead of unloading them, as is customary every night, for the whole country is on fire; but whether by accident or design, I am unable to learn. Our people, who pass this way every summer, say that, almost every year, fire runs over this part of the country, which is, of course, nearly destitute of animals, of any kind.

Thursday, 12. *Sugar Point*. Our people say we have sailed ninety miles during the day.

Friday, 13. GRAND PORTAGE, where we arrived late this evening. This place lies in the 48th degree of north latitude; and is said to be nine hundred miles from the Soult St. Maries, and eighteen hundred from Montreal. The Fort, which is twenty four rods by thirty, is built on the margin of a bay, at the foot of a hill or mountain, of considerable height. Within the fort, there is a considerable number of dwelling houses, shops and stores, all of which appear to be slight buildings, and designed only for present convenience. The houses are surrounded by palisades, which are about eighteen inches in diameter, and are sunk nearly three feet in the ground, and rise about fifteen feet above it. The bay is so shallow that the vessel cannot approach the shore, unless she is almost without lading. There is a considerable island, directly opposite to the fort, which shelters the vessel from the winds that blow from the Lake; and which renders this a tolerably good harbour. There is also another fort, which stands about two hundred rods from this, belonging to the X. Y. Company, under which firm, a number of merchants of Montreal and Quebec, &c. now carry on a trade into this part of the country. It is only three years since they made an establishment here; and as yet, they have had but little success.

This is the Head Quarters or General Rendezvous, for all who trade in this part of the world; and therefore, every summer, the greater part of the Proprietors and Clerks, who have spent the winter in the Interiour come here with the furs which they have been able to collect, during the preceding sea-

son. This, as I am told, is about the time
when they generally arrive; and some of them
are already here. The people who come from
Montreal with the goods, go no farther than
this, excepting a few who take those articles
to the Rainy Lake, which are intended for
Athabasca, as that place lies at too great
a distance from this, to permit people who
reside there to come to this place and return,
before the winter commences. Those who
bring the goods from Montreal, on their
return, take down the furs, &c. from the
north.

Excellent fish, I am informed, are taken
here. White fish are sometimes speared, which
will weigh twenty-two pounds. The water
in the lake is uncommonly clear.

Sunday, 15. The people here pass the
Sabbath, much in the same manner as they
do, the other days of the week. The labouring people have been employed, during the
day, in making and pressing packs of furs,
to be sent to Canada. This appears, not
as it should be, to me, who have been taught
to abstain from labour on the sabbath,
and to consider that it should be employed
in a religious manner. The people, however, who have been long in this savage
country, have no scruples of conscience on
this subject.

Tuesday, 24. I have, for some days past,
been employed, together with several other
clerks, in marking packs of furs. Almost

every day, for some time past, people have been flocking in from the Interiour, with the returns of the season.

Saturday, 28. The last night, a squaw, in a state of intoxication, stabbed her husband, who soon after expired. This afternoon, I went to their tent, where I saw a number of Indians, of both sexes, drinking and crying over the corpse, to which they would frequently offer rum, and try to pour it down his throat, supposing him to be as fond of rum when dead, as he was when alive. The Natives of this place are Chippeways.

Friday, July 4. In the day time, the Natives were permitted to dance in the fort, and the Company made them a present of thirty six gallons of shrub. In the evening, the gentlemen of the place dressed, and we had a famous ball, in the dining room. For musick, we had the bag-pipe, the violin and the flute, which added much to the interest of the occasion. At the ball, there was a number of the ladies of this country; and I was surprised to find that they could conduct with so much propriety, and dance so well.

Sunday, 13. Yesterday, several gentlemen, on their way to their winter quarters, accompanied me to Charlotte, at the other end of this Portage, which is nine miles over. My business was to send off a number of canoes, bound for Fort des Prairies. The country between this and Fort Charlotte, is tolerably level; and the soil appears to be pretty good.

Tuesday, 15. This morning a number of gentlemen, as well as myself, left the Grand Portage, to proceed to winter quarters. I am to accompany John McDonald, Esq. to Fort des Prairies. We left Fort Charlotte, about 3 o'clock P. M. on board of two canoes, each of which will carry about two tons, and is pushed on by six Canadians. This is a small river; and we have passed several places, where the men were obliged to carry the ladings, a short distance, and in some places, to transport the canoes also.

Wednesday, 16. *The Long Cherry Portage*. In the former part of the day, we crossed small lakes and ponds, connected by several portages, and then came over the height of land. Since passing this, we have descended a small river, which, I am informed, after running through several lakes, at length discharges itself into Hudson's Bay, in latitude 51° north. At the mouth of this river, the Hudson Bay Company have a fort, which is called Albany Factory.

Friday, 18. *Great Pines*. We have this day crossed the Flinty Lake, so named from the stones, found on its shore. For some time past, I have had a fit of the ague and fever, every day. It commenced when I was crossing the large Lakes; and, I am told, that it is seldom that a person is attacked with it, in the region where I now am.

Monday, 21. For the last few days, we have been crossing small lakes and ponds, and coming down a small river. The country appears thinly timbered, lies rather low, and the soil is good.

Tuesday, 22. This evening, there came here three canoes, manned by Iroquois, who are going into the vicinity of the upper Red River, to hunt Beaver, for the North West Company. Some of them have their families with them.

Thursday, 24. *Rainy Lake Fort*. This is built about a mile and a half down the river, from the entrance of the Lake, where there is a considerable fall. Here the soil is better than any we have seen, since we left the Ottawa River. The timber, also, is of a very good size. The Lake and River are said to contain excellent fish, such as sturgeon, white-fish, &c. In the vicinity, a considerable quantity of wild rice is gathered, by the Natives, who are Chippeways. This is thought to be nearly as nourishing as the real rice, and almost as palatable. The kernel of the former, is rather longer than that of the latter, and is of a brownish colour.

Friday, 25. In the former part of the day, we overtook several gentlemen, who, like ourselves, are on their way to their winter quarters. This is a beautiful river, and pretty free from rapids.

Saturday, 26. This morning, we met twenty-four canoes from Athabasca. They say they suffered much for want of food, on their way; and during four days, ate nothing. We gave them a dram, which made them almost forget their late sufferings. They will arrive at the Rainy Lake, later than usual.

Monday, 28. We have come down several rapids, at one of which a canoe was broken, the last year, and a man drowned. We are still in the Rainy Lake River, which is about one hundred and twenty miles long, and twelve or fifteen rods broad. The land on each side is low, and is said to be excellent. The timber consists of birch, a species of pine, hemlock, poplar, aspin, cedar, &c.

Tuesday, 29. This day we came across the Woody Lake, which is full of islands. It is about thirty-six miles in length; and the soil about it is much like that, along the Rainy Lake River. We are now in Winipick River, and have passed a rapid where the last year, three men were drowned. One of our men fired at a black bear, but did not kill him.

Wednesday, 30. Passed a number of miry Portages, and a place where, three years since, the Natives, who are Chippeways, fired upon our people, but without killing any of them. One of the Indians was taken, with the intention of carrying him to the nearest Fort, and there punishing him as he deserved. After proceeding a considerable distance, however, and when near a rapid, he jumped

out of the canoe, intending, as was supposed, to swim to the opposite shore, and
thus escape. But the current was too strong;
and he went down the rapid, and was probably drowned.

Thursday, 31. *Mouth of the River Winipick.* Here the North West Company, and
the Hudson Bay Company, have each a
fort. Here the above named river discharges
its waters into Lake Winipick. The River
Winipick, through the greater part of its
course, is a succession of small lakes; and
in several places there are falls, of a considerable height. The country around it is
broken; and occasionally, majestick and
frightful waterfalls are to be seen, particularly where the White River joins this,
about thirty miles above where we now are.
A few miles above this, there is a small
lake, called Lac de Bonne, from which the
Hudson Bay people leave our rout, and proceed toward the Albany Factory. The soil
is good; and among the fruit, I observe the
red plum. The grape, also, grows well in
this vicinity. In the neighbouring woods, a
few moose and deer are found; and the Lake
and River are well supplied with fish.—Our
people are employed in drying the goods
some of which were wet, in coming down the
rapids, yesterday.

Saturday, August 2. When I left the Grand
Portage, it was expected that I should go
up the Sisiscatchwin river, to spend the win-

ter. That river falls into the north western
end of Lake Winipick. But, since our arrival
here, we have received intelligence from the
Swan River Department, which country lies
between Lake Winipick and the Red and
Assiniboin Rivers, that, in the opinion of Mr.
McLeod, who superintends the concerns of
that region, it is necessary to make another
establishment there. It is therefore determined that I shall go and take charge of it;
and I shall accordingly remain here a few
days, to wait for the arrival of the brigade,
destined to the Swan River department.—
The after part of the day, I spent in shooting pigeons, which I found to be numerous,
as at this season, red raspberries, and other
kinds of fruit, are ripe, and exist here in
abundance.

Sunday, 3. In walking in the adjacent
country, I saw the bushes and brambles
loaded with ripe fruit. While partaking of
it, I was led to reflect on the beneficence of
the great Authour of nature, who scatters
his favours with an unsparing hand, and
spreads a table here in the wilderness, for
the refreshment of his creatures.

This is the first day which I have ever
spent, since my infancy, without eating either
bread or biscuit. As a substitute for bread,
we now make use of what the Natives call
pimican, which consists of lean meat, dried
and pounded fine, and then mixed with melted
fat. This compound is put into bags, made

of the skins of the buffaloe, &c. and when cold, it becomes a solid body. If kept in a dry place, it will continue good for years. But, if exposed to moisture, it will soon become musty, and unfit for use. Pimican is a very palatable, nourishing and healthy food; and on it, our Voyagers subsist, while travelling in this country. Sometimes we add to the two above named ingredients, sugar or dried berries, which we procure from the Natives; and the taste of it is thus very much improved.

Monday, 4. I have visited the Hudson Bay people, whose fort is but a few rods from ours. Mr. Miller, the gentleman who has charge of it, informed me, that they obtain their goods from Albany Factory; that, in going down with their barges, they are generally about forty days; but, that they are nearly twice that time in returning, in consequence of the current. The Factory lies to the north east from this.

Wednesday, 6. This morning Mr. McDonell, whom we passed a few days since, overtook, and informed us, that one of his canoes broke, in coming down the rapids, that one of the men was drowned, and most of the property on board was lost.

Friday, 8. This evening, Mons. Mayotte took a woman of this country for a wife, or rather concubine. All the ceremonies attending such an event, are the following. When a person is desirous of taking one of the

daughters of the Natives, as a companion,
he makes a present to the parents of the
damsel, of such articles as he supposes will
be most acceptable; and, among them, rum
is indispensable; for of that all the savages
are fond, to excess. Should the parents
accept the articles offered, the girl remains
at the fort with her suitor, and is clothed
in the Canadian fashion. The greater part
of these young women, as I am informed,
are better pleased to remain with the white
people, than with their own relations. Should
the couple, newly joined, not agree, they
are at liberty, at any time, to separate;
but no part of the property, given to the
parents of the girl, will be refunded.

Sunday, 10. *Lake Winipick.* In the former
part of the day, the people for whom I have
long been waiting, came up; and soon after,
I embarked with them, and came hither.
Although we are not in want of provisions,
yet our people have killed a dog to eat, the
flesh of which, they say, is delicious. The
dogs of this country, which resemble wolves,
differ considerably from the dogs, found in
the civilized part of the world.

Monday, 11. We embarked, early in the
morning; but soon, the wind blew so as to
oblige us to make the land, which we have
done, on a point that projects far into the
Lake. Soon after we reached the shore, a
number of the Indians of this quarter, who
are Chippeways and Muscagoes, came to pay

their respects to us, to whom we gave some rum, tobacco, &c.

Sunday, 17. *Entrance of the River Dauphine.* Lake Winipick, which we now leave to go up this river, is about two hundred and fifty miles in length, and from three to sixty or seventy, in breadth. The country about this lake, for a considerable distance, is low, and is overspread with pretty heavy timber, and the soil appears to be good. Dauphine river is so shallow, at present, that our people are under the necessity of leaving half their ladings, for which they will return, after having proceeded a certain distance with the remainder.

Tuesday, 19. Last night, the wind blew so high, that it drove the water of the Lake to such a distance up the beach, that we were under the necessity of removing our baggage farther into the woods, at three different times. This morning, our people came back for the remainder of the property; and we proceeded up the river, which is about ten rods wide. The country about it is level.

Wednesday, 20. *Lac St. Martin.* The river Dauphine passes through this lake. We here see a great number of swans, bustards, pelicans, &c. The country around is swampy; and I am informed, that Moose are numerous in the vicinity.

Friday, 22. This morning we left Lac St. Martin, and entered the Muddy Lake, where we again find fowls, in great abundance.

Saturday, 23. *North End of the Plain Portage.* This portage is about two miles over, through a beautiful country, and the soil is excellent.

Sunday, 24. *Little Lake Winipick.* Here we find a number of the Natives, who are Chippeways, waiting our arrival, to get rum to drink, and necessaries, to enable them to hunt the beaver.

Monday, 25. We remain still, where we were the last night; and have been employed, during the day, in making out a selection of goods for the establishment at the entrance of the river Dauphine, which falls into the west end of this Lake. At that place, a French missionary resided, before the British obtained possession of Canada. We remained there, but for a short time; and great success, therefore, could not have been expected. I am told, however, that there are some Indians, still living, who recollect prayers, which were taught them by the missionary.

Saturday, 30. *Encampment Island.* Here we arrived, in the fore part of the day; and we have been employed, ever since, in setting aside goods for the Red Deer River, which falls into this lake, at the north end. We are now nearly across the lake, which is about one hundred and twenty miles long, and from five, to thirty broad. There are no mountains, of any magnitude, in this part of the country. The land is generally low, and well covered with timber, which consists of a species of pine, birch, poplar, aspin, willow, &c.

Friday, September 1. In the morning, Mr. McGillis, with most of the people, left us to proceed to the Red Deer River, where they are to pass the ensuing winter. Mr. McLeod, with a number of people in one canoe, has gone to Lac Bourbon, which place lies nearly north west from this. We here take, in nets, the white fish, which are excellent.

Wednesday, 3. I have passed the day in reading the Bible, and in meditating on my present way of living; and, I must confess, that it too much resembles that of a savage.

Sunday, 7. Late the last evening, Mr. McLeod returned from Lac Bourbon; and, this morning they again embarked for Swan River, and left me here, with two men, and as many women, to wait for the arrival of a number of canoes, which are still behind, but which are expected in daily.

Wednesday, 10. Yesterday, a part of the people arrived, for whom I have been waiting, some of whom I sent to the Red Deer River, and others to Swan River.

Sunday, October 4. *North End of Little Lake Winipick.* From the 29th of August, until the morning of this day, I remained on Encampment Island, waiting for the ar-

rival of the people, who were left behind.
But, as they had almost constantly high
winds, which, I am told, are common in this
late part of the season, they did not make
their appearance, until the second instant.

During the long stay which I made at
that unpleasant Island, we had little or nothing to eat, excepting what we took from
the water with our nets. There were times
when we met with little success. When the
wind was high, we could not set our nets;
and consequently took nothing. One night
the wind was so high, that it took the only
canoe which we had, to the other side of
the Lake, a distance of five miles, at least.
We were thus deprived of the means of setting our nets. On the eighth day after this
disaster, Providence sent an Indian to the
place of our encampment, who lent us his
canoe to go in search of ours, which our people found, uninjured. While we had no canoe,
we were under the disagreeable necessity
of living upon the fish which we had left
on the beach, when we took them in plenty.
They had, by this time, become almost pu-
trid. Unsavoury, however, as they were, they
did not last so long as we could have wished;
for, when they were expended, we had nothing to eat, until a kind Providence sent a
black bear near our tents. One of my men
fired, and killed him, which was a blessing,
for which we endeavoured to be thankful.
We considered it sent by Heaven; and felt,

that we deserved not such a favour. But
the rain descends on the unjust as well as
the just.—Yesterday, it snowed, during most
of the day, which prevented us from decamping. But early this morning, without reluctance, we left the solitary Island, where
many a moment of ennui passed over me.
As I had no other book, I read during my
stay there the greater part of the Bible.
This afternoon, we met two men, in a small
canoe, from Swan River, loaded with provisions, for the people of the Red Deer River.
We did not suffer so good an opportunity,
for furnishing ourselves with a sufficiency
of food, to sustain us until we should meet
with another supply, to pass unimproved.
How delicious is food to a person who is
near famishing! But there are thousands,
who know not how to prize abundance, because they have never experienced the distresses of want.

Thursday, October 9. *Little Swan River.*
Yesterday, on account of high winds, we
could not leave our encampment; but early
this morning, we embarked on board of our
canoes, and at twelve, left Little Lake Winipick, and entered this river, which is eight
or ten rods wide, very shallow, and full of
rapids. I therefore debarked, and walked
along on the beach about four miles, in the
snow, mud and water. The people, also,
for want of a sufficiency of water, were
obliged to debark, and drag their canoes

up the shallow places. But we are now encamped around a large fire, with plenty of
food; I have given to each of the people
a dram, and we have all ceased to think
of the fatigue and trouble of the day. To
make a place to lie down, the people scrape
away the snow, and lay down a few branches
of the pine, such as this country in every
part produces; and on this we spread a
blanket or two, and cover ourselves with
another. A day of hard labour, and of great
fatigue, will enable a person to sleep soundly
on such a bed; and to obtain refreshment,
such as a sluggard will seek for in vain, on
a bed of down.

Friday, 10. *Swan River Fort.* In the
morning we crossed Swan Lake, which is
nearly eight miles long, and then entered
the Great Swan River. This river is about
eleven rods wide; there is a sufficiency of
water, and there is no rapid from its mouth
to the fort, a distance of twelve miles. The
country adjoining, is low, and in many places,
swampy, and the soil is rich. Mons. Perigné,
the superintendant of the fort, has a tolerable
kitchen garden. The Hudson Bay people
once came here; but it is several years since
they abandoned the place. As they have
nothing to expect from the Company, but
their salaries, they seem, so far as I can
learn, to make but little exertion to extend
their trade, and, thereby, to benefit their
employers.

Saturday, 11. The day has been employed in fitting out Mons. Perigné, who, with six labouring men, is to go and build a fort, about fifty miles up this river, where they will pass the winter. A few miles from this, there is a salt spring, by boiling down the water of which, tolerable salt is made. It is less strong than that brought from Canada; but, used in sufficient quantity, it will preserve meat very well.

Sunday, 12. The people destined to build a fort up the river, left us to day. I shall remain here until some persons arrive from Alexandria, which is situated nearly one hundred miles to the westward of this, among the Prairies. There I shall pass the winter. with Mr. McLeod, or go and build by the side of the Hudson Bay people, who are about three leagues distant from him.—Our men shoot a few horses and ducks.

Thursday, 16. We have taken a few fish out of this river, with nets. This evening, two men on horses arrived from Alexandria, by whom I received a letter from Mr. McLeod, requesting me to accompany them to that place.

Saturday, 18. *Second crossing place in the Swan River.* In the morning we left the fort. The country which we have passed through, is low; and the timber, consisting of poplar, aspin, birch, willow, pine and an inferiour kind of maple, is small. Of the sap of the maple, sugar is made; but its quality is not equal to that, produced from the real maple.

Monday, 20. *Bird Mountain*. Here Mons. Perigné and others are building a fort. Yesterday and to day, our way has been through prairies, interrupted occasionally, by small groves of wood. Cranes and Pheasants are to be seen in the prairies; and to-day I have also seen and fired at eight Elk, without having killed any of them. They are about the size of a cow, and of a light grey colour. The males, which have long branching horns, are animals of a noble and majestick appearance.

Wednesday, 22. *The Foot of a High Hill and near a Small Lake*. The waters of this lake have a sulphureous taste. In the morning, we left Swan River on our right, after having crossed it on a raft, made by tying several dry trees together. Since leaving that river the country appears more hilly, and almost destitute of timber of any kind. Cranes and pheasants are to be seen, every where.

Thursday, 23. *Alexandria*. We arrived here in the afternoon; and I am happy to find myself, at length, at the end of my journey, and where I hope to pass a few months, at least, in quietness. The fort is built on a small rise of ground, on the bank of the Assiniboine, or Upper Red River, that separates it from a beautiful prairie, about ten miles long, and from one to four broad, which is as level as the floor of a house. At a little distance behind the fort, are small groves of birch, poplar, aspin and pine. On the whole, the scenery around it, is delightful. The fort is sixteen rods in length, by twelve in breadth; the houses, stores, &c., are well built, are plaistered on the inside and outside, and are washed over with a white earth, which answers nearly as well as lime, for white washing. This earth is found, in certain places, in all parts of the country.— Here horses are to be bought of the Natives for a mere trifle. They are well built, strong, and tolerably fleet.

This place lies in Latitude 52° north, and in 103° west Longitude. Mr. McLeod is now gone to fort Dauphine, on horse back, which lies only four day's march from this, over land; yet it is nearly two months, since I passed there in a canoe.

Tuesday, 28. Mr. McLeod and company have just returned from fort Dauphine; and I am happy in meeting him, after so long a separation, and he appears to be pleased to see me, safely here. From the time that I was left at the Encampment Island until now, I have had no person with whom I could converse in English; and I am not yet able to converse in French, though I can read it tolerably well.

Sunday, *November* 9. On the 30th ultimo, I set off, in company with four Canadians, on horse back, for Swan River fort. The day we left this, it snowed and rained, which caused us to pass a very disagreeable night, as we had nothing but our wet blankets with which to cover ourselves. The people went down for goods; and as there is no person there who can read and write, I went to deliver out such articles as we are in immediate want of here.

Sunday, 16. The Indians who come to this establishment are Crees and Assiniboins. The principal part of the former, generally remain in the woody part of the country, and hunt the moose, elk, beaver, &c. and the latter remain in the large prairies, and hunt buffaloes, wolves, &c. Last Wednesday, twelve families of Crees and Assiniboins came from the large prairies, and let us have furs and provisions. Both the men and women have been drinking, ever since, and their noise is very disagreeable; for they talk, sing and cry, at the same time.— Our men play at cards on the sabbath, the same as on any other day. For such improper conduct, I once reproved them; but their reply was, there is no Sabbath in this country, and, they added, no God nor devil; and their behaviour but too plainly shows, that they spoke as they think. It is a lamentable fact, that those who have been for any considerable time in this savage country, lay aside a greater part of the regulations of civilized and christian people, and behave little better than the savages. It is true, we have it not at all times in our power, to observe the sabbath as we ought, as the Natives come to our establishment as often on that day, as any other; and when they do come, they must be attended to, and their wants must be supplied. We are, also, frequently under the necessity of travelling on the Sabbath. But it is likewise true, that, if we were rightly disposed, our minds might, on this day, be almost wholly occupied with divine things. I must, therefore, acknowledge, that we have no reasonable excuse for violating the Sabbath, as we all do.

Wednesday, 19. Last night, there fell about four inches of snow, which is the first that we have had, this season.—Yesterday, eight families of Crees came in. While drinking, one of the women, who had a sharp pointed knife about her, fell down, and drove it nearly two inches into her side; but the wound is not thought to be mortal. To see a house full of drunken Indians, consisting of men, women and children, is a most unpleasant sight; for, in that condition, they often wrangle, pull each other by the hair, and fight. At some times, ten or twelve, of both sexes, may be seen, fighting each other promiscuously, until at last, they all fall on the floor, one upon another, some spilling rum out of a small kettle or dish, which they hold in their hands, while others are throwing up what they have just drunk. To add to this uproar, a number of children, some on their mothers' shoulders, and others running about and taking hold of their clothes, are constantly bawling, the older ones, through fear that their parents may be stabbed, or that some other misfortune may befal them, in the fray. These shrieks of the children, form a very unpleasant chorus to the brutal noise kept up by their drunken parents, who are engaged in the squabble.

Sunday, November 30. This, being St. Andrew's day, which is a fête among the Scotch, and our *Bourgeois*, Mr. McLeod, belonging to that nation, the people of the fort, agreeably to the custom of the country, early in the morning, presented him with a cross, &c., and at the same time, a number of others, who were at his door, discharged a volley or two of muskets. Soon after, they were invited into the hall, where they received a reasonable *dram*, after which, Mr. McLeod made them a present of a sufficiency of spirits, to keep them merry during the remainder of the day, which they drank at their own house. In the evening, they were invited to dance in the hall; and during it, they received several flagons of spirits. They behaved with considerable propriety, until about eleven o'clock, when their heads had become heated, by the great quantity of spiritous liquor which they had drunk, during the course of the day and evening. Some of them became quarrelsome, as the Canadians generally are, when intoxicated, and to high words, blows soon succeeded; and finally, two battles were fought, which put an end to this *truly genteel*, North Western ball.

Tuesday, December 2. As yet, we have only a few inches of snow. Yesterday morning, accompanied by six men on horse-back, I went to the lodge or tent of one of our hunters. The people went for meat, and I, for the pleasure of riding, and seeing the country. We arrived at the place where the Indian was encamped, just as the sun was sinking below the horizon, and when the hunter was about to take a sweat, which is frequently done in the following manner. The women make a kind of hut, of bended willows, which is nearly circular, and if for one or two persons only, not more than fifteen feet in circumference, and three or four in height. Over these, they lay the skins of the buffaloe, &c. and in the centre of the hut, they place heated stones. The Indian then enters, perfectly naked, with a dish of water in his hand, a little of which, he occasionally throws on the hot stones, to create steam, which, in connexion with the heat, puts him into a profuse perspiration. In this situation he will remain, for about an hour; but a person unaccustomed to endure such heat, could not sustain it for half that time. They sweat themselves in this manner, they say, in order that their

limbs may become more supple, and they
more alert, in pursuing animals, which they
are desirous of killing. They, also, consider
sweating a powerful remedy, for the most
of diseases. As they come from sweating,
they frequently plunge into a river, or rub
themselves over with snow. The country
we passed through, is ʾarge prairies, with
here and there a grove of small trees. This
evening we returned to the fort; and the
horses of our people were loaded with the
flesh of the moose and elk. The buffaloes
are as yet a considerable distance farther,
out in the spacious prairies. Nothing but
severe cold weather will drive them into
the woody part of the country, to which
they will then come, in order to be less exposed to the wind and weather, than they
would be, to remain in the open plains.

Sunday, 21. There is now about a foot of
snow on the ground; and, on the 11th instant, I left this place, in company with
seven Canadians, for Swan River fort. Each
man had a sledge, drawn by two dogs,
loaded with one hundred and fifty pounds
weight of furs, besides provisions to serve
man and beast, to perform the trip. On our
return, the sledges were loaded with goods.
We reached our fort, this afternoon, where
I am happy to find Mr. Hugh McGillis, on
a visit from Red Deer River, and also, two
men with letters, from Fort des Prairies, or
Sisiscatchwin River. The former place, lies

about one hundred and fifty miles from this
and the latter, four or five hundred, in nearly
a north direction.

Wednesday, 24. Yesterday, I went to see
the fort of the Hudson Bay Company, which
is situated about nine miles down this river
and is in the charge of a Mr. Sutherland.
He has a woman of this country, for a wife,
who, I was pleased to find, could speak the
English language, tolerably well. I understand, also, that she can both read and
write it, which she learned to do at Hudson's
Bay, where the Company have a school.
She speaks, likewise, the Cree and Sauteux
languages. She appears to possess natural
good sense, and is far from being deficient,
in acquired knowledge.

Friday, January 2, 1801. The weather,
for several days past, has been severely cold.
Yesterday, being the commencement of a new
year, our people, according to a Canadian
custom, which is to get drunk if possible,
spent the day in drinking, and danced in
the evening; but there was neither scratching
nor fighting on this occasion.

Sunday, 4. In the morning, the greater
part of our people, consisting of men, women
and children, were sent away to pass the
remainder of the winter, about two days'
march from this, in the prairie. They will
subsist on the flesh of the buffaloe, which
they will themselves kill in abundance. During their stay there, they will reside in tents

or lodges, made of the skins of the buffaloe, moose or elk. These skins, after having been dressed, are sewed together; and one tent will contain from ten to twenty five of them. These tents are erected on poles, and assume the form of a sugar loaf. Ten or fifteen persons will reside in one of them; for while there, they are either sitting or lying down.

The Indians, who come to this establishment, are, as has been already observed, Crees and Assiniboins; or as some call them, Kinistinoes and Stone Indians. Both of them are numerous tribes; and as they often meet and intermarry, their manners and customs are similar; but there is no resemblance in their languages. Both tribes are well furnished with horses. The Assiniboins, however, are, by far, the best horsemen; they never go any distance on foot, and it is generally on horse back, that they kill their game.

They mount their horses, and run down and kill the buffaloe, and some other animals with bows and arrows, which they find every way as convenient for this purpose, as fire arms. But the Crees, when they can procure them, always make use of guns. Their clothing consists of leggins of cloth or dressed Antelope skins, a shirt or frock of the same materials, and a blanket or dressed Buffaloe skin, which they wrap round their bodies, and tie about their waists. To the above they will often add a cap or bonnet, of the wolf skin, and shoes for their feet.

Last evening, I wrote to two fellow travellers with me from Montreal; and the letters will be taken to them by the winter express, which leaves this, tomorrow, and is to pass by the way of Fort des Prairies, thence to the English River, and thence directly to Athabasca. And, I am informed, there is an express, which every year leaves Athabasca, in the month of December, and passes through the whole country called the North West, and in the latter part of March, reaches the Soult St. Maries. Thus the gentlemen who come up from Montreal, obtain from the interiour, intelligence respecting the transactions of the preceding summer and fall much earlier than they could otherwise do. This information, it is important that they receive, as soon as possible. This conveyance of intelligence, extending to the distance of nearly three thousand miles, is attended with but a trifling expense to the Company.

Thursday, 15. Beautiful weather. On the eleventh, I accompanied six of our people to the tent of one of our hunters; and the day following, they returned with their sledges loaded with meat; but I remained, to go along with the hunter, farther in the prairie. Accordingly, the next day, I proceeded with him, and saw, in different herds, at least a thousand buffaloes, grazing. They would

allow us to come within a few rods of them
before they would leave their places. At
this season, they are tame, and it is not
at all dangerous to go among them. But,
in the fore part of the summer, which is
their rutting season, it is quite the reverse.
Then, if they perceive a human being, the
males will pursue him, and if they can overtake, will trample him under their feet, or
pierce their horns through his body.

The male buffaloe, when fat, will weigh
from one thousand, to fifteen hundred pounds,
and the female, from eight hundred, to a
thousand. Their meat is excellent eating;
but is not generally considered so delicious,
as that of the moose.

Wednesday, February 11. On the 1st
inst. accompanied by eight of our people,
and one of the Natives as a guide, I set
off, with a small assortment of goods, to
go and trade with about fifty families of
Crees and Assiniboins. In going to their
camp or village, we were three days, and at
all times, in an open country. After we
had encamped the first night, there came on
a terrible storm of snow, accompanied by
a strong and cold north wind; and as we
were in an open plain, we had nothing to
shelter us from the violence of the weather.
In the morning, we were covered with snow,
a foot in depth. Our people, however, soon
harnessed the dogs; and we proceeded, hoping to warm ourselves, by running. This

we found it difficult to do, as the wind was strong, and directly in our faces. At the close of the day, after we had encamped, our guide killed a fat buffaloe, which supplied food, both to men and beasts. While eating it around a large fire, we almost forgot the suffering which we endured, by the cold of the preceding night and morning; and, if we were not *thankful* for the blessing bestowed upon us, we were, at least, *glad* to enjoy it. After having passed one or two cold days without eating, there is a relish in food to which the sons of indolence and of pleasure, are perfect strangers; and which they can purchase only, at the expense of toil and hardship.

When we had approached within about a mile of the camp of the Natives, ten or twelve of their Chiefs, or most respectable men among them, came on horseback, to meet, and conduct us to their dwellings. We arrived at them, through a crowd of people, who hailed us with a shout of joy. Immediately after our arrival, the principal Chief of the village sent his son, to invite me and my interpreter to his tent. As soon as we had entered it, and were seated, the respectable old Chief caused meat and berries, and the best of everything which he had, to be set before us. Before we had eaten much, we were sent for to another tent, where we received a similar treatment; and from this, we were invited to another; and so on, till

we had been to more than half a dozen.
At all these, we ate a little, and smoked our
pipes; for, my interpreter informed me, they
would be greatly affronted, and think that
we despised them, if we refused to taste of
every thing which was set before us. Hospitality to strangers, is among the Indian
virtues.—During several days that we remained with these people, we were treated
with more *real* politeness, than is commonly
shown to strangers, in the civilized part of
the world.

While I was at the camp of the Natives, I
was invited to attend and see them dance.
The dancers were about thirty in number,
and were all clothed with the skins of the
Antelope, dressed, which were nearly as white
as snow; and upon their heads they sprinkled
a white earth, which gave them a very genteel appearance. Their dance was conducted
in the following manner. A man, nearly
forty years of age, rose with his tomahawk
in his hand, and made, with a very distinct
voice, a long harangue. He recounted all
the noble exploits which he had achieved,
in the several war-parties with which he had
engaged his enemies; and he made mention
of two persons, in particular, whom he first
killed, and then took off their scalps; and
for each of these, he gave a blow with his
tomahawk against a post, which was set up,
expressly for that purpose, near the center
of the tent. And now the musick began,

which consisted of tambourines, and the
shaking of bells, accompanied by singing.
Soon after, the man who had made the
harangue, began the dance, with great majesty; then another arose, and joined him;
and shortly after, another; and so on, one
after another, until there were twelve or
fifteen up, who all danced around a small
fire, that was in the centre of the tent. While
dancing, they made many savage gestures
and shrieks, such as they are in the habit
of making, when they encounter their enemies. In this course, they continued, for
nearly an hour, when they took their seats,
and another party got up, and went through
with the same ceremonies. Their dancing
and singing, however, appeared, to be a
succession of the same things; and therefore after having remained with them two
or three hours, I returned to my lodgings;
and how long they continued their amusement, I cannot say.

In this excursion, we saw buffaloes in
abundance; and when on a small rise of
ground, I think I may with truth affirm,
that there were in view, gazing on the surrounding plains, at least five thousand of
them. Of these animals, we killed what we
wanted for our own subsistence, and the
support of our dogs; and this evening, we
returned to the fort, well pleased with our
jaunt, loaded with furs and provisions, and
without having received the least affront or

the smallest injury from the Natives, notwithstanding most of them became intoxicated with the spirits, with which we supplied them.

Tuesday, February 17. We have now about a foot and a half of snow on the ground.—Mr. Monteur, accompanied by two Canadians, arrived, with letters from our friends, in Fort des Prairies.—This morning, one of our people killed a buffaloe in the Prairie, opposite to the fort; and another came within ten rods of the fort gate, when the dogs pursued him, and he ran off.

Thursday, 19. This day, I am twenty three years of age, and how rapidly does this space of time appear to have passed away! It seems as if it were but yesterday, that I was a child. The truth is, the time that we are allowed to remain in this fleeting world is so short, even if we should be permitted to reach the utmost boundary of human life, that a person can scarcely have passed the threshold of existence, before he must set his house in order to die.

Friday, 20. During the last night, we sat up to deal out spirits to the Indians. One of them has his own daughter for a wife, and her mother at the same time! Incest, however, is a crime, of which the Indians of this quarter are not often guilty. When one of them does commit it, he is regarded by the rest of his tribe, as void of sense.

Saturday, March 14. The greater part of

the snow is now dissolved. On the sixth inst. accompanied by eighteen of our people, I left this, to go to Swan River fort. We had thirty sledges, some drawn by horses, and some by dogs, which were loaded with furs and provisions.

Saturday, April 4. Swan River Fort. Here I arrived this afternoon, and have come to pass the remainder of the spring. While at Alexandria, my time passed agreeably in company with A. N. McLeod, Esq. who is a sensible man, and an agreeable companion. He appeared desirous of instructing me in what was most necessary to be known, respecting the affairs of this country; and a taste for reading I owe, in a considerable degree, to the influence of his example. These, with many other favours, which he was pleased to show me, I shall ever hold in grateful remembrance.—But now I am comparatively alone, there being no person here, able to speak a word of English; and as I have not been much in the company of those who speak the French language, I do not as yet, understand it very well. Happily for me, I have a few books; and in perusing them, I shall pass most of my leisure moments.

Monday, 6. I have taken a ride on horseback, to a place where our people are making sugar. My path led me over a small prairie, and through a wood, where I saw a great variety of birds, that were straining their

tuneful throats, as if to welcome the return
of another spring; small animals, also, were
running about, or skipping from tree to
tree, and at the same time, were to be seen
swans, bustards, ducks, &c. swimming about
in the river and ponds. All these things
together, rendered my ramble beyond ex-
pression delightful.

Friday, 10. Fine pleasant weather. This
afternoon, I took a solitary, yet pleasing
walk, to the ruins of a fort, which was abandoned, a few years since, by the Hudson Bay
people, to whom it belonged, but who do not
now come into this part of the country.
While surveying these ruins, I could not
avoid reflecting on the short duration of
every thing in this fleeting and perishing
world. I then went to a spot, where a number of their people had been interred, far
from their native country, their friends and
relations! And while I was lamenting their
sad fate, my blood chilled at the thought,
that what had happened to them might,
very probably, befal me also. But my prayer
shall ever be, that a merciful God will, in
due time, restore me to my friends and relations, in good health, and with an un-
blemished character.

Sunday, 19. On Friday last, there fell
nearly a foot of snow, which, however, was
soon dissolved; and it caused the river to
overflow its banks to such a distance, that
our people who were making sugar, were

obliged to leave the woods and return to the fort.

Tuesday, 21. All the snow has left us; and we are again favoured with fine weather. The last night, the ice in this river broke up.

Monday, 27. It has snowed all day, and has fallen to the depth of six inches.—I now begin to feel the want of books, having brought but few with me, on account of the short time that I expect to remain here.

Saturday, May 2. It has rained all day, which is the first time that any has fallen, since the last autumn.—As I have but little business that requires my attention, I employ the greater part of my time in reading the Bible, and in studying the French language.

Sunday, 10. It has rained constantly, during three successive days, which has caused the water in the river, since yesterday, to rise more than four feet.—Yesterday, one of my men went out to shoot ducks, and lost his way, and was therefore under the necessity of passing the night in the woods, without any covering from the cold and the rain, which poured down in torrents. This morning, however, by chance, or rather directed by an all protecting Providence, he fell upon a small foot path, which brought him directly to the fort, where he was not a little pleased to arrive. Experience only can teach us how to value such a deliverance.

Wednesday, 13. The late rains have caused this river to overflow its banks to such an uncommon distance, that when I arose this morning, to my surprise, I found seven inches of water, on the first floor of the house, which is an event that the oldest person here does not remember before to have witnessed. We are obliged to leave the fort, and to pitch our tents on a small rise of ground, at no great distance off, where we shall remain until the deluge is abated.

Friday, 15. Sent five men with a canoe, two days march up this river, for Mr. McLeod and company, as the face of the country extensively lies under water.

Wednesday, 20. The water has left the fort; and with pleasure, we leave our tents, to occupy our former dwellings. This afternoon Mr. McLeod, and company, arrived, and are thus far on their way to the Grand Portage.

Tuesday, 26. Yesterday, our people finished making our furs into packs, of ninety pounds weight each. Two or three of these make a load for a man, to carry across the portages. This morning, all the hands, destined to this service, embarked on board of five canoes, for Head-quarters. To Mr. McLeod, I delivered a packet of letters, to be forwarded to my friends, who reside at Vergennes, in the state of Vermont, and tomorrow, I shall set out for Alexandria, where I expect to pass the ensuing summer, and to superintend the affairs of that place and of this, until the next autumn.

Monday, June 1. Accompanied by two men, I arrived at Alexandria, this afternoon; and I here found six families of Crees, encamped about the fort. I have with me one clerk, two interpreters and five labouring men, also six women and thirteen children, belonging to our people, and a number of women and children belonging to the Natives, whose husbands have gone to make war upon the Rapid Indians, or as they call themselves, Paw-is-tick I-e-ne-wuck. This is a small but brave tribe, who remain a considerable distance out in the large prairies, and toward the upper part of the Missouri river. We shall have nearly one hundred mouths to fill, for the greater part of the summer, out of our store; but to furnish the means, we have hired two of the Natives to hunt for us, during the season; and moose, elk, &c. are considerably numerous in this vicinity. We hope, therefore, that we shall not want for the means of subsistence. Buffaloes have now returned several days' march from this place, into the spacious prairies; but this is no serious loss to us, since, if they were near they would be but indifferent food, as at this season of the year, they are always lean, and consequently, rank and tough.

Wednesday, 10. It is currently reported and believed, that the Rapid Indians are

forming a war-party, in order to come
against the Indians of this quarter, whom
they consider, and I think with sufficient
reason, as their enemies. Should they come
this way, they will as probably fall upon us
as upon the Natives themselves; for they say
that we furnish the Crees and Assiniboins
with what fire arms they want, while they
get but few. I have, therefore, thought it
expedient to direct our people, to build
block-houses over the fort gates, and to put
the bastions in order, that we may be prepared to defend ourselves, in case of an
attack.

Sunday, 14. This afternoon, a number
of the Natives danced in the fort. Their
dance was conducted in the following manner. Two stakes were driven into the ground,
about twenty feet apart; and as one person beat the drum, the others, consisting of
men and women, danced round these stakes.
The men had a different step from that of
the women. The latter placed both feet together, and first moved their heels forward
and then their toes, and thus went twice
round the stakes. But the men rather hopped
than danced, and therefore went twice round
the stakes, while the women went once.
They all kept exact time with the music, for
they have excellent ears. Indeed, I believe
that all their senses are more acute than
those of the white people.

Thursday, July 9. This day, there came

here an American, that, when a small child,
was taken from his parents, who then resided in the Illinois country. He was kid-
napped by the Sauteux, with whom he has
resided ever since; and he speaks no other
language excepting theirs. He is now about
twenty years of age, and is regarded as a
chief among that tribe. He dislikes to hear
people speak to him, respecting his white
relations; and in every respect excepting his
colour, he resembles the savages, with whom
he resides. He is said to be an excellent
hunter. He remains with an old woman
who, soon after he was taken from his relations adopted him into her family; and
they appear to be mutually as fond of each
other, as if they were actually mother and
son.

Thursday, 30. Different kinds of berries
are now ripe, such as strawberries, raspberries, and what the Canadians call paires,
which the Natives denominate Mi-sas-qui-to-
min-uck. The last, if they are not the same
in kind, exactly resemble, in shape and taste,
what in the New England states are called
shad berries. When they are found in the
prairies, they grow on bushes, four or five
feet high; but in a thick wood they often
reach to the height of fifteen or twenty feet.
Of this wood, the Natives always make their
arrows. These berries, when properly dried
by the sun, have an agreeable taste, and are
excellent to mix with pimican. The Natives

generally boil them in the broth of fat meat;
and this constitutes one of their most dainty
dishes, and is introduced at all their feasts.

Mr. A. N. McLeod has a son here named
Alexander, who is nearly five years of age,
and whose Mother is of the tribe of the
Rapid Indians. In my leisure time, I am
teaching him the rudiments of the English
language. The boy speaks the Sauteux and
Cree fluently, for a child; and makes himself understood tolerably well, in the Assiniboin and French languages. In short, he is
like most of the children of this country,
blessed with a retentive memory, and learns
very readily.

We have made about ten tons of hay, to
feed those of our horses which we intend
shall work, during the winter season. The
others live the whole year, upon the grass
which they find in the prairies. In the winter, to procure it, they must scrape away,
with their feet, the snow, which is generally
eighteen inches deep, excepting on the highest
hills, from which the wind drives most of it
into the valleys.

Thursday, August 27. All the provision
which we now have in the fort, consists of
only about fifteen pounds of pimican; and
when we shall be able to add to our supply,
God only knows. All our dependence is on
our hunters; and it is now a considerable
time since they have killed anything, though
moose and elk are numerous in the vicinity.

Sunday, 30. Yesterday, three of our people arrived from the Grand Portage, with letters from Mr. McLeod, &c., which inform me, that the above mentioned people, together with others who remained at Swan River fort, were sent off from head quarters, earlier than usual, with an assortment of goods, supposing, that we might need some articles, before the main brigade arrives.

Sunday, September 6. This is the third day, during which it has rained, without the least cessation.—There are five families of Crees, encamped about the fort, who have been continually drunk, during the last forty eight hours; but now they begin to be troublesome, for they have nothing more to sell, yet they wish to continue drinking.

One of the Indians who was of the party that last spring went to war, has recently come in. When he arrived, his face was painted entirely black, which I am informed, is always their custom, when they return from such expeditions. As he drew nigh to the fort, he began to sing a war song. He states, that his party, the Crees and Assiniboins, have made great slaughter among their enemies, the Rapid Indians, and are bringing a number of their women and children home for slaves. He was sent forward, as he says, to inform us of what they consider glorious news.

Monday, 7. More of the Indians, who have been to war, have reached this place,

and have brought several slaves, and a few
scalps, with them. This afternoon, they
danced and sung their war songs. Agreeably
to the custom of the country, I gave them
a few trifling articles, not as a reward for
having been to war, but because they have
done us honour, as they think, by dancing in
our fort.

Sunday, 27. It has snowed and rained all
day. This afternoon, Mr. McLeod and company, returned from the Grand Portage, and
delivered to me letters from my friends in my
native land; and I am happy in being informed, that they left them blessed with
good health. Self-banished, as I am, in this
dreary country, and at such a distance from
all I hold dear in this world, nothing beside,
could give me half the satisfaction, which
this intelligence affords. I also received several letters from gentlemen in different parts
of the widely extended North West Country.

Friday, October 2. *Montague Aiseau*, or
the *Bird Mountain*. In the morning, I left
Alexandria, on horse back, and arrived here
this evening where, by permission of Providence, I shall pass the ensuing year. I have
with me three interpreters, six labouring men
and two women. The fort is built on the
bank of Swan River, a little more than fifty
miles distant from its entrance into Swan
Lake. The Indians who frequent this establishment are Sauteux, Crees and Mus-ca-
goes, all of whom speak nearly the same

language. Moose and elk are considerably numerous, in this vicinity; but buffaloes seldom come thus far, into the woody country.

Thursday, 29. On the 22nd instant, Mr. McLeod, with ten of his people, arrived on horseback; and on the day following, I accompanied them to the lower fort, where I met Mr. William Henry, a clerk. Mr. McLeod has also brought another clerk into this country, by the name of Frederick Goedike. This evening, Messrs. McLeod, Henry and myself returned, but left the people behind, whose horses are loaded with goods, for this place and Alexandria.

Tuesday, *November* 3. Snow has fallen to the depth of three inches, which is the first that we have had, this fall.

Thursday, 19. A foot and a half of snow has fallen.

Wednesday, *December* 23. Clear and cold. On the 16th inst. I went to Alexandria, where I passed several days agreeably, in the company of Messrs. McLeod, Henry, and Goedike. We have now more snow than we had at any time the last winter. In consequence of lameness, I returned on a sledge drawn by dogs.

Friday, 25. This being Christmas day, agreeably to the custom of the country, I gave our people a dram, and a pint of spirits each.

Monday, 28. Payet, one of my inter-

preters, has taken one of the daughters of
the Natives for a wife; and to her parents,
he gave in rum, dry goods, &c. to the value
of two hundred dollars. No ceremonies attend the formation of such connexions, as I
have before remarked, excepting that the
bridegroom, at the time to retire to rest,
shows his bride where their common lodging
place is; and they continue to cohabit, as
long as both parties choose, but no longer.
One thing is secured by this arrangement,
which is by no means always found in the
civilized world, and that is, while persons
live together, in a state of wedlock, they will
live in harmony.

Friday, January 1, 1802. This being
the first day of the year, in the morning, I
gave the people a *dram* or two, and a pint
of rum each, to drink in the course of the
day, which enabled them to pass it merrily,
although they had very little to eat; for our
hunters say they can kill nothing. One of
them will not go out of his tent; for he
imagines, that the Bad Spirit, as they call
the devil, is watching an opportunity to
find him in the open air, in order to devour
him. What will not imagination do!

Saturday, 9. Several days since, I sent a
number of my people to Alexandria for meat,
as neither of my hunters kill any thing;
though there is no scarcity of animals in
this vicinity. But they have just returned,
without any thing. They say that the buffa-

loes, in consequence of the late mild weather, have gone a considerable distance, into the large prairie. We are therefore under the necessity of subsisting on pounded meat, and dried chokecherries. This latter article, is little better than nothing. When we shall be in a better situation, God only knows. Hope, however, which seldom abandons the wretched, denies us not her comforting aid; and past experience teaches us, that it is possible our circumstances may suddenly change for a better.

Sunday, 17. Last evening, our people brought from the tent of the hunter, the meat of a moose, which lighted up a smile of joy upon our countenances. We were happy to find, that a kind Providence, instead of abandoning, had favoured us with one of the richest dainties, that this country affords. It would be well if our joy was true gratitude to our kind Benefactor.— There are twelve persons in the fort; and yet for the last fifteen days, we have subsisted on what was scarcely sufficient for two people! These were certainly the darkest days that I ever experienced, in this or any other country.

Tuesday, 19. I have taken a walk, accompanied by Payet, a short distance from the fort, where we found hazelnuts, still on the bushes, in such plenty, that a person may easily gather a bushel in the course of a day. I am told, that when sheltered from the wind,

all of them do not fall off, until the month
of May.

Monday, February 1. For several days
past, the weather has been excessively cold;
and this has been, I think, the coldest day
that I ever experienced. In fact, the weather
is so severe, that our hunters dare not venture out of their tents, although they, as
well as ourselves, have little to eat.

Sunday, 7. During the last three days, we
have subsisted on tallow and dried cherries.
This evening, my men returned from Alexandria, with their sledges loaded with buffaloe
meat; and the sight of it, was truly reviving.
Had this favour been withheld from us a
few days longer, we must have all miserably
perished by famine.

Monday, 8. All the Indians of this place,
excepting my hunters, have gone to pass
about a couple of months, as they are accustomed to do, at this season, on their beloved food, the buffaloe.

Friday, 19. At present, thanks to the
Giver of all good, we have a pretty good
stock of provisions in store, and there fore
expect not to want, this season.

Saturday, March 6. I have just returned
from a visit to my friends at Alexandria,
where I passed four days very pleasantly, in
conversing in my mother tongue. This is a
satisfaction that no one knows, excepting
those, who have been situated as I am,
with a people with whom I cannot speak

fluently. And if I could, it would afford me little satisfaction to converse with the ignorant Canadians around me. All their chat is about horses, dogs, canoes, women and strong men, who can fight a good battle. I have, therefore, only one way left to pass my time rationally, and that is reading. Happily for me I have a collection of good books; and mine will be the fault if I do not derive profit from them. I, also, begin to find pleasure in the study of French.

Saturday, 20. The greater number of our Indians have returned from the prairies; and as they have brought little with them to trade, I, of course, give them as little; for we are at too great a distance from the civilized world, to make many gratuities. Yet the Indians were of a different opinion; and at first made use of some unpleasant language. But we did not come to blows, and are now preparing to retire to rest, nearly as good friends as the Indians and traders generally are. With a few exceptions, that friendship is little more, than their fondness for our property, and our eagerness to obtain their furs.

Wednesday, April 21. The most of the snow is now dissolved; and this afternoon the ice in the river broke up.—All our Indians, who for several days past encamped near the fort, have now departed, to hunt the beaver. While they were here, they made a *feast*, at which they danced, cried, sung and howled, and in a word, made a terrible, savage noise. Such feasts, the Crees are accustomed to make, at the return of every spring; and sometimes also at other seasons of the year. By so doing, they say they appease the anger of the Evil Spirit or devil, and thus prevent him from doing them harm, to which they consider him as ever inclined. They have, also, certain places, where they deposit a part of their property, such as guns, kettles, bows, arrows, &c. as a sacrifice to the same Spirit. To the Supreme Being, however, the creator and governor of the universe, whom they call Kitch-e-mon-e-too, that is, Great Spirit, they address their prayers; yet they say there is no necessity of paying him any sacrifice, since he is a good Spirit, and is not disposed to do them injury; whereas the Evil Spirit is malicious, and therefore, it is proper that they should strive to appease his anger.—The above mentioned feast was made by the Chief of the band, whose name is Kâ-she-we-ske-wate, who for the long space of forty eight hours, previous to the entertainment, neither ate nor drank any thing. At the commencement of the feast, every person put on a grave countenance; and the Chief went through a number of ceremonies, with the utmost solemnity. After the entertainment was over, every Indian made a voluntary sacrifice of a part of his property to the devil, or as they call him, Much-e-mon-e-too.

Sunday, May 2. Accompanied by one of my interpreters, I have taken a ride to a place where I intend building a fort, the ensuing summer. The animals in this vicinity are moose, red deer, a species of the antelope, grey, black, brown, chocolate coloured and yellowish bears, two species of wolves, wolverines, polecats or skunks, lynxes, kitts, beavers, otters, fishers, martins, minks, badgers, muskrats and black, silver, cross and red foxes. Of fowls, we have swans, geese, bustards, cranes, cormorants, loons, snipes, several species of ducks, water-hens, pigeons, partridges, pheasants, &c. &c. Most of the above named fowls, are numerous in spring and autumn; but, excepting a few, they retire to the north in the summer, to brood. Toward the fall, they return again; and before winter sets in, they go to the southward, where they remain, during a few of the coldest months of the year.

Thursday, 6. This morning, I received a letter from Mr. McLeod, who is at Alexandria, informing me, that a few nights since, the Assiniboins, who are noted thieves, ran away with twenty two of his horses. Many of this tribe, who reside in the large prairies, are constantly going about to steal horses. Those which they find at one fort, they will take and sell to the people of another fort. Indeed, they steal horses, not unfrequently, from their own relations.

Wednesday, 12. It has snowed and rained,

during the day.—On the 7th inst. I went to
Alexandria, to transact business with Mr.
McLeod. During this jaunt, it rained almost
constantly; and on my return, in crossing
this river, I drowned my horse, which cost
last fall, one hundred dollars in goods, as
we value them here.

Monday, 17. This afternoon, Mr. McLeod
and company passed this place, and are on
their way to the Grand Portage. But I am
to pass, if Providence permit, another summer in the interiour, and to have the superintendence of the lower fort, this place
and Alexandria, residing chiefly at the latter
place.

Tuesday, 18. All the Indians belonging
to this place, have now come in with the
produce of their hunts, which is abundant;
and to reward them for their industry, I
clothed two of their Chiefs, and gave a certain quantity of spirits to them, and to the
others. With this they became intoxicated,
and continued so during the last night, which
prevented our closing our eyes in sleep; for
it is at all times necessary to watch the
motions of the Indians, and especially is this
the case, when reason has been dethroned,
and passion has assumed the sole dominion
over them, through the influence of ardent
spirits. While in that condition, they, like
other people, often do things which they
will regret in their sober moments.

Sunday, 23. It has snowed all day; and

about six inches have fallen. I am waiting the arrival of Mr. Henry to take charge of this post, when I shall proceed to Alexandria. Two women brought me a few hazelnuts, which they this day gathered from the bushes.

Monday, 31. *Alexandria.* Here, accompanied by two of my people, I arrived this afternoon. In crossing Swan River, I was so unfortunate as to drown another horse; and I was therefore obliged to perform the remainder of the journey on foot, with nothing to eat. Here, thanks to the Bestower of all good, I find a tolerable stock of provisions. Mr. Goedike is to pass the summer with me, also two interpreters, and three labouring men, besides several women and children, who together, form a *snug* family.

Wednesday, June 23. On the 16th inst. accompanied by two of my people, I set off for Swan River fort, on horseback. The first night, we slept at Bird Mountain; and the day following we arrived at the lower fort. From that place, I returned in one day, which is a distance of ninety miles. I, however, took a fresh horse at the Bird Mountain. One of my people, who travelled less rapidly, has arrived this evening, and informed me, that he drowned his horse, at the same place where I had before drowned two.

On my return here, those in whose charge I had left the place, had nothing to offer me

5

to eat, excepting boiled parchment skins,
which are little better than nothing, and
scarcely deserve the name of food. I have
therefore sent a part of my people, to endeavour to take some fish out of a small
lake, called by the Natives Devil's Lake,
which lies about ten miles north from this.
If they should not succeed, and our hunters
should not be more fortunate than they
have been for some time past, I know not
what will become of us. All our dependence
is on a kind Providence; and we cannot
but hope for a speedy relief, from our truly
sad condition.

Friday, July 2. For six days, after I
sent the people to fish in the above mentioned lake, we subsisted at the fort on
parchment skins, dogs, herbs and a few small
fish, that we took out of the river opposite
to the fort. But now, we obtain fish in
greater plenty.

One of our hunters has been in, and told
me what he thought to be the cause why
he could not kill. He said that when he
went to hunt, he generally soon fell upon
the track of some animal, which he followed;
but that, as soon as he came nigh to him,
he heard the terrible voice of the Evil Spirit,
that frightened both himself and the animal.
The animal would of course run off, and the
pursuit would end.—I told the hunter, that
I had a certain powerful medicine; and provided he would do with it as I would direct

him, it would not only frighten the Evil
Spirit in his turn, but would also render
him at first speechless, and that shortly
after it would cause him to die. I then took
several drugs and mixed them together,
that he might not know what they were,
which I wrapped in a piece of white paper,
and tied to the but-end of his gun, and thus
armed him to encounter great or little devils;
for they believe in the existence of different
orders. I told him to go in search of a
moose or deer; and as soon as he should
hear the voice of the Evil Spirit, to throw
the paper tied to his gun behind him into
the air, and that it would fall into the mouth
of the Evil Spirit pursuing him, and silence
and destroy him. I warned him not to look
behind him, lest he should be too much
frightened at the sight of so monstrous a
creature, but to pursue the animal, which
he would undoubtedly kill.

The same day, the Indian went to hunting, and fell upon the track of an animal,
which he followed, as he has since told me,
but a short distance, before the Evil Spirit,
as his custom was, began to make horrid
cries. The Indian, however, did with the
medicine as I had directed him, and heard
no more of the frightful voice, but continued
following the animal until, approaching him,
he fired, and killed a fine fat red deer; and
he has since killed several others. Not only
he, but the other Indians place, from this

circumstance, perfect confidence in my medicines. What will not imagination, aided by
great superstition, make a person believe!
It may be caused, however, at times, to remove the evils of its own creation.

Sunday, 4. Mr. William Henry and company arrived from the Bird Mountain, and
inform us, that they are destitute of provision there. They will, therefore, come and
pass the remainder of the summer with us;
for we now have provisions in plenty.

Monday, 17. In consequence of the great
increase of our family of late, we are again
poorly supplied with provisions. In order, if
possible, to obtain a supply, I have sent
seven of my people several different ways, in
search of the Natives, who will be able to
relieve our wants, should our men chance to
find them. For this is the season of the
year, when almost all wild animals are the
fattest; and therefore, it is the best time to
kill them, and make them into dry provisions.

Friday, 23. There are at present, in this
vicinity, grass-hoppers, in such prodigious
numbers, as I never before saw in any place.
In fair weather, between eight and ten
o'clock, A. M. which is the only part of the
day when many of them leave the ground,
they are flying in such numbers, that they
obscure the sun, like a light cloud passing
over it. They also devour every thing before
them, leaving scarcely a leaf on the trees,

or a blade of grass on the prairies; and our
potatoe tops escape not their ravages.

Tuesday, *August* 3. The most of the
mosquetoes and horse flies, which are so
troublesome to man and beast, have left
us, as the nights now begin to be cool.

Yesterday, six families of Crees came to
the fort; and they have been drinking, ever
since. An Indian had a few wrangling words
with a squaw, belonging to another man,
to whom he gave a slight beating. At that
time, the chief, who was the friend of the
Indian, was passing by; and he was so en-
raged at the abusive language given by the
woman to his friend, that he commenced
beating her on the head with a club, and
soon terminated her life. This morning,
the Indian women buried her corpse; and no
more notice is taken of her death, than if a
dog had been killed; for her relations are at
a considerable distance, in another part of
the country.—An Indian is not much regarded or feared by his fellows, unless he
has a number of relations to take part with
him in his contests while in life, or to avenge
his death, in case he should be murdered.
This is true among all the Indian tribes,
with whom I have been acquainted.

Wednesday, 11. On the ninth instant, a
Chief among the Crees, came to the fort,
accompanied by a number of his relations,
who appeared very desirous that I should
take one of his daughters, to remain with

me. I put him off by telling him, that I could not then accept of a woman, but probably might, in the fall. He pressed me however, to allow her to remain with me, at once, and added, "I am fond of you, and my wish is to have my daughter with the white people; for she will be treated better by them, than by her own relations." In fact, he almost persuaded me to keep her; for I was sure that while I had the daughter, I should not only have the father's furs, but those of all his band. This would be for the interest of the Company, and would therefore, turn to my own advantage, in some measure; so that a regard to interest, well nigh made me consent to an act, which would have been unwise and improper. But, happily for me, I escaped the snare.

Saturday, 28. I have sent Primault, one of my interpreters, with a letter, about six days' march from this, where I expect he will meet Mr. McLeod and company, on their way from the Grand Portage. Two of our people, whom I sent a few days since into the large prairie, have just returned with the news, that buffaloes are numerous, within two days' march from this. They say, that the Natives, during the two days that they remained with them, killed upwards of eighty, by driving them into a park, made for that purpose.

Sunday, October 3. Yesterday, a little snow fell, which is the first that we have had this season. We now begin to think some disaster has befallen our people, on their way in, as they do not make their appearance so soon as usual.

Monday, 4. One of our men has just arrived from the Grand Portage, and delivered me a letter from Mr. McLeod, informing me, that he is going to Athabasca, and is to be succeeded here by Mr. Hugh McGillies. The canoe in which this man came, left headquarters alone, some time before the main brigade was prepared to leave.

Thursday, 21. This afternoon, Mr. Hugh McGillies, accompanied by one man on horse back, arrived, and informs me, that they were stopped by the ice, fifteen miles below Swan River fort, whence they will be obliged to bring the goods, on sledges.

Monday, 25. A large band of Indians have been here, who were continually drinking, during the last forty eight hours. They have now taken their departure; but another band has just arrived, and, therefore, we must pass another night without sleep; for when the Natives are at the fort, and have the means of purchasing spirits, they expect to drink both night and day.

Saturday, 30. Several of our people arrived from Swan River, and delivered me letters from my friends in the United States, the perusal of which, has afforded me much satisfaction.

Samuel Holmes, a clerk and interpreter,

and a countryman of mine, has left us, to go and join our opponents, the X. Y. people. [*Soon afterwards, he left the service of the last mentioned company, and went to live with the Natives, the Assiniboins, by whom, a year or two after, he was killed, while he was on his way from the Red River to the River Missouri.]

Monday, November 1. I have taken a ride, accompanied by my interpreter, down to see the Hudson Bay people. A Mr. Miller has charge of the place, and has with him fifteen labouring men, the greater part of whom have just returned from Albany fort, which stands at the mouth of Albany River.

Tuesday, 9. *Bird Mountain.* Here I am to pass another winter; and with me there will be one interpreter and six labouring men, &c. Thus I am continually moving from place to place; and when my residence will be more stationary, God only knows. I cannot, however, but look forward, with pleasing expectation, to the time, when I hope to be permitted to settle down in some part of the civilized world.

Friday, 19. I have just returned from the lower fort, where I have been accompanied with part of my people, for goods. I find here a band of Indians, who have been waiting for my return, in order to procure such articles as they need, to enable

*The remarks included in brackets were added at a later date.

them to make a fall hunt. The Indians in this quarter have been so long accustomed to use European goods, that it would be with difficulty that they could now obtain a livelihood, without them. Especially do they need fire arms, with which to kill their game, and axes, kettles, knives, &c. They have almost lost the use of bows and arrows; and they would find it nearly impossible to cut their wood with implements, made of stone or bone.

Thursday, December 25. Severe cold weather. This day being Christmas, our people have spent it as usual, in drinking and fighting.—My education has taught me, that the advent of a Saviour, ought to be celebrated in a far different manner.—Of all people in the world, I think the Canadians, when drunk, are the most disagreeable; for excessive drinking generally causes them to quarrel and fight, among themselves. Indeed, I had rather have fifty drunken Indians in the fort, than five drunken Canadians.

Thursday, January 27, 1803. I have just returned from Alexandria, where I passed six days, much to my satisfaction, in the company of Messrs. H. McGillies, W. Henry and F. Goedike. While there, I wrote to Messrs. McLeod, A. Henry and J. Clarke, all of Athabasca, which letters will be taken to them, by our winter express.

Sunday, February 20. Yesterday morning, one of the Indian women came to the

fort and said, her husband had cut off her
nose, and was determined to kill her, and
that she therefore thought proper to leave
him, and go to Alexandria, where she would
be out of his reach, at least for the present.
But, after her arrival here, she altered her
mind, and desired my interpreter to put an
end to her life, which he, of course, refused
to do. Then said she, 'I will do the business
myself, for I am resolved that I will live
with my husband no longer.' We did not
believe, however, that she would execute this
determination.—Soon after, she went into
the woods, a short distance, and laid down
her load of the few things which she had
upon her back, and struck and kindled up
a fire, into which she threw the most of her
property. When it was nearly consumed,
she took a little bag of powder and put it
into her bosom, and then set fire to it. The
explosion burned a great part of the hair
from her head, injured her face very much,
and rendered her perfectly blind. She now
commenced running about, in order if possible, to catch her dogs, which she was resolved
next to burn. When we heard her calling out
for them, we went out to see what she was
doing; for at this time, we knew nothing
of what had taken place.—The spectacle was
truly shocking! She was so disfigured, as
scarcely to appear like a human being. We
brought her to the fort, where she remained
very quiet, until we were all in bed and

asleep, when she got up, and went again into the woods. There she tied a cord about her neck, and then fastened it to the limb of a tree. But on throwing herself off, the branch broke, and she fell into the snow, where she remained until morning, when we found her nearly lifeless. On examining, we discovered that she had run a needle its full length, into her right ear. We brought her again to the fort; but her head is very much swollen, and her face is perfectly black; and whether she will recover, is uncertain. [Several years afterward, I saw her with her old husband; and she appeared to enjoy as good health as formerly.]

Wednesday, May 4. *Alexandria.* Here, if Providence permit, I shall pass another summer, and have with me Mr. F. Goedike, one interpreter and several labouring men, besides women and children. As Mr. Goedike will be absent from the fort, during the greater part of the summer, I shall be, in a great measure, alone; for ignorant Canadians furnish little society. Happily for me, I have lifeless friends, my books, that will never abandon me, until I first neglect them.

Thursday, June 2. I have set our people to surround a piece of ground for a garden, with palisades, such as encompass our forts. The X. Y. people are building a fort, five miles up this river.

One of our men, a Canadian, gave me his son, a lad of about twelve years of age,

whom I agree, in the name of the North
West Company, to feed and clothe, until he
becomes able to earn something more. His
mother is a Sauteux woman. He is to serve
me as cook, &c.

Tuesday, 21. This afternoon, we had an
uncommonly heavy shower of hail and rain.

Yesterday, I sent Mr. F. Goedike, accompanied by several of our people, with a small
assortment of goods, to remain at some
distance from this, for several weeks. In the
absence of my friend, this is to me, a solitary
place. At such times as this, my thoughts
visit the land of my nativity; and I almost
regret having left my friends and relatives,
among whom I might now have been pleasantly situated, but for a roving disposition.
But Providence, which is concerned in all the
affairs of men, has, though unseen, directed
my way into this wilderness; and it becomes
me to bear up under my circumstances, with
resignation, perseverance and fortitude. I
am not forbidden to hope, that I shall one
day enjoy, with increased satisfaction, the
society of those friends, from whom I have
for a season banished myself.

Sunday, 26. I have just returned from
an excursion to the large prairies, in which
I was accompanied by two of my people;
and in all our ramble we did not see a single Indian. The most of them, as is their
custom every spring, have gone to war again.
We saw, and then ran down and killed, buf-

faloes, and also, saw red deers and antelopes, bounding across the prairies, as well
as bears and wolves, roving about in search
of prey. In the small lakes and ponds, which
are to be met with occasionally, all over the
prairies, fowls were in considerable plenty;
and with our fire arms, we killed a sufficiency of them, for our daily consumption.
Although it rained during the greater part
of the time that we were absent from the
fort, yet the pleasing variety of the objects
which were presented to our view, made our
ride very agreeable. One night, we slept at
the same place where, a few days before, a
party of the Rapid Indian warriors had encamped. They were probably in search of
their enemies, the Crees and Assiniboins;
and it was happy for us that we did not
meet them, for they would undoubtedly have
massacred us, as they consider us as enemies,
for furnishing their opponents with fire arms.

Monday, August 8. We have now thirty
people in the fort, and have not a supply of
provisions for two days. Our hunters, owing
to a bad dream, or some other superstitious
notion, think they cannot kill, and therefore
make no attempt, notwithstanding animals
are numerous. In the civilized parts of the
world, when provisions are scarce in one
place, they can generally be obtained from
some other place, in the vicinity. But the
case is otherwise with us. When destitute,
we must wait until Providence sends us a

supply; and we sometimes think it rather tardy in coming.

Thursday, 18. An Indian has just arrived, who brings the intelligence, that forty lodges of Crees and Assiniboins, who the last spring, in company with forty lodges of other tribes, set out on a war party, are returning home. They separated at Battle River from their allies, who, the messenger says, crossed that river, to go and make peace with their enemies, the Rapid and Black-feet Indians. The tribes last mentioned, inhabit the country lying along the foot of the Rocky Mountains, between the Sisiscatchwin and Missouri Rivers. Both parties begin to be weary of such bloody wars, as have long been carried on between them, and are much disposed to patch up a peace, on almost any terms. Thus do ruinous wars, waged by restless and ambitious people, in civilized and savage countries, lay waste and destroy the comforts of mankind.

Sunday, *October* 16. This afternoon there fell a little snow, which is the first we have had, this fall.

It is now several days since the X. Y. people arrived from the Grand Portage; but they give us no news of Mr. McGillies and his company; neither would they, were their condition ever so bad. Neither company will convey to the other the least intelligence, that at all concerns their affairs in this country. The North West Company look upon the X. Y. Company as encroachers upon their territories; and, I think, with some reason, since the former company first led the way into this savage country; while the latter people think, that the former have no more right to trade in this part of the world, than themselves. This jarring of interests, keeps up continual misunderstandings, and occasions frequent broils between the contending parties; and to such a height has their enmity risen, that it has, in several instances, occasioned blood shed. But here the murderer escapes without punishment; for the civil law does not extend its protection, so far into the wilderness. I understand, however, that measures are in contemplation in England, which will remedy this evil. If something should not be done soon, I fear many of us may lose our lives.

Wednesday, 19. About six inches of snow have fallen. Mr. McGillies and company arrived from the Grand Portage, and delivered me letters from my friends in the United States; and I rejoiced to hear that they were in health and prosperity.

Saturday, 22. This afternoon, one of our men, an Iroquois, died; and it is thought the foundation was laid for his death, by too great an exertion of his strength at the portages, on his way into the country. The death of our people is not unfrequently occasioned by this circumstance.

Sunday, *November* 6. On the 28th ult.

we sent eight of our men, on horseback, into the plains, to look for buffaloes; and they returned this evening, with their horses loaded with the flesh of those animals. They say that they are still three days' march from this.

Tuesday, December 27. Messrs. Henry and Goedike, my companions and friends, are both absent, on excursions into two different parts of the country. I sensibly feel the loss of their society, and pass, occasionally, a solitary hour, which would glide away imperceptibly, in their company. When they are absent I spend the greater part of my time in reading and writing. Now and then I take a ride on horseback, in the neighbourhood of the fort, and occasionally I visit our neighbours, drawn in a *cariol* by horses, if the snow is light, or by dogs, if it is deep. This afternoon, I accompanied Mr. McGillies, to pay a visit to our X. Y. neighbours.

Wednesday, February 22, 1804. *Lac La Peche*, or *Fishing Lake*. This lies about two days' march into the large plains, west from Alexandria, which place I left on the 15th ultimo, accompanied by twelve of our people. I have come here to pass the winter, by the side of the X. Y. people. For some time after our arrival, we subsisted on rose buds, a kind of food neither very palatable nor nourishing, which we gathered in the fields. They were better than nothing, since they would just support life. When we should procure any thing better, I knew not, as the buffaloes at that time, in consequence of the mild weather, were a great distance, out in the large plains, and my hunters could find neither moose nor deer. We hoped, however, that a merciful God would not suffer us to starve; and that hope has not been disappointed, for we have now provisions in abundance, for which we endeavour to be thankful.

On the 11th instant, I took one of my interpreters and ten labouring men with me, and proceeded several days' march into the wilderness, where we found a camp of upwards of thirty lodges of Crees and Assiniboins, of whom we made a good purchase of furs and provisions. They were encamped on the summit of a hill, whence we had an extensive view of the surrounding country, which was low and level. Not a tree could be seen, as far as the eye could extend; and thousands of buffaloes were to be seen grazing, in different parts of the plain. In order to kill them, the Natives in large bands, mount their horses, run them down and shoot, with their bows and arrows, what number they please, or drive them into parks and kill them at their leisure. In fact, those Indians, who reside in the large plains or prairies, are the most independent, and appear to be the most contented and happy people upon the face of the earth. They subsist upon the flesh of the buffaloe, and of the skins of that animal they make the

6

greatest part of their clothing, which is both warm and convenient. Their tents and beds are also made of the skins of the same animal.

The Crees and Assiniboins procure their livelihood with so much ease, that they have but little to confine them at home. They therefore employ much of their time, in waging war with their neighbours.

Thursday, March 1. *Es-qui-un-a-wăch-a,* or the *last Mountain,* or rather *Hill;* for there are no mountains in this part of the country. Here I arrived this evening, having left Lac La Peche on the 28th ultimo, in company with my interpreter and seven men. The men, I ordered to encamp at a short distance from this, and to join me early to-morrow morning; as it is more convenient and safe, especially when we are not in our forts, to give the Indians spirits to drink in the day time, than in the night. On our arrival, we were invited to the tents of several of the principal Indians, to eat and smoke our pipes.—Indians show great hospitality to strangers, before they have been long acquainted with civilized people, after which, they adopt many of their customs; but they are by no means always gainers, by the exchange.

Monday, 5. On the 2nd, the remainder of our people arrived, and soon after I commenced dealing out spirits to the Natives; and they continued to drink during all that

day and the following night. We were, therefore, prevented from resigning ourselves to
sleep. For though the Indians are naturally
well disposed toward the white people, and
seldom begin a quarrel with us, and will
even receive many insults, before they attempt to defend themselves; yet when drunk,
they often behave like mad men or devils,
and need to be narrowly watched.

This morning, I sent six of my people to
the fort with sledges loaded with furs and
provisions, in order to obtain another supply
of goods, to enable us to go and trade with
another large band of Indians, who are about
two days' march from this, into the plains.

Tuesday, 6. *North side of the Great
Devil's Lake*, or as the Natives call it, *Muche-
e-man-e-to Sa-ky-e-gun*. As I had nothing
of importance to attend to, while our people would be absent in their trip to and
from the fort, and was desirous of seeing
my friend Henry, who, I understood, was
about half a day's march from where I was
the last night, I therefore, set off this morning, accompanied by an Indian lad who
serves as a guide, with the intention of visiting this place. After walking all day, without finding either wood or water, and but
a few inches of snow, just as the sun was
descending below the horizon, we thought
that we descried a small grove, at a considerable distance, directly before us. So
long, therefore, as the light remained, we

directed our course to that object; but as soon as the daylight failed, we had nothing by which to guide ourselves, excepting the stars, which, however, answered very well, until even their faint twinkling was utterly obscured by clouds, and we were inveloped in total darkness. In this forlorn condition, we thought it best to continue our march as well as we could; for we were unwilling to lie down, with little or nothing with which to cover us, and keep ourselves from freezing. There was no wood, with which we could make a fire, nor buffaloe dung, which often serves as fuel, when travelling about in those plains. Neither could we find water to drink; and without fire, we could not melt the snow, for this purpose. We suffered much for want of water, as we had nothing to eat but very dry provisions, which greatly excited thirst. —To be deprived of drink for one day, is more distressing than to be destitute of food for two.—It would not have been safe for us to encamp, without a fire; for we should have been continually exposed to be trodden upon by the large herds of buffaloes, that are perpetually roving about in the plains, or to be devoured by the wolves, which ever follow the buffaloe. We therefore continued travelling, uncertain whither we were going, until at length, the dogs that drew my sledge, suddenly passed by us, as if they saw some uncommon object, directly before us. We did not attempt to impede their motion, but followed them as fast as we could, until they brought us to the place where we now are.—It is almost incredible that my dogs should have smelt this camp at such a distance; for we walked vigorously no less than four hours after they passed us, before we arrived here.

We are happy in finding fifteen tents of Crees and Assiniboins, who want for none of the dainties of this country; and I meet, as usual, with a very hospitable reception. The mistress of the tent where I am, unharnessed my dogs, and put my sledge, &c., into a safe place. She was then proceeding to give food to my dogs, which labour, I offered to do myself; but she told me to remain quiet and smoke my pipe, for she added, "they shall be taken good care of, and will be as safe in my hands, as they would be were they in your own."—Notwithstanding it was near midnight when I arrived, yet at that late hour, the most of the Indians rose, and many of them invited me to their tents, to eat a few mouthfuls, and to smoke the sociable pipe.

But now, all those necessary ceremonies are over; and I am happy in being able to lay myself down on buffaloe robes, by the side of a warm fire, expecting to obtain sweet and refreshing repose, which nature requires, after a day's march so fatiguing. If I was ever thankful for any of God's favours, it is, to find myself here among friends, and in comfortable circumstances, when a few hours before, I expected to wander with weariness, anxiety and danger, during the whole night, in the open plain.

Wednesday, 7. *Canadian's Camp.* This place is so called from the fact, that a number of our people have passed the greater part of the winter here. As there is a good foot path, from the place where I slept last night to this place, I left my young guide and came here alone. Frequently on the way, I met Indians, who are going to join those at the Devil's Lake. I came here in the pleasing expectation of seeing my friend, Henry; but I am disappointed. Yesterday morning, he set out for Alexandria. I hope to have the satisfaction, however, of soon meeting him at the fort.—I here find six Canadians with their families, who have passed the winter in this vicinity, and have subsisted upon the flesh of the buffaloe, which animals are found in plenty. The people appear to be happy in their situation. Indeed, a Canadian, with his belly full of fat meat, is never otherwise.

Friday, 9. *North side of Devil's Lake.* In the morning, I left the Canadian's Camp, and this afternoon reached this place, where I found my young guide, waiting my return. He is the son of a chief, among the Crees and Assiniboins. His grandfather was Monsieur Florimeaux, a Frenchman, who passed a number of years in the Indian country.

When he went to Canada, he took his son, the father of my young guide, along with him, as far as Quebec, intending to send him to France. But the lad, who was then twelve or thirteen years old, did not like to leave his native country. After remaining in Canada for some time, therefore, he deserted and returned to this part of the world, where, he, in time, became a famous warrior, and at length, a chief. He is much respected and beloved by his relatives, and is revered by his own family. As a husband he is affectionate, and as a father he is kind. It was perhaps fortunate for him that he did not go to France; for, I am persuaded he could not have lived more happily and at ease, in any part of the world, than in this independent country, which is abundantly supplied with all of the necessaries, and many of the luxuries of life.

Saturday, 10. *In the middle of an extensive plain.* Early in the morning, accompanied by my young guide, I left our last night's lodgings, to go to the place where I expect to find my people, which is about two days' march further into the great plain, than where I separated from my interpreter, on the 6th inst. After walking all day, without finding either wood or water, at eight o'clock at night, we have concluded to lay ourselves down, in order if possible, to get a little rest. In the day time, the snow melted a little; but in the evening it has frozen

hard, and our feet and our legs, as high as
our knees, are so much covered with ice, that
we cannot take off our shoes; and having
nothing with which to make a fire, in order
to thaw them, we must pass the night
with them on. A more serious evil is, the
risk we must run of being killed by wild
beasts.

Sunday, 11. *Ca-ta-buy-se-pu,* or *the River
that calls.* This steam is so named by the
superstitious Natives, who imagine that a
spirit is constantly going up or down it;
and they say that they often hear its voice
distinctly, which resembles the cry of a human
being. The last night was so unpleasant to
me, that I could not sleep, arising in part
from the constant fear which I was in, of
being torn to pieces before the morning, by
wild beasts. Despondency to a degree took
possession of my spirit. But the light of the
morning dissipated my fears, and restored
to my mind, its usual cheerfulness. As soon
as the light of day appeared, we left the
place where we had lain, not a little pleased,
that the wild beasts had not fallen upon us.
It has snowed and rained all day.—Here I
find my interpreter, and eighty tents, or
nearly two hundred men, with their families.
—Along the banks of this rivulet, there is a
little timber, consisting principally of the
inferiour species of the maple; but no where
else, is there even a shrub to be seen. The
surrounding country is a barren plain, where

nothing grows excepting grass, which rises
from six to eight inches in height, and furnishes food for the buffaloe.

Here, again, as usual, I meet with a kind
reception. These Indians seldom come thus
far into the plains, as the part of the country
where we now are, belongs to the Rapid Indians. A white man was never before known,
to penetrate so far.

Wednesday, 14. Last evening my people
returned from the fort; and as I now had
spirits for the Natives, they, of course, drank
during the whole night. Being so numerous,
they made a terrible noise. They stole a
small keg of spirits from us, and one of
them attempted to stab me. The knife went
through my clothes, and just grazed the
skin of my body. To day I spoke to the
Indian who made this attempt, and he cried
like a child, and said, he had nearly killed
his father, meaning me, and asked me why
I did not tie him, when he had lost the use
of his reason.—My people inform me that
there is little or no snow, for three days'
march from this; but after that, there is an
abundance, all the way to the fort.

Friday, 16. About twelve o'clock, we left
the Indians' camp; but being heavily loaded,
considering there is no snow and our property is drawn by dogs on sledges, we made
slow progress. After we had encamped, we
sent our dogs, which are twenty two in number, after the buffaloe; and they soon stopped

one of them, when one of our party went
and killed him with an axe, for we have not
a gun with us. It is, however, imprudent
for us to venture thus far, without fire arms;
for every white man, when in this savage
country, ought at all times to be well armed.
Then he need be under little apprehension
of an attack; for Indians, when sober, are
not inclined to hazard their lives, and when
they apprehend danger from quarrelling,
will remain quiet and peaceable.

Saturday, 17. *North West end of Devil's
Lake.* The weather is extremely mild, for
the season. The surrounding country is all
on fire; but happily for us, we are encamped
in a swampy place. When the fire passes
over the plains, which circumstance happens
almost yearly, but generally later than this,
great numbers of horses and buffaloes are
destroyed; for those animals when surrounded
by fire, will stand perfectly still, until they
are burned to death.—This evening, we killed
another buffaloe, in the same manner as we
killed one, the last evening.

Sunday, 18. The weather is still mild,
and we see many grass-hoppers, which appear
unusually early in the season. As I found
that we were coming on too slowly with our
heavy loads, about twelve o'clock, I left our
property in charge of three of my people,
and am going to the fort with the others,
for horses to come for it.

This afternoon we met several of the X. Y.

people, who were in search of Indians; but from the information they received from us, they thought them at too great a distance, and they are, therefore, accompanying us to the fort.—The same success has attended us this evening, which we met with the two preceding days, in regard to supplying ourselves with food. Indeed, in these plains where buffaloes are numerous, it is not customary, nor is it needful for people who are travelling, to burden themselves with provisions; for if they have fire arms, they can always kill a sufficiency for the day. This renders travelling cheap and convenient.

Thursday, 22. *Lac la Pêche.* Here we have arrived, and I am happy in reaching a place, where I can take a little repose, after so long and fatiguing a jaunt. Yet it has been in many respects, both pleasant and profitable. The country which I travelled over was beautifully situated, and overspread with buffaloes, and various other kinds of animals, as well as many other delightful objects, which in succession presented themselves to our view. These things made the day glide away almost imperceptibly. But there were times, when my situation was far from being agreeable; they, however, soon passed away, and we all have abundant reason to render thanks to a kind Providence, for his protection, and for our safe return to our home and our families.

At three different times, while performing

the tour above described, I was in great
danger of losing my life, by the evil mach-
inations of the Natives. One escape has been
already mentioned, when one of them attempted to stab me. While I was dealing
out spirits to the Savages, at the last mountain, on the night of the 5th inst. an Indian, who was much intoxicated, told me,
that I should never see another sun arise;
and he, unquestionably, intended to kill me.
The night following, after I arrived at the
north side of the Devil's Lake, I was well
received by the greater part of the Natives
there; but as I have since been informed, one
of them had resolved to take my life. And
yet, this villain invited me to his tent, and
I visited it, without suspicion. He was prevented from executing his purpose by my
host, who was acquainted with his purpose,
and told him that he must first despatch
him; for, he added, 'Kitch-e-mo-cum-mon'
(that is Big Knife, which is the name that
they give me,) 'is my brother, and has
taken up his lodging with me, and it therefore becomes me to defend him and his property.' No Indian will suffer a stranger, if
he be able to defend him, to be injured,
while in his tent, and under his protection.
Therefore, he who had intended to massacre
me, thought it best to remain quiet. This
hostile Indian had nothing against me, but
that I was a friend to a person who he considered had injured him; and as this person

was at a great distance, and therefore beyond his reach, he was resolved to avenge
the affront upon me. It is the custom of all
Savages, not to be very particular on whom
the punishment of an offence falls, whether
the guilty person, or a relation or friend of
this person. The first of these whom he happens to meet, becomes the object of his ven-
geance; and then his wrath is appeased, and
he will not even lift his hand against the
person who has offended him.

Saturday, 24. Yesterday, Mr. F. Goedike
arrived from Alexandria, and delivered me
a letter from Mr. McGillies, requesting me to
abandon Lac la Pêche, and proceed, with
all my people, to Alexandria. In the fore
part of the day, we all left the former place.
There is a woman with us, belonging to one
of our men, who has walked the whole day,
in the snow and water, and who, this evening, gave birth to a son.

Tuesday, 27. *Alexandria.* Here we arrived this afternoon. The woman who, on
the 24th inst. was delivered of a child, took
it on her shoulders the day following, and
continued her march, as though nothing unusual had occurred! It is a very happy circumstance, that the women of this country
are blessed with such strong constitutions,
as they would otherwise be utterly unable
to endure the hardships to which they are
often exposed, and particularly in child-birth.

Monday, April 9. Yesterday, the ice in

this river broke up; and to day, we sent off four men in a boat, loaded with pimican, to be transported as far as the entrance of Winipick River.—The country all around us, is on fire.

Sunday, 29. Yesterday, the greater part of our people set out for Swan River; and to day, Mr. McGillies, and the most of those who were left, have departed for the New Fort, which is distant about forty-five miles, to the north west from the former general rendezvous, the Grand Portage, which the Americans have obliged us to abandon.

It is thought necessary that I should pass another summer at this place; but I am happy in having with me my friends Henry and Goedike. There are here also one interpreter and several labouring men, besides women and children. We are preparing a piece of ground for a garden, the cultivation of which, will be an amusement; and the produce of it, we hope, will add to our comforts. Mr. Goedike plays the violin, and will occasionally cheer our spirits, with an air. But the most of our leisure time, which is at least five sixths of the whole, will be spent in reading, and in meditating and conversing upon what we read. How valuable is the art, which multiplies books, with great facility, and at a moderate expense. Without them the wheels of time would drag heavily, in this wilderness.

Tuesday, May 22. The seeds which we

put into the ground on the 10th inst. have
sprung up, and grow remarkably well.

Tuesday, 29. During the last forty eight
hours, it has rained without cessation; and
I think I never witnessed so great a fall of
water, within the same space of time. The
river has overflowed its banks, to a much
greater distance than is common; and our
garden, which is not far from it, now lies
under water.

Thursday, 31. In the morning, Mr. Goedike, Collin, my interpreter, a young lad
and myself, set off for the purpose of paying
a visit to our X. Y. neighbours. On leaving
the fort, we had the river to cross, which,
in consequence of the late rains, is about
sixty rods broad. Our only means of crossing it was a canoe, made of the skins of buffaloes, which, on account of the length of
time that it had been in the water, began
to be rotten. Before we reached the other
side of the river, the canoe was nearly half
fiilled with water. We drew it on shore,
mounted our horses, visited our neighbours,
and returned to the place where we had left
our canoe, at about three o'clock P. M.
Having repaired it a little, we embarked, for
the purpose of returning to the fort. We
soon perceived that the water came into the
canoe very fast; and we continued paddling,
in hope of reaching the opposite shore, before
it would fill. We were, however, sadly disappointed; for it became full, when we had

gone about one third of the distance; but
it did not immediately overset. The water,
in that place, was about five feet deep; but
the current was strong, and it soon carried
us to a place where we could not reach the
bottom, and the canoe overset. We all clung
to it and, thus drifted a considerable distance, until the canoe was, at length, stopped by a few willows, whose tops rose above
the water. Here I had a moment, in which
I could reflect on our truly deplorable condition, and directed my thoughts to the
means of relief. My first object was, if possible, to gain the shore, in order to free myself from my clothes, which I could not do
where I then was. But my great coat, a
heavy poniard, boots, &c. rendered it very
difficult for me to swim; and I had become
so torpid, in consequence of having been so
long in the cold water, that before I had
proceeded one third of the way to the shore,
I sunk, but soon arose again, to the surface
of the water. I then exerted myself to the
utmost; but, notwithstanding, soon sunk a
second time. I now considered that I must
inevitably drown; the objects of the world
retire from my view, and my mind was in-
tent only upon approaching death; yet I was
not afraid to meet my dissolution.* I however made a few struggles more, which hap-

*For at that time, I was ignorant of my lost con-
dition by nature, and of the necessity of being clothed
in a better righteousness than my own, to prepare me
to appear with safety before a holy God, in judgment.

pily took me to a small tree that stood on
what is usually the bank of the river, but
which is now some rods distant from dry
land. I remained there for some time, to
recover strength, and at length proceeded to
the shore; and as soon as I had gained it,
my mind rose in ardent gratitude to my
gracious Preserver and deliverer, who had
snatched me from the very jaws of death!
I was now safe on shore; but the condition
of my unfortunate companions, was far different. They had still hold of the canoe in
the middle of the river, and by struggling
were just able to keep themselves from sinking. We had no other craft, with which to
go upon the water, nor could any of our
people swim, who were standing on the shore,
the melancholy spectators of this scene of
distress. I therefore took off my clothes,
and threw myself, a second time, into the
water, in order, if possible, to afford some
aid to my companions. When I had reached
the place where they were, I directed the boy,
to take hold of the hair of my head, and I
took him to a staddle, at no great distance,
and directed him to lay fast hold of it, by
which means he would be able to keep the
greater part of his body above water. I then
returned to the canoe, and took Collin to a
similar place. Mr. Goedike had alone proceeded to a small staddle, and would have
reached the shore, had not the cramp seized
him in one of his legs. I next tried to take

7

the canoe ashore, but could not alone effect
it. I therefore, swam to the opposite shore,
caught a horse and mounted him, and made
him swim to the canoe, at one end of which
I tied a cord, and taking the other end in
my teeth and hands, after drifting a considerable distance, I reached the land. After
repairing the canoe a little, I proceeded to
my three wretched fellow creatures, who had,
by this time, become nearly lifeless, having
been in the water at least two hours. By
the aid of a kind Providence, however, they
at last safely reached the shore; and so
deeply were they affected with their unexpected escape, that they prostrated themselves to the earth, in an act of thanksgiv-
ing, to their great and merciful Deliverer.

Sunday, July 1. We now begin to have
strawberries, and the prospect is, that they
will be abundant.

Tuesday, 17. On the 8th instant, some
Indians ran away with three of our horses;
and on the following morning, Mr. Goedike
and myself mounted two others, to pursue
the thieves. We followed them for two days,
and then, ascertaining that they were so far
in advance of us, and travelled so fast, that
it would be impossible to overtake them,
before they would reach their camp, which is
six or seven days' march from this, we ceased
following them. We directed our course another way, for the purpose of finding buffaloe, but without success. We, however,

killed as many fowls, in the small lakes, as we needed for daily consumption; and this evening returned to the fort, having had on the whole a pleasant ride.

We have had a frost, so hard, that it has injured many things in our garden.

Wednesday, 25. An Indian has arrived here with six horses, who states, that he came directly from the territory of the Black feet Indians. He brings the intelligence, that this tribe have concluded a peace with the Crees and Assiniboins; and that forty tents of the latter tribes, who went into that quarter, two years since, are on their way home, and will reach this place before the commencement of winter.

Saturday, *September* 1. This afternoon, Mr. Ferguson and company arrived, from fort Dauphin, bringing the intelligence, that all the Indians who are accustomed to remain in that vicinity, have now gone to the Great Winipick lake.

Thursday, *October* 4. This afternoon, Mr. Francis la Rocque arrived, from Montagne à la Basse, which lies about five days' march from this, down the river. He brought me letters from several gentlemen in this country, one of which is from Mr. Charles Chaboillez, who informs me that this place will be supplied with goods, this season, by the way of the Red River, of which department he has the superintendence. As I am to pass the winter here, he desires me to accompany Mr. La Rocque, down to Montagne à la Basse, and receive such goods as will be necessary for the Indians at this post.

Friday, 26. Agreeably to the instructions of Mr. Chaboillez, in company with Mr. La Rocque, and an Indian, who served as guide, I set out on the 6th instant, for Montagne à la Basse. Our course was nearly south, over a plain country; and on the 9th, we reached Riviere qui Apelle, where the North West and X. Y. companies have each a fort, where we tarried all night, with Monsieur Poitras, who has charge of that post. The next morning, we continued our march, which was always in beautiful plains, until the 11th, when we arrived at the place of our destination. There I found Mr. Chaboillez, C. McKenzie, &c. The fort is well built, and beautifully situated, on a very high bank of the Red River, and overlooks the country round to a great extent, which is a perfect plain. There can be seen, at almost all seasons of the year, from the fort gate, as I am informed, buffaloes grazing, or antelopes bounding over the extensive plains, which cannot fail to render the situation highly pleasant. I spent my time there very pleasantly, during eight days, in company with the gentlemen above mentioned. At times, we would mount our horses, and ride out into the plains, and frequently try the speed of our beasts. On the 19th, I left that enchanting abode, in company with Messrs.

Chaboillez, McKenzie, &c., and the day following, arrived at Riviere qui Apelle, where
we found the people, waiting our arrival.
They came here by water; but at this season,
canoes go up no further, on account of the
shallowness of the river. The goods intended
for Alexandria, therefore, must be taken
from this on horse back. Accordingly, we
delivered out to the people such articles as
we thought necessary, and sent them off;
and the day following, Mr. Chaboillez returned to Montagne a la Basse, and Mr.
McKenzie and myself proceeded to Alexandria,
where we arrived this afternoon, after having made a pleasant jaunt of twenty one
days.

Here I shall pass the winter, having with
me Mr. Goedike, two interpreters, twenty
labouring men, fourteen women and sixteen
children.

Saturday, November 24. Some people
have just arrived from Montagne a la Basse,
with a letter from Mr. Chaboillez, who informs me, that two Captains, Clarke and
Lewis, with one hundred and eighty soldiers,
have arrived at the Mandan Village on the
Missouri River, which place is situated about
three days' march distant from the residence
of Mr. Chaboillez. They have invited Mr.
Chaboillez to visit them. It is said, that
on their arrival, they hoisted the American
flag, and informed the Natives that their
object was not to trade, but merely to ex-

plore the country; and that as soon as the
navigation shall open, they design to continue their route across the Rocky Mountain,
and thence descend to the Pacific Ocean.
They made the Natives a few small presents,
and repaired their guns, axes, &c., gratis.
Mr. Chaboillez writes, that they behave hon-
ourably toward his people, who are there
to trade with the Natives.

Tuesday, January 21, 1805. For nearly
a month, we have subsisted on little besides
potatoes; but thanks to a kind Providence,
the last night, two of my men returned
from the plains, with their sledges loaded
with the flesh of the buffaloe. They bring
us the pleasing intelligence, that there is
a plenty of these animals within a day's
march of us. This supply of provisions could
not have come more opportunely, for our
potatoes are almost gone.

About a month since, I sent Mr. Goedike,
accompanied by ten men, out into the plains,
in hopes that they might fall in with the
Natives, who would be able to furnish us
with food; but we have heard nothing from
them, and I cannot conjecture what should
have detained them so long, as I did not
expect that they would be absent, for more
than ten days, from the fort.

Thursday, February 7. At the most of
the forts in the Swan River department,
they have not a sufficiency of provisions;
and they have therefore, sent the greater

number of their people, to pass the remainder
of the winter here. We now have buffaloe
in abundance, though our family consists
of upwards of seventy persons, who consume,
at least, four hundred and fifty pounds,
daily.

Thursday, 19. On the 8th inst. two men
arrived from Montagne à la Basse, with a
packet of letters, informing me, that a coali-
tion took place, the last autumn at Montreal,
between the North West and the X. Y. companies, which letters I have forwarded to
Fort des Prairies.

On the 16th inst. I left this, in a cariol,
drawn by a horse, to visit a place, about
two days' march from this, into the plains,
where a number of our people have passed a
greater part of the winter; and in the course
of this pleasant ride, I saw thousands of
buffaloes.

Saturday, March 2. People arrived from
Fort des Prairies, with letters from that
place, the English River, and Athabasca.—
Yesterday, swans passed this place, on their
way to the northward.

Monday, 18. A band of Crees and Assiniboins came in, a few days since, consisting
of more than a hundred persons. As they
brought a considerable quantity of furs
and provisions, they were able to purchase
a large supply of spirits for several days,
and of course continued drinking, until their
means were exhausted. During this period,

one of the Assiniboins stabbed one of the Crees. The wound, however, is not thought to be mortal. The injury has been atoned for, therefore, by a horse, presented by the aggressor, to the wounded Indian; and now, they appear to be as great friends, as they were before the quarrel took place.

It is a common thing among all the Natives, for an offender to offer property in satisfaction for an injury; and when this is accepted by the injured party, contention between them entirely ceases. Even murder is, sometimes, in this way, atoned for; but not commonly. In ordinary cases, nothing but the death of the murderer, or of some of his near relations, will satisfy the desire of revenge in an Indian, whose relative has been murdered.

Wednesday, April 10. On the 24th ult. I set out on horse back, accompanied by one man, for Montagne à la Basse. When we arrived there, we were not a little surprised to find the fort gates shut, and about eighty tents of Crees and Assiniboins encamped in a hostile manner, around it, and threatening to massacre all the white people in it. They, in a menacing manner, threw balls over the palisades, and told our people to gather them up, declaring that they would probably have use for them in the course of a few days. After having passed several days there, I set out to return home. Just as I had gotten out of the fort gate, three vil-

lainous Indians approached me, and one
of them seized my horse by the bridle and
stopped him, saying, that the beast belonged
to him, and that he would take him from
me. I told him that he had disposed of
him to Mr. Chaboillez, who had charge of
the post; and that of this gentleman, I had
purchased him, and that I had no concern
with the matter, which was wholly between
him and Mr. Chaboillez. Perceiving, however,
that he was determined not to let go of
the bridle, I gave him a smart blow on his
hand, with the butt end of my whip, which
consisted of a deer's horn, and instantly
striking my horse, I caused him to spring
forward, and leave the Indian behind. Finding myself thus clear of this fellow, I continued my rout; but he with one of his companions, followed us nearly half of the day,
if not longer. After this length of time we
saw no more of them. Apprehensive, however, that they might fall upon us in our
encampment at night, and steal our horses,
and probably massacre us, after it became
dark, we went a little out of the path, and
laid ourselves down; but we dared not make
a fire, lest the light or the smoke should
discover the place where we were.

On my return, I passed four days agreeably, at Riviere qui Apelle, in the company
of a number of gentlemen, whom I found
there. On leaving that place, I was obliged
to cross the river, and at this late season,

the ice was bad. My horse, while I was on
him, fell through the ice twice, and the last
time, I came very near passing under it;
but a kind Providence once more, granted
me deliverance.

While at Montagne à la Basse, Mr. Chaboillez, induced me to consent to undertake
a long and arduous tour of discovery. I am
to leave that place, about the beginning of
June, accompanied by six or seven Canadians, and by two or three Indians. The first
place, at which we shall stop, will be the
Mandan Village, on the Missouri River.
Thence, we shall steer our course towards
the Rocky Mountain, accompanied by a number of the Mandan Indians, who proceed in
that direction every spring, to meet and
trade with another tribe of Indians, who
reside on the other side of the Rocky Mountain. It is expected that we shall return from
our excursion, in the month of November next.

[This journey, I never undertook; for
soon after the plan of it was settled, my
health became so much impaired, that I
was under the necessity of proceeding to
Head Quarters, to procure medical assistance.
A Mr. La Rocque attempted to make this
tour; but went no farther than the Mandan
Village.]

Thursday, 18. We are packing our furs,
in order to send them to the general rendezvous; and a few days hence, I shall abandon this fort, and the Indians in this vicinity

will go either into the region of Riviere
qui Apelle, or up the Sisiscatchwin River,
near Fort des Prairies.

Sunday, May 5. We are now about three
leagues below Alexandria, which place we
abandoned on the 28th ult. All our property is on board of boats; but some of
us travel horse-back. As it has not rained
since the last Autumn, the water in the river
is uncommonly low, on account of which,
our boats make but poor progress. As we
have a pit saw with us, I have directed
some of my people to go into the woods,
and saw a sufficient quantity of boards, to
construct another boat, by means of which,
we may reduce the loading, in those that
we now possess.

Wednesday, 8. *Riviere qui Apelle.* On the
6th Mr. Goedike and several other persons
with myself, left our boats, and proceeded
on horse-back. As the fire has passed over
the plains, this spring, it was with difficulty
that we could find grass, sufficient for the
subsistence of our horses.

Monday, 20. *Montagne à la Basse.* Here
I have been waiting ever since the 15th for
the arrival of our boats. They arrived this
afternoon.

Monday, 27. *Riviere à la Souris,* or *Mouse
River.* This is about fifty miles from Montagne à la Basse. Here are three establishments, formed severally by the North
West, X. Y. and Hudson Bay companies.

Last evening, Mr. Chaboillez invited the
people of the other two forts to a dance; and
we had a real North West country ball.
When three fourths of the people had drunk
so much, as to be incapable of walking
straightly, the other fourth thought it time
to put an end to the ball, or rather *bawl*.
This morning, we were invited to breakfast
at the Hudson Bay House, with a Mr. Mc-
Kay, and in the evening to a dance. This,
however, ended more decently, than the one
of the preceding evening.

It is now more than fifty years, since a
French missionary left this place. He had,
as I am informed, resided here, during a
number of years, for the purpose of instructing the Natives in the Christian religion.
He taught them some short prayers, in
the French language, the whole of which
some of them have not yet forgotten.

The surrounding country consists chiefly
of plains; and the soil appears to be richer,
than that which is farther up the river.

Tuesday, 30. In the morning, I left Mouse
River; and I have with me upwards of forty
men, in five boats and seven canoes.

Saturday, *June* 1. We are now a little
below what was called the Pine Fort. It
is twenty years since this fort was built,
and eleven since it was abandoned. This
River is now so low, arising from the fact
that we have had no rain this spring, and
we have such a number of boats and canoes,

that we drive the sturgeon upon the sand banks, where there is but little water; and we have no difficulty in killing any number of them, that we please. We now subsist entirely on these fish; and they are excellent food.

Thursday, 13. *Portage la Prairie*, or *Plain Portage*. Here the North West company have a miserable fort, the local situation of which, is beautiful, beyond any thing that I have seen in this part of the world. Opposite the fort, there is a plain, which is about sixty miles long, and from one to ten broad, in the whole extent of which, not the least rise of ground is visible.—To this place, the Natives resort every spring, to take and dry sturgeon.

Saturday, 15. We are now encamped under a beautiful range of oaks, which separate the river from a pretty extensive plain. Ever since we left Mouse River, the soil on each side of the Upper Red River, down which we are passing, appears to be excellent, and the timber is very different from what it is near its source. We here find oak, elm, walnut, basswood, &c. and I am informed that there are grapes and plums in this vicinity.

Tuesday, 18. Not far from the place where we are now encamped, there is a considerably large camp of Sauteux. Among them I saw another of my unfortunate countrymen, who, like one of whom I have already spoken, was taken from his parents, when a child. Thus, has many a fond mother, in the frontier settlements, been deprived of her beloved and tender offspring,—but this fellow is lost, beyond recovery, for he now speaks no other language, but that of the Indians, among whom he resides, and he has adopted all their manners and customs; and it would now be as difficult to reconcile him to the habits of civilized life, as it would be, were he a real Indian.

Wednesday, 19. *The Forks*. At this place the Upper and Lower Red Rivers, form a junction. The country around is pleasant, the soil appears to be excellent, and it is tolerably well timbered with oak, basswood, walnut, elm, poplar, aspin, birch, &c. Grape vines and plum trees are also seen.

Friday, 21. We are now encamped at the place, where the Red River enters the Great Winipick Lake. It is now nearly five years since I passed this place, which, at first thought, seems but a moment. But when I deliberately recollect the scenes through which I have passed, during that space of time, it seems as if I had passed the greater part of my days in this country.

Monday, 24. We are now at the entrance of Winipick River, into the Lake of the same name. We, here, find a number of people, who are from their respective winter quarters, and who, like ourselves, are on their way to the New Fort.

Friday, July 5. Rainy Lake. On the margin of the waters, which connect this lake with the Great Winipick Lake, the wild rice is found, of which I have spoken on a former occasion. This useful grain is produced in no other part of the North West Country; though Carver erroneously states, that it is found every where. It grows in water, about two feet deep, where there is a rich muddy bottom. It rises more than eight feet above the water; and, in appearance bears a considerable resemblance to oats. It is gathered about the latter end of September, in the following manner. The Natives pass in among it in canoes. Each canoe has in it two persons, one of whom is in each end, with a long hooked stick, in one hand, and a straight one in the other. With the hooked stick, he brings the heads of the grain over the canoe, and holds it there; while, with the other, he beats it out. When the canoe is thus sufficiently loaded, it is taken to the shore and emptied. This mode of gathering the wild rice, is evidently more simple and convenient, than that which was practised in Carver's day. This grain is gathered in such quantities, in this region, that in ordinary seasons, the North West Company purchase, annually, from twelve to fifteen hundred bushels of it, from the Natives; and it constitutes a principal article of food, at the posts in this vicinity.

I have here received letters from my friends

in Vermont, which left them in April last;
and which have, as usual, afforded me much
satisfaction.

Saturday, 6. *Rainy Lake*. We are about
ten miles from the fort, on this lake; and
have been encamped, during the greater
part of the day, in order that our people
may repair their canoes; for they will soon
be obliged to transport them over a number
of long portages.

Monday, 8. *Cross Lake*. Here we meet
several canoes which, about the beginning of
May last, left Montreal, that have goods
on board, which will be carried in them to
the Rainy Lake fort, and will thence be
transported to Athabasca.—At this lake,
we leave the route which leads to the old
Grand Portage.

Tuesday, 9. During the whole of this
day, we have been crossing small lakes, and
coming down what deserve the name of
brooks, rather than rivers.—We have met
eight canoes, on their way to the Rainy
Lake.

Friday, 12. *The Plain Portage*. In the
former part of the day, we met, A. N. Mc-
Leod, Esq. who is now from the New Fort, on
his way back to Athabasca. We went on
shore, and took breakfast with him. He
has taken with him my friend Mr. F. Goedike, a young man possessed of a good
understanding, and a humane and generous
heart, who has been with me for four years

past, and from whom I could not separate, without regret.

Saturday, July 13. Overtook the Swan River people, and entered Nipignon River, which is nearly ten rods broad. This and Dog's river, excepting a few carrying places, on account of rapids and falls, will carry us to the New Fort. The land in this vicinity is low, and in many places, it is swampy. There are few animals in this region, excepting moose, bears, and a few beavers and martins. This is the rout, by which the French, in former times, passed into the interiour. The Indians in this quarter, are a few Sauteux and Muscagoes. The latter, come from towards Hudson's Bay.

Sunday, 14. *Dog's Portage,* which is about three miles over. After coming down Nipignon River, which is nearly fifty miles long, we entered the Dog's Lake, which may be about forty miles in circumference, and by crossing which, we arrived at this place.

Monday, 15. *The Mountain Portage.* Here the water falls perpendicularly, about seventy feet. The North West company have here a store house, to which they send provisions, &c., from the New Fort, as the river from this to that place is generally shallow, and is full of rapids. Those, therefore, who are going into the interiour, cannot take a full load, until they arrive at this place; and here they usually take their supply of provisions.

8

Tuesday, 16. *New Fort*, or, as it is called by the Natives, *Kâ-mi-ni-ti-qui-â*, is built on the bank of Dog River, which is a considerable stream, that empties into Lake Superiour, about four or five hundred rods below the fort. The vessel that runs on that lake, can come, with a part of her lading, quite up to the quay, before the fort. Here the French, before the English conquered Canada, had an establishment.

We here meet a number of gentlemen, some of whom came this summer from Montreal, and others from different parts of the Interiour. There are also here, one thousand labouring men, the greater part of whom, are Canadians, who answer better in this country, for the service required by the Company, than any other people would probably do.

The country, for some considerable distance round, is covered with heavy timber, consisting of a kind of red pine, poplar, aspin, birch, cedar, &c., but the soil does not appear to be of the first quality. Potatoes, pease, oats, &c., however, grow tolerably well here.

Monday, 22. I have passed several days, not unpleasantly, in the company of a number of young gentlemen. They now begin, however, to leave this, to return to their winter quarters; and to-morrow, I expect to depart, and to proceed for Fort des Prairies. As there will be two other young gentlemen in the same brigade, whom I know to be sociable and pleasant companions, I expect to have a pleasant passage to my winter quarters.

Wednesday, August 28. During nearly a month past we have been coming through a country, which I have already described. We are now at the Grand Rapid, where the Sisiscatchwin River disembogues into the north west part of Great Lake Winipick. This is a noble stream, about two hundred fathoms broad.

Thursday, September 5. *Cumberland House.* This fort stands on the north side of a considerable lake, called by the Natives, who in this vicinity are Muscagoes, Sturgeon Lake. The sturgeon are found in considerable plenty, in this lake. This post was established, thirty three years since, by Mr. Joseph Frobisher. At this place, the people who are destined to Fort des Prairies, and those who are proceeding to Athabasca, separate. The former go up the Sisiscatchwin River, and the latter up the English River The latter, is so called, in honour of Mr. Joseph Frobisher, an Englishman, who was the first trader that ever went into that part of the country.—On the 30th ultimo, we crossed Lac Bourbon, which is about forty miles long, on which the North West Company had a fort, formerly; but it was abandoned, in 1802. There are few mountains or hills to be seen, between this place and Lake Winipick. The country has a pretty heavy growth of timber, and the soil is rich. In the lakes and rivers of this region, excellent fish are taken, such as sturgeon, white-fish, cat-fish, pike, pickerel, &c. This country abounds in fowls, among which are swans, bustards, geese, and many kinds of ducks. Moose are found in considerable plenty; there are a few black bears, otters, muskrats and martins; and rarely, a beaver is found.

Saturday, September 21. South Branch Fort. This is about one hundred and twenty miles above the Fork, or the place where this river forms a junction with the North Branch, after which, it assumes the name of Sisis-catchwin River. Both branches take their rise in the Rocky Mountain, though at a distance of several hundred miles from each other. The South Branch passes through large plains; but the country through which the other runs is woody, particularly on the north side. From Cumberland House to the Fork, the country on both sides of the river is covered with wood. In these woods, and the small plains that are here and there scattered among them, moose, red deer, &c., are to be found.

This fort was put up the last summer, and two stores were built; but the dwelling houses are still to be constructed.—I am informed that buffaloes are in plenty within half a day's march from this. There are four tribes of Indians, who come to trade at this establishment. They are the Crees, Assiniboins,

Sauteux and Muscagoes. A few also of the Black feet Indians resort here.

In coming up this river, we saw many places, where forts have stood, some of which were abandoned thirty years since, and some at a later period. One, which was situated about six miles below this, was abandoned fifteen years since, on account of an attack from the Rapid Indians. The following circumstances, in regard to that affair, were related to me by Mons. Louis Chattellain, who, at that time, had charge of the fort. The Hudson Bay Company had a fort in the same neighbourhood, which was first attacked, by about one hundred and fifty Indians on horse back; and the few people who were in it, excepting one man, who secreted himself, were killed. After they had taken out of the fort all the property which they could conveniently carry away with them, they set fire to the fort, and proceeded to the establishment of the North West Company, which was two hundred rods distant from that of Hudson Bay people, with the intention of treating it in a similar manner.

The fort gates had providentially, been shut, previously to the approach of the Indians. There were in the fort, three men, and several women and children. The men took their stations in the block houses and bastions; and when the Natives had come sufficiently near, fired upon them. The Indians, instantly returned the fire; and the contest continued, until the night approached. The savage assailants, having had several of their party killed, and others severely wounded, while the people in the fort had sustained no injury, thought it best to retreat; and after dragging their dead and dying into the river, they retired. But Mr. Chattellain did not think it prudent to remain there any longer. Accordingly, the day following, they embarked all their property on board of several canoes, and proceeded down the river, about two hundred miles, where they commenced building another fort. The only object of the Indians, in attacking these forts, was plunder.

Mr. William Smith and myself, together with fifteen labouring men, &c. are to pass the winter here; and a few hundred paces from us, the Hudson Bay people have a fort.

Thursday, October 10. This day, a Canadian's daughter, a girl of about fourteen years of age, was offered to me; and after mature consideration, concerning the step which I ought to take, I have finally concluded to accept of her, as it is customary for all gentlemen who remain, for any length of time, in this part of the world, to have a female companion, with whom they can pass their time more socially and agreeably, than to live a lonely life, as they must do, if single. If we can live in harmony together, my intention now is, to keep her as long as I remain in this uncivilized part of the world; and when I return to my native land, I shall endeavour to place her under the protection of some honest man, with whom she can pass the remainder of her days in this country, much more agreeably, than it would be possible for her to do, were she to be taken down into the civilized world, to the manners, customs and language of which, she would be an entire stranger. Her mother is of the tribe of the Snare Indians, whose country lies along the Rocky Mountain. The girl is said to have a mild disposition and an even temper, which are qualities very necessary to make an agreeable woman, and an affectionate partner.

Thursday, November 7. The river froze over the last night; but we have yet had but little snow.

Saturday, March 15, 1806. This evening the northern express arrived; and I am sorry to learn that no letters have come from Athabasca, this season. This failure is owing to the great depth of snow in that quarter.—Buffaloes have been found in plenty, within a few miles of the fort, during the whole winter.

Tuesday, 25. The snow is chiefly dissolved. We have sent four men, about a day's march from this, to make sugar.

Saturday, April 19. The greater part of our Indians have gone to wage war upon the Rapid Indians, their inveterate enemies, with whom they frequently patch up a peace,

which, however, is generally of short continuance.

Monday, 28. This afternoon, the ice in
this river broke up.—A few days since, a
small war party of the Rapid Indians came
and killed several Assiniboins, who were encamped within fifteen miles of our fort. They
also stabbed an old woman in several places,
and scalped her, who, notwithstanding, is
still alive, and, to appearance, likely to recover of her wounds.

Monday, June 2. Last evening, Messrs.
J. Hughes and Alexander Stewart came here,
on horse back, from the North Branch,
which passes within fifteen miles from this.
There, they left their canoes and people;
and on their return, they will continue their
rout to the New Fort.—Mr. Smith and myself, if providence permit, are to pass the
summer at this place, where we have three
interpreters, four labouring men, and a number of women and children. As my companion is a sensible, well informed and sociable young man, I hope to pass my time
both pleasantly and profitably.

Friday, August 8. Six Assiniboins have
arrived, and inform us, that about eighty
tents of Crees and Assiniboins, with about
as many of the Black feet Indians, were on
their way to wage war with the Rapid Indians, their common enemy. But the two
former tribes quarrelled, in their march, respecting a horse, which they both claimed,

and which neither would relinquish. This circumstance occasioned a battle between them, which lasted during a day, in which twenty five of the Black feet Indians, and three of the Assiniboins, were killed. This put an end to the expedition, for this season.

Wednesday, September 3. Two men have arrived from Cumberland House, situated on Sturgeon Lake, who have brought me letters from my friends below, which communicate the melancholy intelligence, that my father, after a severe illness of but a few weeks, expired, on the 25th of June, 1805. The protector and guide of my youth, whom I revered and loved, I shall never more see in this world. It would have afforded me inexpressible satisfaction, could I have seen and conversed with him, previously to his departure. But "the Judge of the earth has done right," and "his will be done." I am not left to mourn, under this severe bereavement, without consolation; for his christian character and profession, afford the comfortable hope, that he has ceased to sin and to suffer, and now participates in blessedness, such as this miserable world cannot afford. May his pious example stimulate me, and his other children, to follow him in the path which conducts to a better world.

I have also received letters from Mr. A. N McLeod, and Mr. J. McDonald, which inform me, that I am to pass the ensuing winter at Cumberland House, for which place, I shall leave this, a few days hence.

Thursday, September 11. *Cumberland House.* I arrived here this afternoon, and find Messrs. J. Hughes, and David Thompson, &c. who have just arrived from the New Fort, and who are on their way to Fort des Prairies. The Hudson Bay people have a fort within a hundred rods of ours, in the charge of Mr. Peter Fidler.

Wednesday, 17. Sent Mons. Perâs and company, with a small assortment of goods, to go and pass the winter at Moose Lake, which is situated about two days' march from this, and nearly west from Lake Winnipick.

The Indians, who resort to this establishment, are Sauteux and Muscagoes. Moose and black bears are pretty abundant in this vicinity; and a few beavers are found. We subsist principally upon sturgeon and white fish, which we take out of the lake. Geese and bustards are numerous, in the fall and spring. The surrounding country is very low and level, so that, at some seasons, much of it is overflowed. This accounts for the periodical influx and reflux of the water, between this lake and the Sisiscatchwin River, which are distant six miles.

Friday, October 3. Hudson Bay people, in three canoes, have just arrived from York Factory. They bring late news from England; and inform us, that war continues to rage as much as ever, on the continent of Europe.

Friday, 24. We have now about four inches of snow; and, the last night, the greater part of this lake froze over.—I have sent people to the other side of this lake to fish for sturgeon, which will weigh from ten to one hundred pounds. They are taken in spread nets, which is the manner in which we generally take all kinds of fish, in this country. Some kinds, however, such as trout, cat fish and pike, we at times take, by setting hooks and lines.

Friday, January 30, 1807. Two of the Hudson Bay people arrived from Fort des Prairies, who were so obliging as to bring me letters from several gentlemen in that quarter. The greater part of the North West and Hudson Bay people, live on amicable terms; and when one can with propriety render a service to the other, it is done with cheerfulness.

Sunday, April 5. The ice in the Sisiscatchwin river, is broken up; and the great quantity of snow which has recently been dissolved, has caused that river to rise so high, as to give another course to a small river, which generally takes its water out of this lake, but which now runs into it.

Saturday, May 23. This lake is free from ice; and we have planted potatoes, and sowed our garden seeds.—Geese have returned from the south, and we now have them in plenty.

Saturday, 30. Mr. John McDonald and others, in seven canoes, have just arrived from Fort des Prairies, and are on their way to the New Fort.

Sunday, June 7. *Grand Rapid.* On the 1st inst. Mr. John McDonald, myself and other people, in seven canoes and one boat, left Cumberland House and arrived here, on the 15th, where we have ever since been, stopped by the ice in Lake Winnipick, which is not yet broken up.—We here spear as many sturgeon as we please, as they are going up or down the rapid, which is about six miles in length.

Monday, 8. *Lake Winnipick.* The last night there arose a strong north west wind, which broke up the ice, and drove it to the north east part of the lake. We, therefore, embarked this morning, and have sailed all day.

Tuesday, 16. *White River.* In the morning we left the fort, at the entrance of Lake Winnipick River, and this afternoon, Mr. A. N. McLeod and company, from Athabasca, overtook us. With this gentleman, to whom I am under many obligations, I am happy to spend an evening, after so long a separation.

Saturday, July 4. *New Fort.* Once more, I have arrived at the general rendezvous, and find myself among my friends and acquaintances, from different parts of the country.—Here I have received letters from my friends below, which inform me of their health and reasonable prosperity. It is a great satisfaction thus to hear from them; but this satisfaction would be greatly increased, could I be permitted to see and converse with them. Although the seven years, for which I was under an engagement to the North West Company, have now expired, I cannot with the least degree of propriety, as I think, gratify the ardent desire which I have of seeing my friends, by going down this year. And when the happy time will come, that I shall visit them, God only knows. It is trying to a person who has the least affection for his friends, to be separated from them, for such a series of years, in such a savage country. My duty and happiness, however, require that I endeavour to make the best of my situation. Notwithstanding the bad examples which we daily witness, a person can be as virtuous in this, as in any other part of the world. True it is, if a person were here to lead a really religious life, he would find but few associates, who would directly encourage him in his course. But this is in a great measure true in every part of the world.

Sunday, July 19. This, which was formerly called the New Fort, is now named Fort William, in honour of William McGilvray, Esq. the head agent of the North West Company. At the time of giving this name, the Company made a present to their Voyagers, of a considerable quantity of spirits, shrub, &c. and also a similar present to the Indians, encamped about the fort.

As I am still in ill health, I shall pass the winter with Doctor McLaughlin, at Sturgeon Lake, in the department of Nipigon, which lies to the north west from this.

Saturday, 25. This afternoon, in company with three canoes, I left Fort William; and we are now encamped on an island, in Lake Superiour.

Monday, August 3. *First long Portage in the Nipigon Road.* We yesterday, separated from Messrs. Chaboillez and Leith, who have gone to winter at the Pic and Michipcotton; and to day, we left Lake Superiour, and have come up a small river.

Tuesday, 4. *South west end of Lake Nipigon.* This lake is said to be one hundred and fifty miles in length, and from one, to twenty, broad. Trout are here taken, superiour to those that are found in any other part of the North West country, which will weigh upwards of seventy pounds, and are of an excellent quality.—The country through which we have passed in coming to this place from Lake Superiour, is rocky and contains but little wood, of any kind. Whortleberries are found in plenty.

Friday, 7. *Fort Duncan, at the north end of Lake Nipigon.* The surrounding country is very rough; but where the ground is arable the soil appears to be good.—Moose and carriboo are found in this vicinity; and there are, also, a few black bears, beavers, otters, muskrats, martins, &c. Great numbers of white fish are taken out of the lake, particularly in the fall of the year. These are hung up by their tails, in the open air, and are preserved good, in a frozen state, during the winter. Most people prefer those that have been thus kept, to fish that are taken immediately out of the water.

Sunday, 9. In the morning, we sent off three canoes, and in the after part of the day, some of the people returned, with the melancholy intelligence, that one of their companions was drowned, in going up a small rapid. The canoe overset, and most of the property on board, was lost. The other persons, who were in it, saved themselves by swimming to the shore.

Thursday, 13. In the morning, Mr. Holdane, the Doctor and myself, with our company, left fort Duncan, where Mr. R. McKenzie will pass the ensuing winter. There, also, we separated from two Messrs. Camerons, whose route is northward, towards Hudson's Bay. Our course is nearly south west.

Monday, 24. *Portage du Fort*, or *Sturgeon Lake*. Here, we arrived, yesterday; and this morning, Mr. Holdane and his company left us, to continue their route to Red Lake. The Doctor and I, with our company,

shall leave this tomorrow, to go and build
at the other end of this lake, which may be
about forty miles long, and from one to five
broad.—The country through which we have
passed, since we left Fort Duncan, is low and
level; no mountains, or even hills, are to
be seen; in many places it is swampy, and
small lakes and ponds and rivers and brooks
are numerous. Where the land is dry, the
soil appears to be principally a black loam.—
This tract of country was formerly well
stocked with beavers and otters; but they
have now become scarce, as they have been
hunted by the Natives, during more than the
last hundred years. Moose and carriboo are
still considerably numerous, in this region.

Tuesday, September 1. Our people are
erecting houses for our winter habitations.
We now take white fish in considerable numbers.—The Indians, who frequent this post,
are Sauteux and Muscagoes.

Saturday, October 3. We sent people to
the other end of this lake, to make a fall
fishery. They will take white fish, trout,
pike, carp, &c., which constitutes the principal food for those who are in the Nipigon
country. In this country, which is at least
seven hundred miles long and five or six
hundred broad, more people have starved to
death, than in all the rest of the Indian
country. At this lake, several years since,
eleven Canadians lost their lives for want of
food. We experience at present, no difficulty

in this respect; and I am of opinion that the distresses of our predecessors were, in a considerable measure, owing to the want of good management.

Monday, November 9. Our people have returned, and inform us, that they have caught only fourteen hundred fish of all descriptions. These, however, with what corn, flour, wild rice and meat we have, together with the trout which we hope to take with set hooks and lines, as soon as the lake is frozen over, will, we expect, furnish us with a comfortable subsistence, during the winter. We are in a solitary place, where we see no one, excepting the Natives; and they are few in number, compared with those, among whom I have formerly been. Happily for us, we have a few good books; and in perusing them, we shall pass the greater part of the time. The Doctor, who is of about the same age with myself, is an excellent companion, and fond of conversation; and I trust, that a friendly intercourse will mutually cheer our spirits, and that we shall spend the winter in a manner, that will be both pleasant and profitable.—We have now about four inches of snow, which will probably remain with us through the winter.

Sunday, 15. The last night, this lake froze over.

Friday, December 4. We now take great numbers of excellent trout from under the ice, with hooks and lines.

9

Early this morning, the woman whom I have taken to reside with me, became the mother of a boy, whom I name George Harmon.

Monday, December 28. Doctor McLaughlin, accompanied by two Canadians and one of the Natives, has gone to visit Mr. Holdane, at Red Lake.

Friday, February 19, 1808. The Doctor and company have returned, from their long jaunt; and I am happy in again enjoying his society, after a season of comparative loneliness.

Another year of my life is gone, which makes me thirty years of age. This anniversary leads me to reflect on the rapid flight of time, and the brevity of human life. When I attentively consider these things, it seems surprising that we should encounter so much difficulty and labour in the acquisition of property, which, if it could minister more effectually to our enjoyment than it does, we must very soon relinquish forever.

Friday, May 13. The Doctor, with one man in a small canoe, has set off for Fort William, where he will be wanted, as soon as he can arrive, to attend on the sick. Among the great number who visit that rendezvous every summer, there are always some, who need medical aid; though I firmly believe, that no part of the world is more healthy than this.—The Doctor has not been able to learn, to his satisfaction, what my complaint is. I think that the medicines, which I have taken, in the course of the winter, have been of essential service to me; and I hope, before long to regain my former state of good health.

The Indians of this place have subsisted, during the greater part of the past winter, upon hares.—There is an old Sauteux woman here, who compels her own son to have criminal intercourse with her.

Thursday, June 9. *Portage du Fort.* Here, we shall wait the arrival of the people of this department; and we shall then continue our route, with them to Fort William. It is nine months and fifteen days since I passed this place, the last autumn, in going into the country, which evinces that our winter has been long; and I may add too, that it has been dreary. But we have reason to be thankful to God, that we have not suffered at all, for the want of the means of subsistence.

Wednesday, 22. *Fort Duncan.* The people for whom we were waiting at Portage du Fort, arrived on the 12th, and the day following, we set out for this place, which we reached this afternoon.

Saturday, 25. Yesterday, we left fort Duncan, and came to an island in Lake Nipigon, on which we are now encamped, and where we intend to pass a few days, in fishing for trout, which are here in plenty, and are of an excellent quality.

Thursday, July 7. Yesterday morning, I arrived at Fort William, where I had only time to read my letters from my friends below, and answer them, and prepare myself for a long journey. This afternoon I embarked for Athabasca, in company with Mr. J. G. McTavish; and both of us are to remain at the place of our destination, for three years, at least.

Wednesday, 20. *Rainy Lake.* We here find all the Athabasca people, excepting one brigade, which is expected daily.

Saturday, 22. Ever since my arrival here, we have been busily employed in preparing to leave this place, for our winter quarters.

Tuesday, 26. *Rainy Lake River.* In the morning, I left the fort in company with Mr. Archibald McGillivray. Our brigade consists of ten canoes.

Friday, 29. *Portage de L'Isle,* in Winnipick River. In the morning, we met Mr. David Thomson and company from the Columbia River.

Monday, August 1. *Lake Winnipick.* This morning, we arrived at the fort on this lake, where we remained until noon. While there, I wrote to my old friend Mr. William Henry, who is at the Lower Red River. I also received a letter from him, in which he informs me, that his fort was attacked this summer, by a considerable party of Sieux. Two shots, from cannon in the block houses,

however, caused them to retire, in doing
which, they threatened that they would before long, return and make another attempt
to take the fort.—The Sieux are a numerous
tribe of Indians, who are scattered over a
large tract of land, that lies between the
Mississippi and Missouri rivers; and they are
said to be the greatest villains, in this part
of the world. They are the same tribe that
Carver distinguishes, by the name of Naudo-
wesseis.

Saturday, 6. *Grand Rapid*, at the north
west end of Lake Winnipick. The wind has
been high, during the day; and in the latter
part of it, one of our canoes filled with water.
Happily, it was near an island, when this
disaster happened. The people were, however, under the necessity of throwing a part
of their property overboard.

We find here Mons. Perigné, who was formerly a clerk to the North West Company,
but who, as he informs me, has lately been
to Canada, and has come up on his own
account. He has brought up a few goods,
to enable him to carry on a small traffick
with the Natives. He, also, intends, occasionally to hunt the beaver, &c., himself. But
I am convinced, that, at this great distance
from the place of market for furs, the trade
cannot be profitably carried on, unless it
be done on a large scale, which requires a
greater capital than an individual can embark in this undertaking. The experiment

has been made, in a number of instances; and it has uniformly failed.

Friday, 12. *Cumberland House.* From this place, I shall take a route, which I have never before travelled.

Saturday, 13. *Entrance of River Maligne,* or *Bad River.* This is a considerable river, which runs into Sturgeon Lake.

Sunday, 14. *Beaver Lake.* The greater part of the day, we have employed in coming up the river last mentioned, which, through its whole course, has a continual succession of rapids. The country around is low, and the timber, like that of the North West country generally, is small.

Tuesday, 16. *Pelican Lake.* Most of the day has been passed in crossing Lac Martin.

Wednesday, 17. *Portage du Forte de Traite,* or *Trading Fort Portage.* This was so named, from a circumstance which occurred here, thirty four years since. Mr. Joseph Frobisher and company, who were the first traders who ever came into this quarter, here met a large band of Natives, whose canoes were loaded with furs, which they were taking to York Factory, at Hudson's Bay. He succeeded in bartering his goods for their furs, which amounted to more than he could take to headquarters, the next season. He therefore built a fort, and, with his people passed several winters here; and at that time, it was the most northern post, belonging either to the North West, or the Hudson Bay Company.

All the waters from this side of the portage, pass through Lake Winnipick, and finally fall into Hudson's Bay, at York Factory. But, on the other side of the portage, which is about half a mile over, the stream, which is called Mis-sin-ni-pi or Great River, runs in a different direction, and enters Hudson's Bay, at Churchill Factory, which is the most northern post belonging to the Hudson Bay Company. The river last mentioned, is called, by the Hudson Bay people, Churchill River, and by the people from Canada, English River.

Thursday, August 18. This afternoon we obtained some dried meat from the Natives, which we find much more palatable than the salted provisions, on which we have subsisted, ever since we left Fort William. In the Interiour we never make use of salted provisions; not, however, for want of salt, which is found in most parts of the country, and which can be obtained in plenty, at all our establishments.

Tuesday, 23. *Isle à la Cross Lake.* Ever since we left Portage du Forte de Traite, we have been in what may with propriety, be called the English River, though it passes through several small lakes; and in this river, our way has been obstructed by thirty six portages.

Thursday, 25. *Isle la Cross fort.* This

fort stands on the north side of the lake of
the same name, is well built and has at-
tached to it an excellent kitchen garden.
Out of the lake, the best of white fish are
taken, during the whole year; and it is the
only place in this country, in which these
fish can be taken, at all seasons.—The Indians who come to this establishment, are
Chippewyans, in considerable numbers, and
a few Crees. I am informed that there are,
in this vicinity, many moose and cariboo,
and a few black bears, beavers, otters, cats,
&c. The country is low; and scarcely any
mountains are to be seen.

Tuesday, 30. *East end of Portage la
Loche*, or *Loach Portage*. This is so named,
from a neighbouring lake, where these fish are
taken, in abundance. This portage is twelve
miles over; and across it, the people are
obliged to transport both canoes and lading.
The road, however, is excellent, through a
level country, thinly wooded with cypress.
In coming here from Isle la Cross, we have
passed two considerable lakes, and come up
a small river, which is between those lakes.
The country through which we have passed,
is generally level, and the soil is tolerably
good. The streams, before we cross this
portage, discharge themselves into Hudson's
Bay at Churchill Factory; but afterward,
the water, after passing through Athabasca,
Great Slave, and other lakes, enters the
North Sea.

Saturday, September 3. *North west end of Portage la Loche.* We here find a small band of Chippewyans, who assist our people in transporting our property across the portage, and who supply us with provisions, which we very much need, since our former stock is nearly exhausted.

About a mile from this end of the portage is a hill, which towers majestically, to the height of a thousand feet, above the plain below; and which commands a most extensive and delightful prospect. Two lofty and extensive ridges, enclose a valley, about three miles in width, which stretches, far as the eye can reach. The Little River, which is, also, by different persons, denominated Swan, Clear water, or Pelican River, winds, in a most delightful manner, along this charming valley. The majestick forests, which wave upon these ridges, the delightful verdure of the intervening lawn, and the beautiful stream, which wanders along through it, giving a pleasing variety to the scene, until these objects become blended with the horizon, form, on the whole, the most delightful, natural scenery, that I ever beheld.

Sunday, 4. In the morning, we left the Portage; and are now in Little Athabasca River; which is about twenty rods wide.

Tuesday, 6. We are now in the Great Athabasca River, which is about three quarters of a mile in breadth. In the early part of the day, we passed the Fork, where Little

Athabasca river and Red deer, or as some call it, Elk river, form a junction.—At a small distance from Portage la Loche, the navigation of the river is interrupted by several carrying places, in about the middle of which, are some mineral springs, that are evidently impregnated with sulphur, as appears by the incrustations on their margins. At about twenty miles from the Fork, several bituminous fountains are found, into which a pole of twenty feet in length, may be plunged, without the least resistance. The bitumen, which is in a fluid state, is mixed with gum, or the resinous substance collected from the spruce fir, and is used for gumming canoes. When heated, it emits a smell, like that of sea coal.—There are some places, along this river, which are of many miles in extent, where there is scarcely a tree standing. They were killed by the fire, and were then thrown down by the winds. At these places, a few buffaloes, moose and cariboo, are found.

Wednesday, 7. *Fort Chippewyan*. This fort stands on a rocky point, at the south western end of Athabasca Lake, or, as some call it, the Lake of the Hills.—This is the general rendezvous for all Athabasca. Here the goods are set apart for all the different posts, in this extensive department; and to this place, the greater number of persons who have the charge of these posts, come every fall, to receive their merchandise from those, who have brought it from the Rainy

Lake.—This place is in N. Lat. 58° 40' and W. Long. 111°.

A few Crees, and a greater number of Chippewyans, resort to this establishment. The latter tribe were accustomed, formerly, to take their furs to Churchill Factory, at Hudson's Bay. They were, generally, six months in performing the journey; and many of them have actually starved to death, on their return home, as the country through which they passed, is almost destitute of game.—This lake is, in no part of it, more than fifteen miles wide; but it is, at least, two hundred miles long, and extends eastwardly, toward Churchill Factory.

About sixty miles from this, down Slave River, there are several places, where almost any quantity of excellent, clean, white salt may be taken, with as much ease, as sand, along the sea shore. From these places, the greater part of the North West is supplied with this valuable article.

The country around this place, is low and level, and, in the spring of the year, much of it is covered with water. A few moose are found, in this vicinity; but, the fish of the lake form the principal dependence for food, and they are abundant, and of an excellent quality.—Every fall and spring, bustards and geese are found in greater numbers, than in any other part of the North West.

Wednesday, 21. Ever since my arrival in this place, people, from almost every corner of this extensive department, have been flocking in, some of whom are from more than a thousand miles down McKenzie's River, which is nearly north west from this. Others are from Great Slave Lake and Peace River. Mr. Simon Frazer has just returned from the Pacific Ocean. The last spring, accompanied by two other gentlemen, twelve Canadians, and two of the Natives, he set out from New Caledonia, on the west side of the Rocky Mountain, on this tour. Mr. Frazer states, that his party met with some ill treatment from the Indians who live along the sea coast, but that they were hospitably received by those who reside farther up the country. The Indians in that quarter, he says, are less scattered than those who live on this side of the Rocky Mountain, and reside, not in tents, but in houses or huts, constructed of wood. He also reports, that the country through which they passed, is far from being well stocked with beavers, or any other kind of animals; and that the Natives subsist principally upon fish.

Thursday, 22. This afternoon, in company with a number of persons, in several canoes, I left Fort Chippewyan; and, after coming two miles in Athabasca Lake, we entered a small river, which is about thirty six miles long, and which now runs out of that Lake into Peace river; but, when this river is high, it discharges itself into the Lake.

Friday, 23. *Peace River*. This river is about seventy rods in breadth, and has a gentle current. It rises on the west side of the Rocky Mountain, at the distance of nearly a thousand miles from this. Below this, it assumes the name of Slave River; and, after a course of one hundred and forty or fifty miles, it discharges itself into Great Slave Lake.

Sunday, October 2. *Fort Vermillion*. To this post, great numbers of Beaver Indians bring their furs; and there are a few Iroquois, also, from Canada, who hunt in this vicinity.—About sixty miles below this, where the river is about thirty rods wide, there is a fall, of about twenty feet. Through the whole course, from this fall, nearly to the Rocky Mountain, at a little distance from the river, on each side, there are plains of considerable extent, which afford pasture for numerous herds of the buffaloe, the red deer or elk, and a few moose. Great numbers of black bears are found, that feed on the berries, which are abundant on the hills, on both sides of the river.

Friday, 7. *Encampment island Fort*. This place is, also established, for the purpose of trading with the Beaver Indians. They are the only Indians who live along this noble river, excepting a few Crees, who occasionally come to this quarter, from the Lesser Slave Lake.

Monday, 10. *Dunvegan*. This is a well

built fort, pleasantly situated, with plains on each side of the river, in N. Lat. 56° and W. Lon. 119°.

About the Fort a number of Iroquois hunters and a band of Beaver Indians, have encamped, who have been waiting our arrival, in order to obtain the articles which they need. At this place I expect to pass the ensuing winter. There will, also, be here, Messrs. D. McTavish, J. G. McTavish, J. McGillivray, thirty two labouring men, nine women and several children, which renders this place very different from my solitary abode the last winter.

Our principal food will be the flesh of the buffaloe, moose, red deer and bear. We have a tolerably good kitchen garden; and we are in no fear that we shall want the means of a comfortable subsistence. We have, also, a provision for the entertainment and improvement of our minds, in a good collection of books. The gentlemen who are to remain with me, are enlightened, sociable and pleasant companions; and I hope, therefore, to spend a pleasant and a profitable winter.

Friday, 14. This morning, my old friend Mr. F. Goedike, whom I have been happy to meet at this place, left us, with his company, for St. Johns, which is about one hundred and twenty miles up this river, where he is to pass the ensuing winter.

Saturday, November 12. About a foot of snow has fallen.

Tuesday, December 20. During the last night, this river froze over; and, at nine o'clock this morning, the thermometer was at 40 degrees below 0.

Wednesday, January 4, 1809. Sent the express to the Lesser Slave Lake, which lies about two hundred and fifty miles to the south east from this, whence it will be forwarded to Fort des Prairies.

Wednesday, March 1. A band of our Indians have come in, who went a considerable distance to the northward, the last autumn, in search of beavers. They state, that where they were, the snow fell to an extraordinary depth, in consequence of which, they suffered greatly for want of provisions. In this vicinity, the snow was, at no time, more than two feet and an half deep.

Monday, 20. The snow is fast dissolving.— Mr. A. R. McLeod and company, have just arrived from the Encampment Island; and they bring the melancholy intelligence of the death of Mr. Andrew McKenzie, natural son of Sir Alexander McKenzie. He expired at Fort Vermillion, on the 1st inst. The death of this amiable young man, is regretted by all who knew him.—They, also, inform us, that several Canadians have lost their lives by famine, in the vicinity of Great Slave Lake. Those who survived, were under the necessity of subsisting, several days, upon the flesh of their dead companions. It is reported, that one man killed his wife and child, in order to supply himself with food, who, afterwards, himself starved to death. These Canadians came up into this part of the world, *free*, to hunt the beaver, &c. and they were at too great a distance from our establishments, to receive any aid from us, until it was too late, for the greater part of them.

It is not unfrequently the case, that, the surviving part of a band of the Natives, subsist upon the flesh of their dead companions, when compelled to do it for want of other food, sufficient to sustain life. I know a woman who, it is said ate of no less than fourteen of her friends and relations, during one winter. In the summer season, the Indians can find food, almost any where; but the case is far otherwise, when the ground is covered with snow, to the depth of several feet.

Wednesday, 22. Sent people to look for birch bark, to make canoes, to take out our returns to the Rainy Lake. The greater part of the canoes, in which we bring our merchandise into the country, will not answer to transport our furs below.

Thursday, April 6. The weather is mild. The people, whom we sent for bark, have returned, with one hundred and eighty fathoms, which will make nine canoes, that will carry about two tons burthen, each. Two men will easily transport one of them on their shoulders, across the portages.

Tuesday, 11. Geese and bustards begin to come from the south.

Tuesday, 18. This morning, the ice in this river broke up.

Saturday, May 6. The surrounding plains are all on fire.—We have planted our potatoes, and sowed most of our garden seeds.— Our people are preparing to set out for the Rainy Lake.

Thursday, 11. We, yesterday, sent off eleven canoes, loaded with the returns of this place and of St. John's; and, early this morning, Messrs. D. McTavish, J. G. McTavish, F. Goedike and J. McGillivray, embarked on board of two light canoes, bound for the Rainy Lake and Fort William. But I am to pass the ensuing summer, at this place.—The last winter was, to me, the most agreeable one that I have yet spent in this country. The greatest harmony prevailed among us, the days glided on smoothly, and the winter passed, almost imperceptibly, away.

Tuesday, 16. In the morning, Messrs. Simon Frazer and James McDougall and company, arrived, in four canoes. The former gentleman came from the Rocky Mountain Portage, which is about one hundred and eighty miles, up this River. The later is from New Caledonia, on the west side of the Rocky Mountain, which is distant from this, about four hundred and fifty miles. After passing the most of the day with me, they continued their route toward the Rainy Lake.

Friday, June 2. The seeds which we sowed in the garden, have sprung up, and grow remarkably well. The present prospect is, that strawberries, red raspberries, shad berries, cherries, &c., will be abundant, this season.

This river since the beginning of May, has risen twelve feet perpendicularly; and it still continues to rise. This circumstance arises, in part, from the large quantity of rain, which has lately fallen, but more, I presume, from the dissolving of the snow, on and near the Rocky Mountain.

Tuesday, 13. An Indian has come here, who says, that one of their chiefs has lately died; and he requests that we furnish a chief's clothing to be put on him, that he may be decently interred; and, also, that we would supply a small quantity of spirits, for his relations and friends to drink, at his interment; all of which I have sent, for the deceased was a friendly Indian. Nothing pleases an Indian better, than to see his deceased relatives, handsomely attired; for he believes that they will arrive in the other world, in the same dress, with which they are clad, when they are consigned to the grave.

Wednesday, July 19. A few days since, Mr. John Stuart and company, came here, from New Caledonia, for goods; and to day, they set out on their return home. During the few days which that gentleman passed here, I derived much satisfaction from his society. We rambled about the plains, conversing as we went, and now and then stopping, to eat a few berries, which are every where to be found. He has evidently read and reflected much. How happy should I be to have such a companion, during the whole summer. But such is our mode of life in this country, that we meet but seldom; and the time that we remain together, is short. We only begin to find the ties of friendship, binding us closely together, when we are compelled to separate, not to meet again perhaps for years to come.

Baptiste La Fleur, my interpreter, will accompany Mr. Stuart and his men, as far as St. John's, in hopes of obtaining some information respecting his brother, who, it is supposed, was killed by an Indian, the last spring, while on his was from the Rocky Mountain Portage to St. John's.

Wednesday, July 19. Baptiste La Fleur has returned from St. Johns, without having been able to obtain the least intelligence, respecting his poor brother, and the two Indians, who were coming down the river, in the same canoe with him. We are, therefore, apprehensive that all three of them have been drowned, in coming down the rapids, as their canoe was made of the bark of the spruce fir tree, and was, therefore, very weak.

Friday, 21. We have cut down our barley; and I think it is the finest that I ever saw in any country. The soil on the points of land, along this river is excellent.

The mother of the chief, who died this summer, and who is far advanced in years, now remains in a tent, at the distance of a few rods from the fort. Many of the Natives, of both sexes, when they become old and infirm, and unable to travel with their relations, who depend upon the chase for subsistence, and are frequently moving from place to place, settle down near our fort; and it is easy for us to render them more effectual aid, than their friends could possibly afford them.

Almost every day, just as the sun is sinking below the horizon, the old lady, above mentioned, goes to the place where her deceased son, when alive, was accustomed to encamp, when he came to the fort, and there weeps, and sings a mournful kind of song, of which the following is a translation. "My dear son, come to me! why do you leave me, my son?" This she repeats for two hours together, in the most plaintive and melancholy tone imaginable.

It is customary for the women, among the Beaver Indians, when they lose a near relation, to cut off a joint of one of their fingers; and, in consequence of so barbarous a custom, we frequently see some of their aged women, who want the first two joints of every finger, on both hands. The men content themselves, on such occasions, by cutting off their hair, close to their heads, and by scratching or cutting their faces and arms, frequently in a most barbarous and shocking manner.

The Beaver Indians are a peaceable and quiet people, and, perhaps, the most honest of any, on the face of the earth. Theft is rarely committed among them; and when one of their tribe is known to have stolen, he is regarded with a detestation, like that which follows a highwayman in civilized countries.

Formerly, their clothing was made of the skins of the buffaloe, moose, and red deer, and their arms were bows and arrows; but the greater part of them, are now clothed with European goods, and are supplied with fire arms. They have, also, iron axes and knives, in the place of those which were made of stone and of bone.

Friday, September 1. Fowls begin to leave the north, to go to the southward.

Friday, October 6. As the weather begins to be cold, we have taken our vegetables out of the ground, which we find to have been very productive.

Saturday, 7. Mr. A. R. McLeod and company, passed this place, to-day, in three canoes, which are on their way to the Rocky Mountain Portage, and thence to New Caledonia. This gentleman delivered me letters, not only from different persons in this country, but also from my relatives below. To be informed, in this way, of the health and

prosperity of the latter, to attend to the ef-
fusions of their hearts, and a detail of many
of the circumstances of their lives, transports
me in imagination, for a short season, into
the midst of their society, and communicates a pleasure resembling that of personal
intercourse. Excellent invention of letters!
thus to enable us to keep up a kind of conversation with beloved friends, while separated from them by thousands of miles.

Sunday, February 25, 1810. On the evening of the 15th inst. my woman was delivered of two living boys. They appear,
however, to have been prematurely born;
and, from the first, little hope was entertained that they would long survive.
One of them died on the morning of the
22d, and the other the last night; and to-
day, they were both buried in the same
coffin. He who gave them life, has taken
it away. He had an undoubted right so
to do; and though his ways are to us,
inscrutable, he has the best reasons for whatever he does. It becomes us, therefore, humbly to acquiesce in this afflictive dispensation.

Thursday, May 3. This day, the ice in the
river broke up.

Tuesday, 15. Early this morning, Mr. D.
McTavish and company, set out for Fort
William; and this afternoon, Mr. J. Clarke
and company, from St. John's, passed this,
on their way to the Rainy Lake. But I

shall remain, if providence permit, at this place, during another summer. The local situation is pleasant; and we have good horses, by means of which, I can, at pleasure make excursions into the surrounding plains, over which are scattered buffaloes, moose, red deers, antelopes, black and grey bears, &c. I shall have no intelligent companion, with whom to converse. But this deficiency will be in a measure supplied, by a good collection of books, with which I am furnished. Were it not for this resource, many a dreary day would pass over me.

Tuesday, 22. Messrs. J. Stuart, and H. Faries and company, passed this place in four canoes, with the returns of New Caledonia and Rocky Mountain Portage; and, like many others, they are on their way to the Rainy Lake.

Saturday, June 23. The last night was so cold, that the tops of our potatoes were frozen. This morning, as several red deer were crossing from the opposite side of the river, one of our people leaped into a canoe, and pursued them, and succeeded in killing one of them.

Thursday, September 13. Two men have arrived from New Caledonia, who bring the disagreeable intelligence, that salmon, this season, do not come up the rivers of that region, as usual. As this kind of fish forms the principal article of food, both for the Natives and white people, it is apprehended

that they will all be under the necessity of
proceeding towards the Pacific Ocean, until
they find a people who have been more
favoured by Providence.

Wednesday, October 3. We have taken
our potatoes out of the ground, and find,
that nine bushels, which we planted the 10th
of May last, have produced a little more
than one hundred and fifty bushels. The
other vegetables in our garden have yielded
an increase, much in the same proportion,
which is sufficient proof, that the soil of the
points of land, along this river, is good.
Indeed, I am of opinion, that wheat, rye,
barley, oats, pease, &c. would grow well in
the plains around us.

Saturday, October 6. Mr. John Stuart
and company, in four canoes, have arrived
from Fort Chippewyan, having on board,
goods for the establishment at the Rocky
Mountain Portage and New Caledonia. This
gentleman delivered me a packet of letters
from home, and also a number of others
from gentlemen in this country, one of which
is a joint letter, signed by three of the partners, requesting me to go and superintend
the affairs of New Caledonia; or, if I prefer
it, to accompany Mr. Stuart, as second in
command to him, until the next spring, at
which time it is presumed, that I shall have
learned sufficient of the state of things in
that country, to assume the whole management myself. As Mr. Stuart has passed

several years in that part of the country, the information which his experience will enable him to afford me, will be of great service. I prefer, therefore, accompanying him, to going alone, especially in view of the late unfavourable reports from that country, in regard to the means of subsistence.

Wednesday, October 10. *St. John's.* On the 7th Mr. Stuart and myself, with our company, left Dunvegan; and this evening, we arrived here. The current in the river begins to be much stronger than we found it below Dunvegan. On both sides of the river, are hills of a considerable height, which are almost destitute of timber of any kind. At different places, we saw buffaloes, red deer, and bears. During our passage to this place, the weather has been bad. The snow and rain have been very unpleasant, unprotected against them, as we are, in our open canoes.

Thursday, 11. In the early part of the day, our people were busily employed in preparing provisions to take with us to New Caledonia. This afternoon, Mr. Stuart and company embarked in three canoes, for the Rocky Mountain Portage. Having a little business still to transact, I shall pass the night here.

Monday, 15. *Rocky Mountain Portage Fort.* We here find nearly eight inches of snow. Mr. Stuart and company reached here yesterday; and I arrived this morning. Be-

tween this place and St. John's, the river is
very rapid, its banks are high, and the country, on both sides of it, is generally clothed
with small timber. Ever since our arrival,
we have been employed in delivering goods
for this place, and dividing the remainder
among our people, to be taken on their
backs, to the other end of the portage, which
is twelve miles over, through a rough and
hilly country. We leave our canoes and
take others, at the other end of the carrying
place.

From the Great Slave Lake to this place,
there are few rapids, and only one fall; but
at several places, the current is very strong.
Yesterday, we came up one of these places;
and as our progress was very slow, I went
on shore alone, to walk along the beach.
Having proceeded some distance, I arrived
at a place which I could not pass, without
making a considerable turn into the woods.
I, therefore, left the side of the river, and,
after having walked a mile or two, I fell upon a well beaten footpath, which I supposed
would take me directly to the fort. After I
had followed it for several miles, I perceived
that it had been trodden by wild animals,
and was as I thought, leading me in a different direction from that which I ought to
have taken. I was unwilling to retrace my
steps; and I, therefore, proceeded in a different direction, hoping soon to come to the
river, farther up than the place where I left

it. I marched a good pace, for a considerable time, through the snow, eight inches in depth, until I found myself in a swampy country, thickly wooded, when the sun was just sinking below the horizon. Even while the light lasted, I knew not which way to steer; but it soon became so dark, that I could not distinguish any object, at the distance of more than ten yards from me. I had no means of striking fire; and without this cheering element, it would have been uncomfortable and unsafe encamping. I must have suffered severely with the cold; and might have been torn in pieces by wild beasts, which are numerous in this region. I concluded it best, therefore, to continue walking, until the light of the morning should enable me to find the bank of the river. Contrary to my expectation, however, a kind Providence directed my way, out of that dreary swamp, where at every step, I sunk up to my knees in snow, mud and water.

With great joy, about ten o'clock, I reached the river side, which I followed down, some distance, where I found our people, encamped around a large and cheering fire. During the greater part of this excursion, the rain poured down in torrents.

Wednesday, 17. *North West end of the Rocky Mountain Portage.* In the morning, Mr. S. myself and our company, left the fort; and, this evening, we reached this

place, where we find some of our people,
repairing four, crazy, old canoes, in
which, I should suppose that no one
would be willing to embark, who attaches
much value to life. The remainder of our
hands are employed in transporting our
baggage, which is still behind, to this place.
They are assisted in doing this, by some of
the Natives, who are Sicannies. They have
just returned from the other side of the
Rocky Mountain, where they go to pass the
summer months. During the winter season,
they remain on this side of the Mountain,
where they find buffaloes, moose and deer.
On the other side, none of these animals,
excepting a few straggling ones, are to be
found.

The Sicannies are a quiet, inoffensive people, whose situation exposes them to peculiar difficulties and distresses. When they
proceed to the west side of the mountain,
the Natives of that region, who are Tâcullies
and Atenâs, attack and kill many of them;
and when they are on this side, the Beaver
Indians and Crees, are continually making
war upon them. Being thus surrounded by
enemies, against whom they are too feeble
successfully to contend, they frequently suffer
much for want of food; for when on the
west side, they dare not, at all times, visit
those places, where fish are in plenty, and
when on the east side, they are frequently
afraid to visit those parts, where animals

abound. They are compelled, therefore, often-
times to subsist upon the roots, which they
find in the mountains, and which barely
enable them to sustain life; and their emaci-
ated bodies frequently bear witness, to the
scantiness of their fare.

We here begin to see lofty mountains at a
distance. This place is in the 56° of North
Latitude, and 121° of West Longitude.

Monday, 22. It has snowed and rained,
during the whole of this day.—We are now
in the heart of the Rocky Mountain, the
lofty summits of which, on each side of the
river, tower majestically toward the heavens,
and are perpetually whitened by snows,
that are never dissolved, by solar heat.
They are by far the highest mountains that
I have ever seen. The timber, which grows
upon them, is chiefly spruce fir, birch and
poplar. It is a curious fact, in the geog-
raphy of North America, that so many of
the lakes and rivers, on the west side of this
lofty range of mountains, discharge their
waters through one narrow passage, in this
great barrier, and eventually enter the North
Sea.

Wednesday, 24. Although we have found
the current in this river very strong, ever since
we left the Rocky Mountain Portage, yet,
until this day, we have found no place where
we were under the necessity of unloading our
canoes, in order to stem the current. This
afternoon, just as we got through the moun-

tain, we passed Finlay's or the North Branch,
which appears to be of about the same magnitude as the South Branch, which we are
following. These two branches take their
rise in very different directions. The source
of the South Branch, is in the Rocky Mountain, at the distance of nearly two hundred
miles from the place where we now are. The
North Branch runs out of a very large lake,
called by the Natives Musk-quâ Sâ-ky-e-gun,
or Bears Lake. This lake, which is so large
that the Indians never attempt to cross it in
their canoes, and which, those who reside at
the east end of it, affirm, extends to the
Western Ocean, is situated nearly west from
the place where the two branches form a
junction, at the distance, as is thought of
about one hundred and fifty miles. Both
branches, before their junction, run along
the foot of the mountain, as if in search of
a passage through.

Thursday, November 1. *McLeod's Lake
Fort.* This place is situated in 55° North
Latitude, and 124° West Longitude. The
country lying between this place and Finlay's Branch, is thickly covered with timber,
on both sides of the river; and, on the right,
in coming up, the land is low and level.
Mountains, it is true, are to be seen; but
they appear at a considerable distance. We
have not seen a large animal, nor even the
track of one, since we left the Rocky Mountain Portage. About twenty miles from this

place, we left Peace River, and have come up a small river, of five or six rods in breadth, which, a little below this, passes through a small lake. Here, we leave our canoes, and take our goods by land, to the establishment at Stuart's Lake, which place is situated nearly one hundred miles to the west from this. There is a passage by water to that lake; but it is so circuitous, that we could not make it in less than twelve or fifteen days.

McLeod's Lake may be sixty or seventy miles in circumference. Small white fish and trout are here taken; but those who reside here subsist, during the greater part of the year, on dried salmon, which are brought in the winter, on sledges, drawn by dogs, from Stuart's Lake.

The Indians who frequent this establishment, are Sicannies, and belong to the same tribe with those who take their furs to the Rocky Mountain Portage. Their dialect differs but little from that of the Beaver Indians. They appear to be in wretched circumstances, frequently suffering much for want of food; and they are often driven to the necessity of subsisting on roots. There are but few large animals, in this part of the country; and when the snow is five or six feet deep, as is frequently the case in the winter, few beavers can be taken, nor can many fish be caught, in this cold season of the year. Yet after all the difficulties which these people encounter, in procuring a subsistence, such is their attachment to the country that gave them birth, that they would not willingly exchange it, for any other part of the world.

Wednesday, 7. *Stuart's Lake.* This lake is called by the Natives Nuck-aws-lay, and the establishment on it, where we now are, is situated in 54° 30' North Latitude, and in 125° West Longitude. On the third instant, I left Mr. Stuart at McLeod's Lake, where he designs to pass the winter; and, accompanied by thirteen labouring men, I arrived at this place, this afternoon. In coming here, I passed over an uneven country, which is in general thickly covered with timber. We saw, on our way, several lakes or ponds, one of which was about six miles long.

This fort stands in a very pleasant place, on a rise of ground, at the east end of Stuart's Lake, which I am informed, is at least three hundred miles in circumference. At the distance of about two hundred rods from the fort, a considerable river runs out of the lake, where the Natives, who call themselves Tâcullies, have a village or rather a few small huts, built of wood. At these they remain during the season for taking and drying salmon, on which they subsist, during the greater part of the year.

Monday, 12. I have sent J. M. Quesnel, accompanied by ten labouring men, with a small assortment of goods, to Frazer's Lake, to reestablish the post there. That lake lies nearly fifty miles due west from this. We understand that the Indians, this fall, have taken and dried a considerable quantity of salmon, in that vicinity. I have also sent people to the other side of this lake, hoping they will take a few white fish, although the season, in which we usually take them, is nearly past.

Wednesday, 14. The lake, opposite to the fort, froze over the last night. To day Mr. Stuart and company, arrived from McLeod's Lake.

Saturday, 17. We have now about eight inches of snow on the ground.

Sunday, 18. Mr. Stuart and company, have gone to Frazer's Lake. I accompanied them to the other side of this lake, where I saw all the Indians belonging to the village in this vicinity. They amount to about one hundred souls, are very poorly clothed, and, to us, appear to be in wretched circumstances; but they are, notwithstanding, contented and cheerful. My interpreter informs me, that their language strongly resembles that spoken by the Sicannies; and no doubt they formerly constituted a part of the same tribe, though they now differ from them, in their manners and customs. The Sicannies bury, while the Tâcullies, burn their dead.

Monday, 26. The corpse of a woman of this place, who died on the 20th instant, was burned this afternoon. While the ceremony

II

was performing, the Natives made a terrible savage noise, by howling, crying, and a kind of singing.

Saturday, December 29. *Frazer's Lake.* In coming to this place, I passed through a country, which is very rough, and thickly covered with timber, consisting of spruce, fir, poplar, aspin, birch, cypress, &c. We crossed one considerable mountain, and several small lakes.

This establishment is at the east end of Frazer's Lake, which received its name from that of the gentleman, who first built here, in 1806. At the distance of about a mile from this, there runs out of this lake, a considerable river, where the Natives have a large village, and where they take and dry salmon. This lake may be eighty or ninety miles in circumference, and is well supplied with white fish, trout, &c.

Tuesday, January 1, 1811. This being the first day of another year, our people have passed it, according to the custom of the Canadians, in drinking and fighting. Some of the principal Indians of this place, desired us to allow them to remain at the fort, that they might see our people drink. As soon as they began to be a little intoxicated, and to quarrel among themselves, the Natives began to be apprehensive, that something unpleasant might befal them, also. They, therefore hid themselves under beds, and elsewhere, saying, that they thought the white people had run mad, for they appeared not to know what they were about. They perceived that those who were the most beastly in the early part of the day, became the most quiet in the latter part, in view of which, they exclaimed, "the senses of the white people have returned to them again," and they appeared not a little surprised at the change; for, it was the first time, that they had ever seen a person intoxicated.

Sunday, 27. This day the Natives have burned the corpse of one of their chiefs, who died in the early part of this month. Shortly after his death, one of his nieces painted her face with vermillion; and, in other respects arrayed herself in the gayest manner possible. Her mother, observing this unbecoming conduct, reproved her in the following manner. "Are you not ashamed, my daughter," said she, "to appear so gaily clad, so soon after the decease of your uncle? You ought rather to daub your face with black, and to cut your hair short to your head." This reproach for the apparent destitution of natural affection, so afflicted the girl, that, soon after, she went into a neighbouring wood, and hung herself, from the limb of a tree. Happily for her, however, some people passed that way, before she had long been in this situation, and took her down. She was, at first, senseless; but soon after recovered.— Instances of suicide, by hanging, frequently occur, among the women of all the tribes, with whom I have been acquainted; but the men are seldom known to take away their own lives.

Wednesday, 30. Two nights since, an Indian cut a hole in a window in my room, which is made of parchment, at the distance of not more than two feet from the foot of my bed, where I lay asleep, and took from a table, near it, several articles of clothing. The next morning, two other Indians brought back to me a part of the stolen property, and informed me who the thief was, and where he could be found. Soon after, accompanied by my interpreter, I went, and found the young villain, in a hut under ground, along with about twelve others, who are as great thieves as himself. I told him, that, as he was young, I hoped this was the first time he had ever been guilty of theft; and, provided he would return all the property which he had taken away, I would forgive this offence; but if he should ever in future be guilty of any misconduct toward us, he might depend on being severely punished. I then returned to our house; and, shortly after, two Indians brought me the remainder of the property which had been stolen, and I gave them a little ammunition, for having made known the thief.—Nearly all the Tâcullies, or Carriers as we call them, are much addicted to pilfering; but there are few among them who dare steal from us.

Friday, *February* 15. Yesterday and to-day, we found the cold to be more intense, than at any other time this season.

Monday, 18. Baptiste Bouchè, my interpreter, has taken the daughter of one of the Carrier chiefs, as a wife. She is the first woman of that tribe, ever kept by any of the white people.

Friday, April 5. *Stuart's Lake.* In the morning, I left and abandoned the post at Frazer's Lake, and arrived here this evening.

Monday, 15. The weather is pleasant, and seems to presage an early spring.—Swans and ducks of several kinds, have passed the winter with us; but bustards and geese, now first begin to make their appearance.

Sunday, 21. A few days since, I sent the greater part of my people to McLeod's Lake, to prepare for the voyage from that place to the Rainy Lake. Tomorrow, I shall leave this place myself, in company with Mr. Quesnel and others, for McLeod's Lake. I shall take with me my little son George, who was three years old last December, for the purpose of sending him to my friends in the United States, in order that he may receive an English education. Mr. J. M. Quesnel will have the care of him, until he shall arrive at Montreal.

Wednesday, 24. *McLeod's Lake.* I find Mr. Stuart and the men very busy, in preparing for the voyage to the Rainy Lake.— The spring here is less advanced, by fifteen days, than it was at Stuart's Lake. This great difference of climate, I conclude, is owing to the fact, that this place lies nearer the mountains.

Wednesday, May 8. People have just arrived from Stuart's Lake, who inform me that the mother of my son was delivered on the 25th ultimo, of a daughter, whom I name Polly Harmon.

As the ice in Peace River begins to be bad, it is expected that a few days hence the navigation will be opened, when Messrs. Stuart, Quesnel, and their company, will embark, with the returns of this place, for the Rainy Lake. Tomorrow, I design to return to Stuart's Lake, where I expect to pass the ensuing summer. But my attention is chiefly taken up with the separation, which is soon to take place between me and my beloved son. A few months hence, he will be at a great distance from his affectionate father; and, it may be, I shall never more see him, in this world. No consideration could induce me to send him down, especially while he is so young, excepting the thought, that he will soon be under the fostering care of my kind relatives, who will be able to educate him much better than it would be possible for me to do, in this savage country. As I do that which I apprehend will be for the benefit of my little son, so I earnestly pray, that God would graciously protect him, in his absence from me.

Sunday, 12.   *Stuart's Lake.*   Here, I arrived this afternoon, after having passed four of the most disagreeable days that I ever experienced. My spirits were dejected, in view of the departure of my child; the snow, which was three feet in depth, had become softened by the late warm weather, so that walking was attended with great fatigue; I broke my snow shoes, on the way, which the Indian lad with me mended as well as our circumstances would permit, though but poorly; and finally we had scarcely any thing to eat. I am happy, therefore, to find myself at a place where I can enjoy a little repose, after such an unpleasant jaunt.

Tuesday, 21. This afternoon, the ice in this lake broke up. Musquetoes begin to come about; and troublesome companions they are in the wilderness.

Wednesday, 22. As the frost is now out of the ground, we have planted our potatoes, and sowed barley, turnips, &c. which are the first that we ever sowed, on this west side of the mountain.—We now take trout in this lake, with set hooks and lines, in considerable numbers; but they are not of a good kind.— It is, perhaps, a little remarkable, that pike or pickerel have never been found in any of the lakes and rivers, on the west side of the Rocky Mountain.

Tuesday, June 11. Three Indians have arrived from Sy-cus, a village, lying about one hundred and thirty miles down this river, who say, that it is reported by others, from farther down, that there is a very extraordinary and powerful being on his way here, from the sea, who, when he arrives, will transform me into a stone, as well as perform many other miraculous deeds; and the simple and credulous Natives fully believe this report.

Sunday, 16. A number of Indians have arrived, in six large wooden canoes, from the other end of this lake; and among them are two, a father and his son, who say, that they belong to a tribe, who call themselves Nâte-ote-tains. These are the first of that nation, whom we have ever seen here. They state, that their tribe is numerous, and scattered, in villages, over a large extent of country, lying directly west from this; and that it is not more than five or six days' march, to their nearest village. They, also, inform us, that a large river passes through their country, and at no considerable distance from it, enters the Pacific Ocean. They, likewise, say, that a number of white people come up that river, in barges, every autumn, in order to trade with the Indians, who reside along its shores. But I could not learn from them, to what nation those white people belong. I imagine, however, that they are Americans, who come round Cape Horn, to carry on, what is called a coasting trade; for, I cannot learn that they ever attempted to make establishments, along the sea coast.

Tuesday, July 2. Yesterday, five Sicannies

came here, from McLeod's Lake, who form a small war party. Their leader, or war chief desired me to allow them to go where they might think proper; upon which, I inquired of them, whither they wished to direct their course, and what their business was. The speaker replied, that, when they left their lands, their intention was to go and try to take a scalp or two from the Indians of Frazer's Lake, "who," he added, "have done us no injury. But we have lost a relation; and we must try to revenge his death, on some one."—This is a custom common to a greater or less extent to all the tribes.

I asked him whether he supposed that we supplied them with guns and ammunitions, to enable them to destroy their fellow creatures, or to kill the beaver, &c. I added, that should they, in the fall, bring in an hundred scalps, they could not, with them all, procure a pint of rum, or a pipe full of tobacco; but, if they would bring beaver skins, they would able to purchase the articles which they would need. After reflecting for some time on what I had said, the speaker informed me, that they would, in compliance with my advice, return and hunt the beaver; and they performed their promise, by proceeding immediately to their own lands.

Monday, 29. Several days since, one of our men, who remains at McLeod's Lake, came here with the information, that there were Indians lurking around that fort, wait-

ing, as was supposed, for a favourable opportunity to attack it. I, accordingly, went
over, hoping that I should be able to ascertain who they were; but I have not been
able to obtain the least information respecting them. Probably, they had not courage
to make the attack, and have returned to
their own lands.

Shad berries begin to ripen, which is about
twenty days later than they ripen, in the
same Latitude, on the east side of the Rocky
Mountain.

Friday, August 2. Our whole stock of
provisions in the fort, for ten persons, consists of five salmon, only. It is impossible,
at this season, to take fish out of this lake
or river. Unless the salmon from the sea,
soon make their appearance, our condition
will be deplorable.

Saturday, 10. Sent all our people, consisting of men, women, and children, to
gather berries at Pinchy, a village about
twelve miles distant from this, toward the
other end of this lake. At no great distance
from that village, as I am informed, there is
a small lake, out of which the Natives take
small fish, which very much resemble a salmon in shape and in flavour, which are not
more than six inches long. They are said to
be very palatable; but, if they were not so,
they would be very acceptable to us, in our
present circumstances.

Thursday, 22. One of the Natives has

caught a salmon, which is joyful intelligence
to us all; for we hope and expect, that, in a
few days, we shall have them in abundance.
These fish visit, to a greater or less extent,
all the rivers in this region, and form the
principal dependence of the inhabitants, as
the means of subsistence.

Monday, September 2. We now have the
common salmon in abundance. They weigh
from five to seven pounds. There are, also,
a few of a larger kind, which will weigh
sixty or seventy pounds. Both of them are
very good, when just taken out of the water.
But, when dried, as they are by the Indians
here, by the heat of the sun, or in the smoke
of a fire, they are not very palatable. When
salted, they are excellent.

As soon as the salmon come into this lake,
they go in search of the rivers and brooks,
that fall into it; and these streams they
ascend so far as there is water to enable
them to swim; and when they can proceed
no farther up, they remain there and die.
None were ever seen to descend these streams.
They are found dead in such numbers, in
some places, as to infect the atmosphere,
with a terrible stench, for a considerable
distance round. But, even when they are in
a putrified state, the Natives frequently
gather them up and eat them, apparently,
with as great a relish, as if they were fresh.

Tuesday, 17. Between nine and ten
o'clock, this forenoon, the sun was eclipsed,

for nearly half an hour, which event alarmed the Natives greatly; for they considered it as foreboding some great calamity, about to fall upon them. They therefore cried and howled, making a savage noise. Their priests or magicians took their hands full of swan's down, and blew it through their hands toward the sun, imploring that great luminary to accept of the offering, thus made to him, to be put on the head of his sons, when engaged in dancing, and to spare the Indians. They suppose that the sun has children, who, like those of the Carriers, are fond of putting swan's down on their heads, when they dance.—I explained to them the cause of the darkness; at which they appeared both pleased and astonished, and acknowledged that my account of the subject was rational, but wondered how I could obtain a knowledge of such hidden and mysterious things.

Monday, 23. Bustards and geese begin to come from the north.

In the early part of the day, I found it necessary to chastise the chief of this village, with considerable severity. He is the first Indian that I have ever struck during a residence of eleven years, in this savage country.

The following circumstances attended this transaction. The name of the Indian, who was chastised, was Quâs. He had a friend, who was a worthless fellow, to whom he wished me to advance goods on credit, which

I declined doing for two reasons. The first was, that I did not believe that the Indian would ever pay me for them. The other was, that Quâs wished to make the Indians believe, that he had a great deal of influence over us, which would be prejudicial to our interest, if he should effect it. He tried every method, which he could devise, to persuade me to advance the goods, but to no purpose; for I perceived what was his object. He then told me, that he saw no other difference between me and himself, but this only: 'you,' said he, 'know how to read and write; but I do not. Do not I manage my affairs as well, as you do yours? You keep your fort in order, and make your slaves,' meaning my men, 'obey you. You send a great way off for goods, and you are rich and want for nothing. But do not I manage my affairs as well as you do yours? When did you ever hear that Quâs was in danger of starving? When it is the proper season to hunt the beaver, I kill them; and of their flesh I make feasts for my relations. I, often, feast all the Indians of my village; and, sometimes, invite people from afar off, to come and partake of the fruits of my hunts. I know the season when fish spawn, and, then send my women with the nets which they have made, to take them. I never want for any thing, and my family is always well clothed."—In this manner, the fellow proceeded, for a considerable time.

I told him that what he had said, concerning himself and his family, was true; yet,
I added, 'I am master of my own property,
and shall dispose of it as I please.' 'Well,'
said he, 'have you ever been to war?' 'No,'
replied I, 'nor do I desire to take the life of
any of my fellow creatures.' 'I have been to
war,' continued he, 'and have brought home
many of the scalps of my enemies.' I was
now strongly tempted to beat him, as his
object manifestly was, to intimidate me. But
I wished to avoid a quarrel, which might be
evil in its consequences; and especially to
evince to the Indians, who were spectators of
what passed between us, that I was disposed
to live in peace with them.—Quâs proceeded
to try me another way. He asked me if I
would trust him with a small piece of cloth, to
make him a breech cloth? This I consented
to do, and went into the store, to measure it
off. He followed me together with my interpreter, and ten or twelve other Indians. I
took up a piece of cloth, and asked him, if he
would have it from that? He answered, no.
I then made a similar inquiry, respecting another piece, to which he made a similar reply.
This persuaded me, that his only object was
to provoke me to quarrel with him. I, therefore, threw down the cloth, and told him, if
he would not have that, he should have
this, (meaning a square yard stick which I
had in my hand) with which I gave him a
smart blow over the head, which cut it, con-

siderably. I then sprang over the counter,
and pelted him, for about five minutes, during which time, he continually called to his
companions, all of whom had knives in their
hands, to come and take me off. But, they
replied that they could not, because there
were two other white people in the room, who
would prevent them. It was happy for us
that these Indians stood in such fear of us;
for there were only four white men, at this
time in the fort, and they could easily have
murdered us.—As Quâs and his company left
us, he told me that he would see me again
tomorrow, when the sun should be nearly in
the south, meaning between ten and twelve
o'clock.

Monday, October 7. The next day after I
chastised the Indian, as above described, he
sent one of his wives to request me, either to
come and see him, or to send him some
medicine. I, therefore, sent him some salve,
with which to dress the wound in his head.—
A few days after, he became so well as to be
able to hunt; and he killed and brought
home a number of beavers, with which he
yesterday made a feast. He sent an invitation to me to attend this feast; and I concluded that it would be necessary for me to
go, or he might think that I was afraid of
him. I, accordingly, put a brace of pistols in
my pocket, and hung a sword by my side,
and directed my interpreter to arm himself in
a similar manner, and to accompany me. We

proceeded to the house of the chief, where we found nearly an hundred Indians, assembled. As soon as we arrived, he requested us to be seated. He then rose, and stood in the middle of the circle, formed by the guests, and with a distinct and elevated voice, made a long harangue, in which he did not forget to make mention of the beating which he had lately received from me. He said, if it had been given to him by any person but the Big Knife (the name which they give to me) he would have either lost his own life, or have taken that of the person attacking him. But now, he said, he considered himself as my *wife;* for that was the way, he said, that he treated his women (of whom he has four) when they behave ill. He said, that he thanked me for what I had done, for it had given him sense.—To this I replied, that, in a remote country, I had left my friends and relations, who wanted for none of the good things of this world, and had come a great distance, with such articles as the Indians greatly needed, and which I would exchange for their furs, with which I could purchase more; and in this way, I could always supply their necessities; that I considered the Indians as my children, and that I must chastise them when they behaved ill, because it was for their good. 'You all know,' said I, 'that I treat good Indians well, and that I strive to live in peace with you.'—'Yes,' replied the father-in-law to the chief, 'Big Knife speaks the truth. My son had no sense, and vexed him, and therefore deserved the beating which he has received.'—Quâs then told the Indians, that if he ever heard of any of them laughing at him for the beating which he had received, he would make them repent of their mirth.

After this the feast was served up in a manner, which I shall describe in another place.—It will be seen, by this account, that the white people have a great ascendency over the Indians; for, I believe that this chief is not destitute of bravery. But it is very necessary, in order to secure ourselves from aggression, that we manifest that we are not afraid of them.

Saturday, 12. During the last three days, it has snowed continually; and it has fallen to the depth of nearly two feet.

Monday, 21. We have now in our store, twenty five thousand salmon. Four in a day are allowed to each man.—I have sent some of our people to take white fish.

Thursday, 31. Two men have arrived from McLeod's Lake, and have delivered me several letters, one of which, from Mr. James McDougall, who accompanied our people from the Rainy Lake, informs me, that the canoes were stopped by the ice, on the 12th inst. about three days' march below McLeod's Lake, where they still remain, together with the property which they had on board.

Saturday, November 16. Our fishermen

have returned to the fort, and inform me
that they have taken seven thousand white
fish. These fish, which, singly, will weigh
from three to four pounds, were taken in nine
nets, of sixty fathoms each.

Sunday, 17. Clear and cold. The last
night, the lake, opposite to the fort, froze
over.—The greater part of the snow, which
fell in October, is now dissolved.

Friday, December 13. On the 20th ult. I
set off, accompanied by twenty of my people,
for the goods which were stopped by the taking of the ice in Peace River, the last October.
We all returned this evening accompanied by
Mr. McDougall, who has come to pass the
holidays with us. Our goods were drawn on
sledges by dogs. Each pair of dogs drew a
load of from two hundred, to two hundred
and fifty pounds, besides provisions for themselves and their driver, which would make the
whole load about three hundred pounds. I
have seen many dogs, two of which would
draw on a sledge, five hundred pounds,
twenty miles, in five hours. For a short distance, two of our stoutest dogs will draw
more than a thousand pounds weight. In
short, there is no animal, with which I am
acquainted, that would be able to render half
the service that our dogs do, in this country,
where the snow is very deep in the winter
season. They sink but little into it, in following a person on snow shoes.

Wednesday, January 1, 1812. This being

the first day of the year, Mr. McDougall and I dined with all our people, in the hall. After our repast was ended, I invited several of the Sicanny and Carrier chiefs, and most respectable men, to partake of the provisions which we had left; and I was surprised to see them behave with much decency, and even propriety, while eating, and while drinking a flagon or two of spirits.

After they had finished their repast, they smoked their pipes, and conversed rationally, on the great difference which there is, between the manners and customs of civilized people, and those of the savages. They readily conceded, that ours are superior to theirs.

Tuesday, 7. On the 4th inst. accompanied by several of our people, I set off for Tachy, a village, toward the other end of this lake. We there saw a number of Indians, who appear to be very indolent, and who are, of course, wretchedly clad, and not better fed. From that place, we proceeded up a considerable river, about half a day's march, to another village, inhabited chiefly by Sicannies, who appear to be more industrious than the inhabitants of the former village; and, therefore, they are better clothed, and live more comfortably. Their principal food consists of salmon, white fish, and trout; and they, at times, kill a beaver, or a cariboo. The country around the lake is hilly; but, on both sides of this river, it is level; and from the appearance of the timber which grows on it, I should think that the soil is not bad.

Monday, 13. On the 9th inst. a Sicanny died at this place; and the following circumstances attended his incineration, to day.—The corpse was placed on a pile of dry wood, with the face upwards, which was painted and bare. The body was covered with a robe, made of beaver skins, and shoes were on the feet. In short, the deceased was clothed in the same manner as when alive, only a little more gaily. His gun and powder horn, together with every trinket which he had possessed, were placed by his side. As they were about to set fire to the wood, on which the deceased lay, one of his brothers asked him if he would ever come among them again; for, they suppose that the soul of a person, after the death of the body, can revisit the earth, in another body. They must, therefore, believe in the immortality, though they connect with it the transmigration, of the soul.

The deceased had two wives, who were placed, the one at the head, and the other at the foot of the corpse; and there they lay until the hair of their heads was nearly consumed by the flames, and they were almost suffocated by the smoke. When almost senseless, they rolled on the ground, to a little distance from the fire. As soon as they had recovered a little strength, they stood up, and began to strike the burning corpse with both their hands alternately; and this disgusting, savage ceremony was continued, until the body was nearly consumed. This operation was interrupted by their frequent turns of fainting, arising from the intensity of the heat. If they did not soon recover from these turns, and commence the operation of striking the corpse, the men would seize them by the little remaining hair on their heads, and push them into the flames, in order to compel them to do it. This violence was especially used toward one of the wives of the deceased, who had frequently run away from him, while he was living.

When the body was nearly burned to ashes, the wives of the deceased gathered up these ashes, and the remaining pieces of bones, which they put into bags. These bags they will be compelled to carry upon their backs, and to lay by their sides, when they lie down at night, for about two years. The relations of the deceased will then make a feast, and enclose these bones and ashes in a box, and deposit them under a shed, erected for that purpose, in the centre of the village. Until this time, the widows are kept in a kind of slavery, and are required to daub their faces over with some black substance, and to appear clothed with rags, and frequently to go without any clothing, excepting round their waists. But, at the time of this feast, they are set at liberty from these disagreeable restraints.

Thursday, 30. On the 17th inst. accompanied by Mr. McDougall, twelve of my men and two carriers, I set out on a journey to the territory of the Nâte-ote-tains, a tribe of Indians, who have never had any intercourse with white people, and few of whom have ever seen them. After travelling, with all possible expedition, during seven days, generally on lakes, we arrived at their first village. The inhabitants were not a little surprised and alarmed to see people come among them, whose complexion was so different from their own. As their village stands on a rise of ground, near to a large lake, they saw us coming, when we were at a considerable distance from them; and the men, women and children came out to meet us, all of whom were armed, some with bows and arrows, and others with axes and clubs. They offered no offence; but, by many savage gestures they manifested a determination to defend themselves, in case they were attacked. We soon dissipated their fears, by informing them, that we came not to make war upon them, but to supply them with articles which they needed, and to receive their furs in exchange. They treated us with much respect and with great hospitality.

The day following, we proceeded on our route, and, during our progress, we saw four more of their villages. At the second of these, we found the two men who, the last summer, visited my fort. These people were not, therefore, surprised at seeing us among them; for, I had promised these two men, that, in the course of the winter, I would visit their country. They gave us the same account as they had before given at the fort, of the white people, who come up a large river, already mentioned. And to convince us of the truth of the account, they showed us guns, cloth, axes, blankets, iron pots, &c. which they obtained from their neighbours, the Atenâs, who purchase them directly of the white people.

The five villages which we visited, contain about two thousand inhabitants, who are well made and robust. They subsist principally on salmon, and other small fish. The salmon here have small scales, while those at Stuart's Lake, have none.—The clothing of these people, is much like that of the Carriers. I procured from them vessels, curiously wrought, of the smaller roots of the spruce fir, in different shapes. Some of them are open, like a kettle, and will hold water. They also, let me have a blanket or rug, which was manufactured by the Atenâs, of the wool of a kind of sheep or goat. These animals are said to be numerous, on the mountains, in their country.—They told us that we had seen but a small part of the Nâte-ote-tains, who, they say, are a numerous tribe. They speak a language peculiar to themselves, though the greater part of them understand that, spoken by the Carriers.

The country, which we travelled over, in this route, is generally level. Few mountains are to be seen. A heavy growth of timber evinces, that the soil is good.—We saw no large animals, excepting the cariboo; but we were informed, that black bears, and other kinds of the larger animals, exist in considerable numbers, in that region.

Sunday, February 23. I have just returned from a jaunt of eight days, to Frazer's Lake and Stillâ. The latter place lies about twenty miles beyond the former. Wherever we went, the Natives, as usual, appeared to be pleased to see us, and treated us hospitably.

Monday, April 6. Six Indians have arrived from Frazer's Lake, who delivered to me a letter, written by Mr. David Thompson, which is dated August 28th, 1811, at Ilk-koy-ope Falls, on the Columbia River. It informs me, that this gentleman, accompanied by seven Canadians, descended the Columbia River, to the place where it enters the Pacific Ocean, where they arrived on the 16th of July. There they found a number of people, employed in building a fort for a company of Americans, who denominate themselves the Pacific Fur Company. He also writes, that Mr. Alexander McKay and others, have proceeded to the northward, in the vessel that brought them there, on a coasting trade.—Mr. Thompson, after having remained seven days with the American people, set out on his return to his establishments, which

are near the source of the Columbia River.
From one of these posts, he wrote the letter
above mentioned, and delivered it to an Indian, to bring to the next tribe, with the
direction, that they should forward it to the
next, and so on, until it should reach this
place. This circumstance accounts for the
great length of time, that it has been on the
way; for the distance that it has come, might
be travelled over, in twenty five or thirty
days.

Monday, May 11. This morning I returned
from McLeod's Lake, where I have been to
send off my people, who are to go to the
Rainy Lake. While there, one of my men,
Pieere Lambert, while crossing a small lake
on a sledge, fell through the ice; and, before
his companions who were near could ex-
tricate him, he was drowned. The day following, his corpse was brought to the fort and
interred.

On my way home, the walking was exceedingly bad. The snow was three feet deep,
and the weather was so mild, that it had
become very soft. About ten miles from this
place, I left my guide, and came on forward
of him. I had not proceeded far, before I
wandered from my proper course. I might
have followed my tracks back; but this I was
unwilling to do, and I continued, therefore
to wander about during the remainder of the
day. The night came upon me, while I was
in a thick wood; and, as I had nothing to

eat, I could only kindle up a fire, and endeavour to solace myself, by smoking my
pipe.—I passed the greater part of the night
in melancholy reflections on the unpleasant
condition, into which I had brought myself,
by leaving my guide. Very early in the morning, I left my fire, and commenced travelling,
without knowing what direction to take.
The sun was concealed by clouds, and the
rain fell copiously. Before I had gone far, I
perceived, at no great distance from me, a
pretty high hill, which I at length ascended,
with much difficulty. From its summit, I was
cheered by a prospect of this lake, at a considerable distance from me. Having ascer-
tained the course which I must take, I descended into the valley, and took the following method to keep in the direction to the
fort. I at first marked a tree; and from
that, singled out one forward of me, to
which I proceeded; and by means of these
two fixed upon another, in a straight line
ahead; and continued the same operation,
for several hours, until, with great joy, I
reached the fort. And now, therefore, I desire
to return thanks to kind Providence, for
having once more directed my steps to my
home and my family.

Thursday, 21. The last night, an east
wind drove the ice to the other end of the
lake.

Tuesday, 23. This morning, the Natives
caught a sturgeon that would weigh about

two hundred and fifty pounds. We frequently see in this lake, those which are much larger, which we cannot take, for the want of nets, sufficiently strong to hold them.

Saturday, August 15. Salmon begin to come up this river. As soon as one is caught the Natives always make a feast, to express their joy at the arrival of these fish. The person, who first sees a salmon in the river, exclaims, Tâ-loe nas-lay! Tâ-loe nas-lay! in English, Salmon have arrived! Salmon have arrived! and the exclamation is caught with joy, and uttered with animation, by every person in the village.

Wednesday, September 2. Mr. McDougall and company, who came here on the 25th ult. set out this morning, on their return home, to McLeod's Lake. This visit has afforded me much satisfaction. In this lonely part of the world, we enjoy the pleasures of social intercourse, when we are permitted to spend a little time with a friend, with the highest relish.

Sunday, October 25. Early this morning, my people returned from the Rainy Lake. By them I have received letters from home, which have given me more satisfaction than I can express. My friends are in good health, and my beloved son George has arrived safely among them. For these blessings, I cannot be sufficiently thankful, unless a merciful God is graciously pleased to change my heart of stone into a heart of flesh.

Friday, November 6. We have now about six inches of snow on the ground.—On the 27th ult. I set out for McLeod's Lake, where I arrived on the 29th. I there found Mr. John Stuart, who, with his company, arrived the day before, from Fort Chipewyan. His men are on their way to the Columbia River, down which they will proceed under Mr. J. G. McTavish. The coming winter, they will pass near the source of that river. At the Pacific Ocean, it is expected that they will meet Donald McTavish, Esq., and company, who were to sail from England, last October, and proceed round Cape Horn to the mouth of Columbia River. This afternoon Mr. Stuart and myself, with our company, arrived at this place, (Stuart's Lake) where both of us, God willing, shall pass the ensuing winter. With us, are twenty-one labouring men, one interpreter, and five women, besides children.

Saturday, January 23, 1813. On the 29th ult. Mr. Stuart and myself, with the most of our people, went to purchase furs and salmon, at Frazer's Lake and Stillâs. The last fall, but few salmon came up this river. At the two places, above mentioned, we were so successful as to be able to procure a sufficient quantity. While at Frazer's Lake Mr. Stuart, our interpreter and myself, came near being massacred by the Indians of that place, on account of the interpreter's wife, who is a native of that village. Eighty or

ninety of the Indians armed themselves, some
with guns, some with bows and arrows, and
others with axes and clubs, for the purpose
of attacking us. By mild measures, however,
which I have generally found to be the best,
in the management of the Indians, we succeeded in appeasing their anger, so that we
suffered no injury; and we finally separated,
to appearance, as good friends, as if nothing
unpleasant had occurred. Those who are
acquainted with the disposition of the Indians
and who are a little respected by them, may,
by humouring their feelings, generally, controul them, almost as they please.

Sunday, February 21. *Rocky Mountain
Portage Fort.* Here I arrived this afternoon,
accompanied by five Canadians and one
Carrier. We left Stuart's Lake on the 6th
inst. and are on our way to Dunvegan, where
I am going to transact some business with
Mr. John McGillivray, who is there. As the
mountains, on both sides of the river, for
the distance of seventy or eighty miles, are
very lofty, there is generally a strong wind
passing, either up or down the stream, which,
at this season, renders it extremely cold and
disagreeable travelling. On the 18th, we
were in the heart of those mountains; and
we had to encounter such a strong head
wind, that my upper lip became very much
frozen, without my having perceived it at
the time. It is now much swollen, and very
painful. We all caught severe colds, in con-

sequence of a fall of snow upon us, to the
depth of eight inches, after we had encamped
and resigned ourselves to sleep, the second
night after leaving Stuart's Lake; and I have
become unable to speak, excepting in a
whisper. It requires indeed, a strong con-
stitution, to conflict with the hardships,
incident to our mode of life.

We here find no person, excepting two Canadians. Mr. A. R. McLeod, who has charge
of this place, is now absent on a visit to his
hunter's tent, which is five days' march from
this. From such a distance, provisions are
obtained for this post, as there are very few
large animals at this season, in this vicinity,
in consequence, I presume, of the great depth
of snow, which always falls in places, so near
the mountain, as this. The people who are
here say, that the hunters had such difficulty
in finding animals of any kind, the last fall,
that they all passed five days, without any
kind of food.

Monday, March 1. *Dunvegan.* I have, at
length, reached this place, where I passed the
years 1809 and 1810, and revisiting it, many
a pleasing scene is recalled by memory, and
many hours of agreeable conversation, which
I passed, with the gentlemen who were then
here, rise fresh to my recollection.—Mr. Mc-
Gillivray is now absent, on a visit to the
Lesser Slave Lake; and Mr. Collin Campbell
has charge of the fort.

Sunday, 14. Mr. McGillivray returned, on

the 10th inst. He is an amiable and excellent man; and I have enjoyed his society, during my short stay here, very highly. Having completed my business here, I shall set out tomorrow, on my return to Stuart's Lake. I here received the intelligence, that Niagara and Makana had surrendered to the British forces; but not before many valuable lives were lost, on both sides.

Sunday, April 4. Stuart's Lake. We left Dunvegan on the 16th ult. and arrived here this evening, without having experienced any disaster by the way.

Saturday, May 1. Present appearances justify the expectation, that the ice in the river will soon break up, so that our people will be able to commence their journey to the Rainy Lake with our returns, all of which we have sent to McLeod's Lake, together with letters to people in this country, and to our friends in the civilized part of the world.

Thursday, 13. The weather is fine. In the early part of the day, Mr. J. Stuart, accompanied by six Canadians and two of the Natives, embarked on board of two canoes, taking with him a small assortment of goods, as a kind of pocket money, and provisions sufficient for a month and a half. They are going to join Mr. J. G. McTavish and his company, at some place on the Columbia River; and to proceed with them to the ocean. Should Mr. Stuart be so successful as to discover a water communication, between

this and the Columbia, we shall, for the
future, obtain our yearly supply of goods
by that route, and send our returns out that
way, to be shipped directly for China, in
vessels which the company, in that case,
design to build on the North West coast.
While the execution of this comprehensive
plan is committed to others, my more humble
employment, in which, however, I am quite
as sure of being successful, is to be, the superintendence of the affairs of New Caledonia.

No other people, perhaps, who pursue business to obtain a livelihood, have so much
leisure, as we do. Few of us are employed
more, and many of us much less, than one
fifth of our time, in transacting the business
of the Company. The remaining four fifths
are at our own disposal. If we do not, with
such an opportunity, improve our under
standings, the fault must be our own; for
there are few posts, which are not tolerably
well supplied with books. These books are
not, indeed, all of the best kind; but among
them are many which are valuable. If I were
deprived of these silent companions, many a
gloomy hour would pass over me. Even with
them, my spirit at times sinks, when I reflect
on the great length of time which has elapsed,
since I left the land of my nativity, and my
relatives and friends, to dwell in this savage
country. These gloomy moments, thank
God, occur but seldom, and soon glide away.
A little reflection reconciles me to the lot,

which Providence has assigned me, in the world.

Saturday, June 12. A Sicanny has just arrived, who states, that a little this side of McLeod's Lake, where he was encamped with his family, an Indian of the same tribe, rushed out of the wood, and fired upon them, and killed his wife. Her corpse he immediately burned upon the spot; and then, with his son and two daughters, he proceeded directly to this place.—All the savages, who have had a near relation killed, are never quiet until they have avenged the death, either by killing the murderer, or some person nearly related to him. This spirit of revenge has occasioned the death of the old woman, above mentioned, and she undoubtedly, deserved to die; for, the last summer, she persuaded her husband to go and kill the cousin of her murderer, and that, merely because her own son had been drowned.—The custom, which extensively prevails among the Indians, of revenging the natural death of a relative, by the commission of murder, seems to arise from a superstitious notion entertained by them, that death, even when it takes place n this manner, has, in some mysterious way, been occasioned by a fellow creature.

Sunday, 20. Yesterday, an Indian of this village killed another, who was on a visit from the other end of this lake, just as he was entering his canoe to return. The former approached the latter, and gave him five stabs with a lance, and ripped open his bowels, in such a shocking manner, that his entrails immediately fell upon the ground; and he, of course, instantly expired. The murderer made his escape; and the chief of the village, wrapped the corpse in a moose skin, and sent it to his relations. Notwithstanding this conciliatory act, the people of this place are apprehensive, that the relations of the person murdered, will make war upon them; and they will, therefore, set out to-morrow, to go a considerable distance down this river, where they will pass a greater part of the summer, until harmony is restored between the two villages.—This murderer has a wife, who is known to be a worthless woman, with whom he supposed that the person murdered had had improper intercourse; and it was to revenge this, that the act was committed.—All the Carriers are extremely jealous of their wives; while, to their unmarried daughters, they cheerfully allow every liberty!

Thursday, August 12. Salmon begin to make their appearance in this river, which is a joyful event to us; for the stock of provisions which we have in the fort, is sufficient, but for a few days, and the Natives, for some time past, have suffered greatly for the want of food. We ought to be thankful to our merciful Preserver and Benefactor, who continually watches over us, and supplies our wants. Often has he appeared for our relief, when we were in urgent need, and taught us, that he is the proper object of our confidence.

Wednesday, September 1. A few days since, Mr. McDougall arrived here from McLeod's Lake, and took all the people, belonging to this fort, with him to Pinchy, to gather berries. Having been left entirely alone, I have had a favourable opportunity for serious reflection, and for self examination; and I have been disposed to employ it for this purpose. On reviewing the exercises of my heart, and the course of my conduct, during my past life, I have been filled with astonishment and with grief, in view of my wide departures from the path of duty. My sins have risen in gloomy array before me, and I have been led to feel, that I am, indeed, the chief of sinners; and that, on account of my transgressions, I deserve to be banished forever from the gracious presence of God, and to be consigned to the world of future misery. This view of my guilt would have been overwhelming, had not God been graciously pleased, as I trust, to reveal the Saviour to me, in his glorious fullness, as an all sufficient and an accepted Mediator between sinful men and the offended majesty of heaven. He has appeared to me amiable in himself, and entirely suited to my necessities; and I humbly hope that I have committed my soul to him, to be washed from the defilement of sin in his blood, to be accepted of God through his intercession, and to be sanctified by his

Spirit. The change in my views and feelings, is certainly great; and it is surprising to myself. What I once considered as the foibles and follies of my youth, now appear to be grievous sins, against a righteous and a long suffering God; and a religious course of life, I regard as the path, not only of wisdom, but of happiness; and by the aid of Divine grace, it is my resolution, for the time to come, to labour after a compliance with every Divine requirement.

Until this day, I have always doubted whether such a Saviour as the scriptures describe, ever really existed, and appeared on earth! So blind was I, that I could see no necessity for an atoning Mediator between God and men. Before I left the civilized part of the world, I had frequently heard the cavils of infidelity urged; and these cavils followed me into the wilderness, frequently came fresh to my recollection, and contributed to overshadow my mind with the gloomy doubts of infidelity. My intention, however, was, by no means to cast off all religion; but, I attempted to frame to myself a religion, which would comport with my feelings, and with my manner of life.—For several years past, however, my mind has not been at rest. I was taught in early life, by parents whom I respected and loved, the truths and duties of christianity; and I had a wish to believe in the same religion which they professed, and from which, I have frequently heard them say, they derived the most substantial consolation. I, therefore, some time since, commenced reading the Bible, with more attention than I had before done; for, from my youth up, I had been accustomed to read it. I also read all other books that I could find, which treated of the christian religion. Some excellent notes, respecting the Saviour, in the Universal History, affected my mind much; as did, also, the serious letters which I received, every year, from my brother Stephen. I also prayed a gracious God to enable me to believe on his Son, the Lord Jesus Christ. As I was praying to-day, on a sudden, the faith, respecting which I was so solicitous, was, I trust, graciously granted to me. My views of the Saviour, underwent a total change. I was enabled, not only to believe in his existence, but to apprehend his superlative excellency; and now he appears to be, in truth, what the scriptures describe him to be, the chiefest among ten thousand, and one altogether lovely. May the grace of God enable me to follow his heavenly example through life, that I may dwell with him in glory, forever!

As I seem to myself to have hitherto led a more wicked life than the rest of my fellow creatures, I deem it proper, for the time to come, to devote the first day of every month to religious fasting, employing it in reading the scriptures, in devout meditation, and in prayer, that I may keep in mind the great business of life, which I now consider to be, a preparation for eternity. My prayer shall ever be, that a gracious God would be pleased to blot out my numberless and aggravated transgressions, for the sake of the atonement which Jesus has made; and that he would keep me, by his grace, without which, I am convinced I can do nothing acceptable to him, in the path of holiness, until it shall terminate in heavenly glory.

Tuesday, 7. I have this day composed two prayers, which I design to use regularly and devoutly, morning and evening. It is not only a duty, but a privilege, thus to approach the mercy seat of the great Sovereign of the Universe, in the name of a prevalent Intercessor, and to supplicate the numerous blessings which we need, as well as to give thanks for those which we are continually receiving.

Saturday, 25. An Indian has arrived, from a considerable distance down this river, who has delivered to me three letters from Mr. J. Stuart. The last of them is dated at O-ke-nâ-gun Lake, which is situated at a short distance from the Columbia River. Mr. Stuart writes, that he met with every kindness and assistance from the Natives, on his way to that place; that, after descending this river, during eight days, he was under the necessity of leaving his canoes, and of taking his property on horses, more than one hundred and fifty miles, to the above mentioned Lake. From that place, he states, that they can go all the way by water, to the Ocean, by making a few portages; and he hopes to reach the Pacific Ocean, in twelve or fifteen days, at farthest. They will be delayed, for a time, where they are, by the necessary construction of canoes.

Friday, October 1. The first of my appointe l days of religious fasting, has arrived; and I have endeavoured to observe it, agreeably to my resolution.

Sunday, November 7. This afternoon, Mr. Joseph La Roque and company arrived from the Columbia River. This gentleman went, the last summer, with Mr. J. G. McTavish and his party, to the Pacific Ocean. On their return, they met Mr. Stuart and his company. Mr. La Roque, accompanied by two of Mr. Stuart's men, set off thence, to come to this place, by the circuitous way of Red Deer River, Lesser Slave Lake, and Dunvegan, from which last place, they were accompanied by my people, who have been, this summer, to the Rainy Lake. By them I have received a number of letters from people in this country, and from my friends in the United States.

Tuesday, December 14. On the 1st inst. I set out for McLeod's Lake; and I there received several letters from my brothers below, which announce the truly afflicting intelligence, that my beloved son George is no longer to be numbered among the living!

He was in good health on the second of
March last, and a corpse on the eighteenth
of the same month.—For some time, I could
scarcely credit this intelligence; though I had
no reason to doubt its truth. This dispensation of divine providence is so unexpected,
and so afflictive, that at first, I could scarcely bear up under it, with a becoming christian resignation. My tenderest affection was
placed upon this darling boy; and I fondly
hoped, that he would be the solace of my declining years. But how delusive was this expectation! How frail and perishing are all
earthly objects and enjoyments. A few days
since, in my imagination, I was often wandering with delight, to the remote land of my
kindred, and parental love centered in this
promising son, for whom, principally, I wished
to live, and for whom I would have been
willing to die. Perhaps this child occupied
a place in my heart, which my God and
Saviour only may of right occupy. I hope
that this affliction may be the means of dis-
engaging my affections from an inordinate
attachment to earthly objects; and that it
may induce me to fix my confidence and hope
on things, which will never disappoint my expectation. The Judge of all the earth has
done right; and it becomes me to be still
and know, that he is God. I, too, must soon
die; and this dispensation is, perhaps, a sea-
sonable warning to me, to be prepared to
meet my own dissolution. I desire that the

Holy Spirit may sanctify this affliction to me, and make it subservient to this important end.

On my return from McLeod's Lake, I was accompanied by Mr. McDougall and family, who came to mourn with me, and the mother of my departed son, the loss of this dear object of our mutual affection.—Her distress, on receiving this intelligence, was greater, if possible, than my own. I endeavoured, by some introductory remarks, on the uncertainty of earthly things, to prepare her mind for the disclosure, which I was about to make. Her fears were alarmed, by these remarks; and, probably, she discovered in my countenance, something to confirm them. When I informed her that our beloved son George was dead, she looked at me, with a wild stare of agony, and immediately threw herself upon the bed, where she continued, in a state of delirium, during the succeeding night.

Saturday, January 22, 1814. On the 4th inst. Mr. McDougall and family, left this place, to return home. They were accompanied by two men, who have gone to Peace River, with letters.—The same day, Mr. La Roque and myself, accompanied by fourteen of my people, went to Frazer's Lake. On the 9th I sent him, accompanied with two Canadians and two Indians, with letters to the people, who are on the Columbia River. After having purchased what furs I could, and a sufficient quantity of salmon, I set out on my return home, where I arrived this evening.

Friday, February 4. This evening, Mr. Donald McLeunen and company, arrived here from the Columbia Department, with a packet of letters. One of these is from Mr. John Stuart, informing me that the last autumn, the North West Company purchased of the Pacific Fur Company, all the furs which they had bought of the Natives, and all the goods which they had on hand. The people who were engaged in the service of that company, are to have a passage, the next summer, to Montreal, in the canoes of the North West Company, unless they choose to enter into our service.

Sunday, April 17. As the ice appears to be out of this river, I have sent Mr. McLeunen, accompanied by two Canadians, in a small canoe, with letters to the gentlemen on Columbia River. I am, therefore, deprived of an agreeable companion, who, I expected until lately, would pass the summer with me. —Happy are those, who have an amiable and intelligent friend, with whom they can, at pleasure, converse.

Friday, 22. Sent off my people to McLeod's Lake, in order that they may be in readiness to embark for the Rainy Lake, as soon as the navigation opens. By them I have, as usual, forwarded my letters, and accounts of the place. If God permit, I shall

pass another summer at this place, havi
with me ten persons.

As this is the only season of the year wh
we can leave this country, now it is, that we
have the most ardent desire of visiting the
land of our nativity. At other seasons, the
impossibility of a departure, suppresses the
rising wish to go, stern necessity binds us to
our situation, and we rest in quietude until
the return of another spring. Then all the
finer feelings of affection take possession of
our souls; and their strength seems to be
increased, by the previous restraint, which
had been laid upon them.

Saturday, May 7. The weather is fine
and vegetation is far advanced, for the season. This lake is clear of ice; and the frost
is chiefly out of the ground. Swans,
bustards, and ducks, are numerous in the
rivers and lakes; and, during the last ten
days, an incredible number of cranes have
passed this, on their way to the north; but
none of them stopped here.

Three Indians have come to this place
from Frazer's Lake, to obtain the piece of a
garment, belonging to an Indian of that
place, which they say, was cut off by an
Indian of this village. They are so superstitious as firmly to believe, that, by virtue
of this piece of garment, the Indian, who has
it in his possession, is able to destroy the life
of its owner, at pleasure.

Friday, August 5. Salmon begin to come

up this river. They are generally to be taken, in considerable numbers, until the latter part of September. During about a month, they come up in multitudes; and we can take any number of them that we please.

Tuesday, September 20. We have had but few salmon here, this year. It is only in every second season, that they are very numerous; the reason of which, I am unable to assign.

I have sent an Indian, with letters, to Dunvegan, on Peace River, which is distant from this place, at least, five hundred miles.

Friday, 30. We have had but a few salmon in this river, during the past season. We hope, however, that a kind Providence has sent them to some of our neighbouring villages, where we shall be able to purchase what will be necessary, in addition to the white fish, which we expect to take, for our consumption, during the ensuing winter. But let my condition be ever so deplorable, I am resolved to place all my dependence on that Being, who depends on no one.

Tuesday, October 18. This afternoon, I was agreeably surprised by the arrival of Mr. J. La Roque and company, in two canoes, laden with goods, from Fort George, at the mouth of the Columbia River, which place they left, the latter part of last August. Our vessels arrived there, in the months of March and April; and, soon after, one of them set sail again, loaded with furs, for Canton in China.—Mr. La Roque brings the melancholy intelligence, that Messrs. D. McTavish, Alexander Henry, and five sailors were drowned, on the 22d of May last, in going out in a boat, from fort George, to the vessel called the Isaac Tod, which lay at anchor without the bar, in going over which, this disaster befel them. With the former gentleman, I passed two winters at Dunvegan, on Peace River. He stood high in my esteem, and I considered him as one of my best friends; and I shall ever lament the sad catastrophe, which has thus suddenly removed him from my society, and from all earthly scenes. I hope that I may not be regardless of the admonition, addressed to me by this providence, to be also ready for my departure, to the world of spirits.

Monday, 24. Sent Mr. La Roque, and the people who came up with him, to re-establish the post at Frazer's Lake.

Saturday, 29. My people have returned from the Rainy Lake, and delivered me letters from my relatives below. They afford me renewed proof of the uncertainty of earthly objects and enjoyments, in the intelligence, that a brother's wife has been cut down by death, in the midst of her days, leaving a disconsolate husband, and two young children, to mourn over her early departure. I ought, however, to be thankful, that the rest of my numerous relatives, are blessed with health, and a reasonable portion of earthly comforts. I have also received a letter from Mr. John Stuart, who has arrived at McLeod's Lake, desiring me to go and superintend the affairs at Frazer's Lake, and to send Mr. La Roque, with several of the people who are there, to this place, that they may return to the Columbia department, where it is presumed they will be more wanted, than in this quarter. Tomorrow, therefore, I shall depart for Frazer's Lake.

Thursday, November 3. Frazer's Lake. Here we arrived this afternoon, and found Mr. La Roque and his people, busily employed, in bartering with the Natives, for furs and salmon, and in constructing houses. With this gentleman, I have spent a pleasant evening; and I am happy to find that, from having been thoughtless and dissolute, he now appears to be the reverse of this. It is manifest, that he has recently reflected much, on the vanity of this world, and on the importance of the concerns of eternity; and he now appears determined, by the aids of God's Holy Spirit, on a thorough reformation. May he be enabled to persevere in this important undertaking.

Tuesday, December 20. Messrs. Stuart and McDougall, with a number of men, have arrived from Stuart's Lake, for the purpose of proceeding with me to Stillâ, in order to purchase salmon. The Indians of this village have not a sufficiency for themselves and for us, owing to the scarcity of salmon at several neighbouring villages, whose inhabitants flock to this place, in hopes of obtaining a subsistence, during the winter.

Saturday, January 7, 1815. On the 29th ult. I accompanied my two friends to Stuart's Lake, where we passed the holidays together, in the intercourse of an intimate and endearing friendship. Each related how he had passed his youthful days, and even in what manner he had lived to the present hour; and we all readily acknowledged, that our lives had been very different from what we then wished they had been. I hope and believe, that we all parted, fully determined on a thorough reformation of conduct. May none of us fail to carry this resolution into effect.

Friday, February 3. During the whole of the last month, it has been the coldest weather, by far, that I have ever experienced, in New Caledonia.

On the 11th ult. accompanied by six of my people and two of the Natives, I set out to visit the lands of the Nas-koo-tains, which lie along Frazer's River. This river Mr. Stuart followed some distance, when he left this place to proceed to the Columbia River. The above mentioned Indians never had any intercourse with the white people, until I went among them. We reached their first village, on the 19th; but as they were nearly destitute of provisions, and we had expended those which we took with us from this place, we passed only one night with them. The next morning, we continued our route down the river, every day passing one or two small villages, until the 22d, when we met people from the Columbia River, with letters, &c.

Frazer's River is about fifty rods wide, and has a pretty strong current. On the north side, the bank is generaly high; but, on the other, it is low, and the country is level. In going from this, to the place where we fell upon the river, we occupied nine days, and the country which we passed over, is very uneven. We, however, crossed several ponds and small lakes, which were from one to fifteen miles in length. At these waters, the Natives pass the greater part of the summer, and subsist on excellent white fish, trout and carp; but, towards the latter part of August, they return to the banks of the river, in order to take and dry salmon, for their subsistence during the succeeding winter.

Sunday, 12. As salmon are becoming rather scarce among the Indians of this village, they are preparing to visit the neighbouring lakes, in order to obtain a subsistence, from the fish that they hope to be able to take out of them.

Monday, 27. The weather is serene and cold; and thus far, this has been much the coldest winter that I have experienced in this part of the country.—The winters are, generally milder here, than in most parts of the North West. Mr. Stuart has just left me, on his return home. The few days which he has spent here, were passed much to our mutual satisfaction; and I hope that we shall reap some benefit from this visit. Religion was the principal topic, on which we conversed, because, to both of us, it was more interesting than any other. Indeed, what ought to interest us so much, as that which concerns our eternal welfare? I, at times, almost envy the satisfaction of those, who live among christian people, with whom they can converse, at pleasure, on the great things of religion, as it must be a source of much satisfaction, and of great advantage, to a pious mind.

Thursday, April 6. About ten days since, an Indian of this place lost his wife, after a lingering illness of several months; and, shortly after, the disconsolate husband hung himself from the limb of a tree. For several days previous to the fatal act, he appeared to be much cast down, which being observed by his companions, they endeavoured to cheer his spirits, by the consideration, that what had befallen him, had been suffered by multitudes of others, and was the common lot. He replied that he should conduct as his own feelings dictated; and that he had not forgotten the request of his dying companion, which was, that he would accompany her.

14

Not long after, he was missing; and, search being made for him, he was found in the situation above mentioned. The strength of conjugal attachment is not an unfrequent cause of suicide, in every part of the Indian country.

Monday, 24. The snow is fast leaving us, and fowls begin to come from the south.

Wednesday, 26. I have sent letters to my friends below, to Stuart's Lake, which place they will leave, on their way, the first of next month. I expect to pass the ensuing summer here, having but a few people with me. But, by dividing my time between reading, meditation and exercise, I hope that it will pass not unpleasantly, away.

Wednesday, May 10. We have surrounded a piece of ground with palisades, for a garden, in which we have planted a few potatoes, and sowed onion, carrot, beet and parsnip seeds, and a little barley. I have, also, planted a very little Indian corn, without the expectation that it will come to maturity. The nights in this region are too cool, and the summers are too short, to admit of its ripening. There is not a month in the whole year, in which water does not congeal; though the air in the day time, in the summer, is warm, and we even have a few days of sultry weather.—The soil, in many places in New Caledonia, is tolerably good.

Tuesday, May 30. I have just returned from a visit to Mr. Stuart, who passes the summer at Stuart's Lake. On the mountain, which I crossed in going there, I found snow, two feet, at least, in depth.

Friday, June 16. Soon after the Natives left their village, last February, to go to the small lakes, for the purpose of taking fish, four of their number deceased. Their corpses were kept, by their relations, to the present time, when they are bringing them to the village in order to burn them. Little else but the skeletons, now remain.—In the winter season, the Carriers often keep their dead in their huts during five or six months, before they will allow them to be burned. At this season, the coldness of the weather enables them to keep the bodies, without their becoming offensive; and they are unwilling that the lifeless remains of the objects of their affection, should be removed forever from their sight, until it becomes a matter of necessity.

Sunday, 18. This afternoon eight of the Nâte-ote-tains came to pay a visit to the Indians of this village, by whom they were, at first, treated in a friendly manner. Soon after their arrival, they began to play, as is the custom of the Indians, whenever the people of different villages meet. Things proceeded smoothly, until the strangers began to be winners, when disputes arose. An open contest was prevented, by the restoration of the property won; but a coolness between the parties, was visible. The stran-

gers soon set out, to return home; but as they
were embarking in their canoes, a worthless
fellow fired upon them, and killed one of
them. This disaster caused them to hasten
their departure, uttering at the same time
the threat, that they would soon return,
with a large band of their relations, to
revenge the death of their companion.—
Human life is often sacrificed for a trifle,
among the savages; and he only may feel
secure, who is prepared to oppose strength
to aggression.

Monday, July 24. Fruits, of various
kinds, now begin to ripen. Of this delicious
food, the present prospect is, that we shall
soon have an abundance; and for this favour,
it becomes us to be grateful to the Bestower.
The person who is surrounded with the comforts of civilized life, knows not how we
prize these delicacies of the wilderness. Our
circumstances, also, teach us to enjoy and
to value the intercourse of friendship. To
be connected, and to have intercourse, with
a warm and disinterested friend, who is able,
and will be faithful, to point out our faults,
and to direct us by his good counsel, is
surely a great blessing. Such a friend, I
have, in my nearest neighbour, Mr. Stuart.
For some time past, he has frequently written to me long, entertaining and instructive
letters, which are a cordial to my spirits,
too often dejected, by the loneliness of my
situation, and more frequently, by reflections

on my past life of folly and of sin. Mr. James McDougall, also, another gentleman in this department, is equally dear to me. His distance from me, renders intercourse less practicable; but when we meet, we endeavour to make up in conversation, for our long separation.

Friday, August 4. The holy scriptures contain the most abundant instruction, in regard to the duties which we owe to God, and to our fellow creatures. To aid me in keeping these instructions, habitually and distinctly in view, that my life may thereby be more exemplary, I think proper to form the following resolutions, which I hope, by the aid of the Holy Spirit, to be enabled to observe, during my life.

Resolved, that the scoffs of the wicked, directed against serious religion, shall never have any other effect upon me, than to make me strive, the more earnestly, to lead the life of a sincere christian.

Resolved, to be in the company of the wicked, as little as possible; and when among such people, to endeavour to persuade them in such a way as may be consistent with propriety, to forsake their evil courses.

Resolved, to assist the poor and needy, so far as may be consistent with my means; hoping that avarice may never prevent me from judging correctly, in regard to this subject.

Resolved, never to let a day pass, when

at home, or when convenient, abroad, without reading a portion of the holy scriptures, and spending half an hour or more, in meditating on what I have read; and that the whole of the Sabbath, when it is not in my power to attend publick worship, shall be spent in prayer, reading the bible, or sermons, or some other religious book, in self examination, and in meditating on the eternal world.

Resolved, to offer up daily prayers to the throne of grace, for a right temper of mind, that I may be constant and diligent, in strictly observing the above resolutions. And I pray that my humble endeavours may, by the blessing of God, keep me in the path of holiness, so that I may, from day to day, become better prepared to enter the world of bliss, whenever my Maker and Redeemer shall see fit to terminate my mortal course. Amen.

Monday, 7. At half past seven, A. M. we had an earthquake, which lasted about twenty seconds. At that time I was sitting in a chair, in the house, and the agitation put me, and the whole house, in a motion like that of a canoe when rolled about by considerable swells. The Natives say, that a similar shaking of the earth occurs, almost yearly, at this place.

Sunday, 13. Salmon begin to come up this river, which lights up joy in the countenances, both of ourselves and of the Natives;

for we had all become nearly destitute of
provisions, of any kind. A kind Providence
will not allow us to suffer want, though we
so little deserve favours.

Monday, October 2. Within a few days
past, we have caught, in nets made for the
purpose, of strong twine, three sturgeon, one
of which measured ten feet and three inches
in length, and four feet and one inch round
his middle, which might weigh about four
hundred pounds. All that we have taken,
were uncommonly fat, and of the best flavour
of any that I have ever eaten.

Friday, 13. This afternoon, the Natives
sent for me to come and see one of their
young women, who lay at the point of death,
at their village; and, merely to please them,
I went, without expecting to render her any
service, especially with the medicines which
we have here. I found her so far gone that
I thought it would not be proper to give her
any thing. I told the Indians, moreover,
that if she should die, shortly after taking
our medicines, they would say, as they ever
do in such cases, that I was the cause of
her death. They assured me however, to
the contrary; and I gave her a simple medicine, which I supposed could do her neither
good nor harm, with which they were
satisfied.

I understood that her relations had said,
that a certain Indian, by his magic, had caused
her illness, and that he would finally take

her life. I, therefore, took this opportunity of repeating again, what I had often told them before, that God, the infinitely powerful being, who made every thing, had alone the power of causing their dissolution, whenever he thought proper. Upon this, one of the chiefs, who thought himself more knowing than the others, observed, that it was the God of the salmon, who remained at the sea, who was taking the girl's life. I replied, that God is in heaven above; but that, so searching are his eyes, he can easily see what takes place on the face of the whole earth. They said, it might be so; but they could not conceive, by what means I came to have a knowledge of these things. This, I endeavoured to explain to them.

Wednesday, November 1. This afternoon, three of our men arrived from the Rainy Lake, who say that they left the remainder of their company at McLeod's and Stuart's Lakes. They delivered me letters from people in this country; but none from home. By the men in the other canoes, I hope to receive letters from my friends below. We are happy to be informed, that peace has taken place between Great Britain and the United States. My earnest desire is, that they may long continue to enjoy this blessing.

Thursday, 16. We have now about three inches of snow on the ground.

Sunday, March 17, 1816. In consequence of the late arrival, at fort Chipewyan, of the men who went to the Rainy Lake, two canoes, which were expected last fall, could not then proceed here, which is the reason why I have but just received the letters that I then expected, from my friends below. They bring me the distressing intelligence, that two of my brothers are brought, by a consumption, to the borders of the grave. Happy should I consider myself, could I once more see them in this world. But, if this may not be, the will of the Lord be done. By this affliction I have renewed proof, that this world cannot be my rest; and I pray God to prepare me, and my dying brothers, for that happy abode, where a separation of friends never causes the heart to bleed.

Monday, April 15. My desire to return to my native country has never been so intense, since I took up my abode in the wilderness, as it is now, in consequence of the peculiar situation of my friends; yet, I cannot think of doing it this season, as it is absolutely necessary that I should pass the ensuing summer at this place.

I shall write to my friends below, a few days hence; and as we live in a world of disappointment and death, I am resolved to forward to them by Mr. John Stuart, a copy of my Journal, in order that they may know something of the manner in which I have been employed, both as it respects my temporal and spiritual concerns, while in the wilderness, if I should never enjoy the inexpressible pleasure of a personal intercourse with them.

Wednesday, 24. I have just returned from Stuart's Lake. While there, I agreed with Mr. George McDougall to remain in this country two years or more, as clerk to the North West company. He came out the last summer from Canada, with Lord Selkirk's party, without having obligated himself to continue with them, for any definite time. After they arrived at Fort Vermilion on Peace River, he was treated by his superiour, Mr. John Clarke, in so unbecoming a manner, that he left them, and had come into this quarter to visit his brother, Mr. James McDougall, before he should return to Canada, which he designed to do the ensuing summer.

Saturday, *July* 20. Strawberries begin to ripen, and we have the prospect of an abundance of them, as well as of other kinds of fruit.

I now pass a short time every day, very pleasantly, in teaching my little daughter Polly to read and spell words in the English language, in which she makes good progress, though she knows not the meaning of one of them. In conversing with my children, I use entirely the Cree, Indian language; with their mother I more frequently employ the French. Her native tongue, however, is more familiar to her, which is the reason why our children have been taught to speak that, in preference to the French language.

Tuesday, September 9. Salmon begin to come up this river.

Thursday, October 3. We have taken our vegetables out of the ground. We have forty-one bushels of potatoes, the produce of one bushel planted the last spring. Our turnips, barley, &c. have produced well.

Saturday, November 23. By our people who returned this afternoon from the Rainy Lake, I have received letters, which announce the afflictive intelligence, that two of my brothers, of whose decline I had before been informed, are gone into eternity. The happy days that I had fondly hoped that I should pass in their society on earth, I shall never enjoy. Such is the uncertainty of all earthly expectations. But the Judge of all the earth has done right.—My departed brothers gave evidence, to those around them, that they died in the faith and hope and peace of the gospel. They are gone, I trust, to a world where sin and suffering cannot follow them.

When the cold hands of death shall have been laid upon a few more of my relatives, there will be nothing remaining on the earth to console me for their loss. Nothing revives my drooping spirits in view of the departure of my friends, one after another, from year to year, into eternity, like the hope that, through rich grace, I may be at length permitted to join their society, in a world of perfect purity and of uninterrupted and everlasting joy.

We rarely prize our blessings in a suitable manner, until we learn their value by being deprived of them. I feel the force of this truth, in regard to my deceased brothers. To one of them in a particular manner, I am deeply indebted; and I have never been fully sensible of his worth, until now. During the whole period of my residence in this country, he has written to me annually, long, affectionate, and instructive letters. For a number of years past, religion was the great subject of them. He was tenderly concerned for my spiritual welfare; and doubtless learned from my letters, that I was lingering on the gloomy confines of infidelity, and little disposed to heed, as I ought to have done, his friendly admonition. So far from being discouraged by this circumstance, it only rendered him more vigorous and persevering in his efforts; and his letters stand chief among the means, which have been blessed, as I would hope, to my conversion from the love and practice of sin, to the fear and service of God. These letters have also been of use to the few friends, to whom I have shown them. It would have given me great pleasure to have acknowledged, in person, the obligation which I am under to him; but it becomes not me to dictate to infinite wisdom.

I have, also, received letters from gentlemen in different parts of this country, which inform me of the many disasters that befel the people whom Lord Selkirk sent the year before, from Scotland, the Orkney Islands, and Canada, some of whom were destined to form a colony on the Red River, and others to traffic with the Natives, in different parts of the Indian country. They consisted at first, as I am informed, of two or three hundred men, together with a few women and children. Those, who went to establish themselves on the Red River, at a short distance from its entrance into the great Winnipick Lake, began, soon after their arrival, to behave in a hostile manner toward the people of the North West Company, who have establishments in that quarter. Of some of our forts, they actually took possession, and carried away the property which they found in them; and, in some instances, they set fire to the forts, and reduced them to ashes. They also took Duncan Cameron Esq. a partner of the North West Company, and another gentleman, who is a clerk, whom they carried, in the spring, to Hudson's Bay, with the intention, as they stated, of taking them to England.— In the course of the winter, as the Express of the North West Company was passing that way, destined to the Soult St. Maries, they took possession of that also, perused the letters and other papers which had been

sealed up, and finally carried them to York
Factory, at Hudson's Bay.

All this unmerited treatment, at length so
provoked the people of the North West Company, that they proceeded to retake their
own forts, which had not been burned, as
well as some property belonging to those
disturbers of the peace.

In June, a number of the Brulés, that is,
people whose fathers were white men, and
whose mothers were Indian women, proceeded
from the upper part of Red River, toward
the place of its entrance into the Lake, in
order to guard some property there belonging to the N. W. Company. On their
way, they were obliged to pass, for about
two miles, over an open plain, directly behind
Lord Selkirk's establishment. As soon as
they were observed, his people came out in
a body, and fired upon them, twice. This
was unexpected by the Brulés; neither were
they prepared for such an encounter, as
many of them had neither gun nor ammunition. Perceiving however, that they must
defend themselves or be cut off, those who
had arms returned the fire; and the contest
continued, until twenty two of the noble
Earl's people fell, and some others were
wounded. The Brulés had only one man
killed, and one wounded.—This unhappy
affair broke up the colony. Some of the
people went to Hudson's Bay; but the
greater number returned to Canada.

Those of Lord Selkirk's people who came to the English River and Athabasca, suffered greatly for the want of provisions. Out of nearly one hundred who came to Athabasca, twelve actually lost their lives by starvation; and all the others must have shared the same unhappy fate, had not the people of the North West Company supplied them with provisions. In short, Lord Selkirk lost the last year, in fight and by starvation, sixty eight of his men! and still, with the phrenzy of a madman, he is resolved on pursuing his wild projects.

Wednesday, December 4. There is now about a foot and an half of snow on the ground.

I have sent fifteen men, with each a sledge drawn by two dogs and loaded with salmon, to McLeod's Lake, for the subsistence of the people who are to pass the winter there and for the additional number who will be there in the spring, to make up the furs into packs. Salmon are our chief subsistence here; and they are taken only in the waters which are discharged into the Pacific Ocean. The outlet of McLeod's Lake enters Peace River, whose waters, are finally discharged into the North Sea.

Thursday, January 2, 1817. I have just returned from a neighbouring village, where my interpreter gave one of the natives a decent drubbing, for having stolen from us. Soon after, the Indian who had been beaten,

with a number of his relations, flew to arms,
and surrounded our camp; but they proceeded at first no farther than to gesticulate
in a threatening manner. This I permitted
them, for a short time, to do, when I ordered
my men to load their guns; though I was
determined that they should not fire, unless
it became a matter of necessity. I then told
the Natives that we were prepared to defend
ourselves, and, if they intended to fire upon
us, to begin; or otherwise, to walk off, and
lay aside their arms, which if they would
not do, we should fire upon them. They
concluded to retire, and shortly after came
back without their arms, and began to trade,
as if nothing had happened.

Monday, February 10. This evening the
mother of my children, was delivered of a
daughter, whom I name Sally Harmon.

Wednesday, 19. I am this day thirty
nine years of age. When I reflect on the
events of my past life, and recollect, especially, in how many instances a merciful God has
snatched me from the very jaws of death,
when it would undoubtedly have delivered
me over to everlasting destruction, I am
grieved and ashamed, in view of the in-
gratitude with which I have requited such
infinite kindness. My past life now appears
to me to have been a continual course of
sins, committed against a merciful Creator,
Benefactor and Redeemer. I have even de-
nied the Lord that brought me, and that

because I could see no need of that atonement for sin, which is the only thing that has stood between me and hopeless perdition! If I have indeed been rescued from such a wretched condition, if I have been effectually convinced of my sinfulness, and have been led, in the exercise of faith, to apply unto the Lord Jesus Christ for pardon and for sanctification, surely, it can be attributed to nothing but the grace of God. Much of my life has been spent in the service of sin; the little that remains, ought to be sacredly devoted to God and the Redeemer. May the Holy Spirit enable me to live in the time to come, as a disciple of the blessed Saviour.

Monday, September 1. *Stuart's Lake.* On the 8th of May last, I left New Caledonia, and went as far as Fort Chipewyan, on the Athabasca Lake. This afternoon, I returned to this place. While I was at that lake, the Indians who were encamped about the fort, to the number of about one hundred, rose up in arms against us, on account of a quarrel between one of their people and one of our men. We did not, however, come to blows; and, after a parley, the Indians were persuaded to lay down their arms.—Those Chipeways are a savage people; and they have as I believe, killed more white men, than any other tribe in the North West country. A few years since, they burned one of our forts, and killed every person belonging to it.

On the 21st of June, I left Athabasca Lake, at which period, there was still ice floating about in it. In coming up Peace River, we saw many of the buffaloe and red deer, and killed as many of them as we wanted for our own consumption. Black bears, also, were in plenty; and of them, we killed eleven. One day as I was walking along the beach alone without my gun, a black bear, that had cubs, pursued me for nearly a mile. Happily for me, I could out-run her; and I therefore escaped from her terrible paws.

A little below the Rocky Mountain Port-age, along the side of the river, there is a kind of marsh where earth, of a beautiful yellow colour is found, which when burned, becomes a pretty lively red. The natives use it as paint, for which it answers tolerably well. We, also, use it to paint our forts and houses.

Saturday, October 4. This evening, an Indian arrived from Frazer's Lake, bringing the disagreeable intelligence, that yesterday in the afternoon, our fort there was con-sumed by fire. We have reason to be thank-ful, however, that most of the property which was in it, was saved.

Thursday, 16. We have taken our vegeta-bles out of the ground. In consequence of the very dry summer, they have yielded but poorly. There were months, during which not a drop of rain fell.—Fruit of all kinds has been uncommonly abundant this season.

Wednesday, February 18, 1818. I have just returned from a jaunt of twenty three days, to a place down Frazer's River. While there, the Natives had concerted a plan to massacre us all; but I discovered it, and kept my people on their guard. The Indians, perceiving this, dared not attempt to execute their bloody and unprovoked purpose.

Saturday, May 2. Expecting that the ice in Peace River will soon break up, I have sent off the last of our people who are going to the Rainy lake; and by them I have forwarded, as usual, my accounts of the place, and letters to my friends below. I look forward, with pleasing anticipation, to the return of another spring, when I hope, if my life is spared, I shall myself leave this country on a visit to the civilized world.

Thursday, September 3. Last night, there fell about four inches of snow, which is earlier than I have ever before seen it fall, in this part of the country. On the 6th ult. salmon began to come up this river; but they are not very numerous.

In the month of June, we took out of this lake twenty one sturgeon, that were from eight to twelve feet in length. One of them measured twelve feet two inches, from its extreme points, four feet eleven inches round the middle; and would weigh from five hundred and fifty, to six hundred pounds. All the sturgeon that we have caught, on this side of the mountain, are far superior in flavour, to any I ever saw in any other part of the world.

A few days since, we cut down and threshed our barley. The five quarts, which I sowed on the first of May, have yielded as many bushels. One acre of ground, producing in the same proportion that this has done, would yield eighty four bushels. This is sufficient proof that the soil, in many places in this quarter, is favourable to agriculture. It will probably be long, however, before it will exhibit the fruits of cultivation. The Indians, though they often suffer for the want of food, are too lazy to cultivate the ground. I have frequently tried to prevail on some of them to hoe and prepare a piece of ground, promising them that I would give them potatoes and turnips, with which to plant it; but I have not succeeded. Having been from their infancy trained up to privation, the fear of want is a much less powerful stimulus to excite them to industry, than it is to those who have always been accustomed to the comforts of civilized life.

Tuesday, October 13. We have several inches of snow on the ground.

For several years past, Iroquois from Canada, have been in the habit of coming into different parts of the North West country, to hunt the beaver, &c. The Natives of the country, consider them as intruders. As they are mere rovers, they do not feel the same interest, as those who permanently reside here, in keeping the stock of animals good, and therefore they make great havock among the game, destroying alike the animals which are young and old. A number of Iroquois have passed several summers on this side of the mountain, which circumstance they knew to be displeasing to the Indians here, who have often threatened to kill them, if they persisted in destroying the animals on their lands. These menaces were disregarded. A month since, an Iroquois, with his wife and two children, were all killed, while asleep, by two Carriers of this village, which melancholy event, I hope, will prevent any of the Iroquois from coming into this region again.

Saturday, November 7. We have now about a foot of snow on the ground.—To-day our people returned from the Rainy Lake, and say that, on account of the large quantities of ice that was drifting in Peace River, they were obliged to leave the greater part of the goods, which they had on board of the canoes, but a short distance this side of the Rocky Mountain Portage. We shall be obliged, therefore, to bring these goods on sledges, drawn by dogs from that place, which is distant from this, about two hundred and eighty miles.

Saturday, February 28, 1819. Mr. George McDougall has arrived here from Frazer's Lake, to remain, as I am going to McLeod's

Lake, to prepare for a departure for Head Quarters; and my intention is, during the next summer, to visit my native land. I design, also, to take my family with me, and leave them there, that they may be educated in a civilized and christian manner. The mother of my children will accompany me; and, if she shall be satisfied to remain in that part of the world, I design to make her regularly my wife by a formal marriage. It will be seen by this remark, that my intentions have materially changed, since the time that I at first took her to live with me; and as my conduct in this respect is different from that which has generally been pursued by the gentlemen of the North West Company, it will be proper to state some of the reasons which have governed my decision, in regard to this weighty affair. It has been made with the most serious deliberation; and, I hope, under a solemn sense of my accountability to God.

Having lived with this woman as my wife, though we were never formally contracted to each other, during life, and having children by her, I consider that I am under a moral obligation not to dissolve the connexion, if she is willing to continue it. The union which has been formed between us, in the providence of God, has not only been cemented by a long and mutual performance of kind offices, but, also, by a more sacred consideration. Ever since my own mind was turned effectually to the subject of religion, I have taken pains to instruct her in the great doctrines and duties of christianity. My exertions have not been in vain. Through the merciful agency of the Holy Spirit, I trust that she has become a partaker with me, in the consolations and hopes of the gospel. I consider it to be my duty to take her to a christian land, where she may enjoy Divine ordinances, grow in grace, and ripen for glory.—We have wept together over the early departure of several children, and especially, over the death of a beloved son. We have children still living, who are equally dear to us both. How could I spend my days in the civilized world, and leave my beloved children in the wilderness? The thought has in it the bitterness of death. How could I tear them from a mother's love, and leave her to mourn over their absence, to the day of her death? Possessing only the common feelings of humanity, how could I think of her, in such circumstances, without anguish? On the whole, I consider the course which I design to pursue, as the only one which religion and humanity would justify.

Mr. McDougall informs me, that, not long since, an Indian died at Frazer's Lake, and left behind him a widow, who had been in similar circumstances before, by the loss of a former husband. A day or two before the corpse was to be burned, she told the relations of her late husband, that she was

resolved not to undergo a second slavery.
She therefore left the tent, secretly, in the
evening, and hung herself from a tree.

Among the Carriers, widows are slaves to
the relations of their deceased husbands, for
the term of two or three years from the
commencement of their widowhood, during
which, they are generally treated in a cruel
manner. Their heads are shaved, and it belongs to them to do all the drudgery, about
the tent. They are frequently beaten with a
club or an axe, or some such weapon.

Saturday, May 8. *McLeod's Lake.* I arrived here about two months since. Yesterday, the most of our people embarked with
the returns of this place, in three canoes; and
a few hours hence, I shall, with my family,
proceed in another, which will be pushed on
by six Canadians.

It is now eight years and an half, since I
came to the west side of the Rocky Mountain.
My life, which has often been in jeopardy, is
still preserved; my family have generally enjoyed, in a high degree, the comforts, which
this part of the world affords; and, especially,
they have been extensively blessed with
health of body, and contentment of mind.
Our worldly affairs have prospered, to as
great an extent as we could reasonably expect. For all these blessings, it becomes us
to return unfeigned thanks, to the great
Giver of every good gift.

Friday, 14. *Rocky Mountain Portage.*

All the way to this place, we have drifted down, amidst great quantities of ice, by which, at five different places, the river was completely blocked up, so that we were obliged to tarry, until the water rose so high, as to remove these barriers. This is the reason why we have been so long in coming to this place. Had the river been high, and yet clear from ice, the current is so strong, that we might have reached here in two days.

Wednesday, August 18. *Fort William.* I have at length arrived at head quarters. In coming from New Caledonia to this place, which is a distance of at least three thousand miles, nothing uncommon has occurred. A few days hence, I shall leave this place, to proceed to Canada. As I have already described the country between this, and Montreal, I shall here conclude my Journal.

CHARACTER

OF THE CANADIAN VOYAGERS.

———

LIKE their ancestors the French, the Canadian Voyagers possess lively and fickle dispositions; and they are rarely subject to depression of spirits, of long continuance, even when in circumstances the most adverse. Although what they consider good eating and drinking constitutes their chief good, yet, when necessity compels them to it, they submit to great privation and hardship, not only without complaining, but even with cheerfulness and gaiety. They are very talkative, and extremely thoughtless, and make many resolutions, which are almost as soon broken as formed. They never think of providing for future wants; and seldom lay up any part of their earnings, to serve them in a day of sickness, or in the decline of life. Trifling provocations will often throw them into a rage; but they are easily appeased when in anger, and they never harbour a revengeful purpose against those, by whom they conceive that they have been injured. They are not brave; but when they appre-

hend little danger, they will often, as they
say, play the man. They are very deceitful,
are exceedingly smooth and polite, and are
even gross flatterers to the face of a person,
whom they will basely slander, behind his
back. They pay little regard to veracity or
to honesty. Their word is not to be trusted;
and they are much addicted to pilfering, and
will even steal articles of considerable value,
when a favourable opportunity offers. A
secret they cannot keep. They rarely feel
gratitude, though they are often generous.
They are obedient, but not faithful servants.
By flattering their vanity, of which they have
not a little, they may be persuaded to undertake the most difficult enterprises, provided
their lives are not endangered. Although
they are generally unable to read, yet they
acquire considerable knowledge of human
nature, and some general information, in
regard to the state of this country. As they
leave Canada while they are young, they
have but little knowledge of the principles of
the religion, which their Priests profess to
follow, and before they have been long in the
Indian country, they pay little more attention to the sabbath, or the worship of God,
or any other Divine institution, than the
savages themselves.

AN

ACCOUNT OF THE INDIANS

LIVING WEST OF THE

ROCKY MOUNTAIN.

ACCOUNT, &c.

As the Indians living on the west side of the Rocky Mountain, differ greatly in their language, manners, customs, religion, &c. from those on the east side, it may be proper to give concisely a separate account of them, and of the country which they inhabit. In doing this, I shall dwell more particularly on those things which are peculiar to these people, as I design, in another place, to give a general description of the Indians, which shall have a principal reference, however, to the more numerous tribes on the east side of the Mountain. I shall, I hope, be pardoned, if some repetition shall be found, of things contained in my journal, as it cannot easily be avoided.

That part of the country, west of the Rocky Mountain, with which I am acquainted, has, ever since the North West Company first made an establishment there, which was in 1806, gone by the name of New Caledonia; and may extend from north to south, about five hundred miles, and from east to west, three hundred and fifty or four

hundred. The post at Stuart's Lake, is
nearly in the centre of it, and lies, as already
mentioned in my Journal, in 54° 30' North
Latitude, and in 125° West Longitude from
Greenwich. In this large extent of country,
there are not more than five thousand Indians, including men, women and children.

New Caledonia is considerably mountainous. Between its elevated parts, however,
there are pretty extensive valleys, along
which pass innumerable small rivers and
brooks. It contains a great number of small
lakes, and two which are considerably large.
These are Stuart's Lake, which is about three
hundred miles in circumference, and Nâte-
ote-tain Lake, which is nearly twice as large.
I am of the opinion that about one sixth
part of New Caledonia, is covered with water.
There are but two large rivers. One of these
I denominate Fraser's River, which may be
sixty or seventy rods wide. It rises in the
Rocky Mountain, within a short distance of
the source of Peace River; and is the river
which Sir Alexander McKenzie followed a
considerable distance, when he went to the
Pacific Ocean, in 1793, and which he took to
be the Columbia River; but it is now known
to be several hundred miles north of that noble
stream. The other large river of New Caledonia, arises near Great Bear's Lake; and
after passing through several considerable
lakes, it enters the Pacific Ocean, several
hundred miles north of Fraser's River.

The mountains of New Caledonia, in point of elevation, are not to be compared with those which we pass through in coming up that part of Peace River, which lies between the Rocky Mountain portage and Finlay's Branch. There are some, however, which are pretty lofty; and on the summits of one in particular, which we see from Stuart's Lake, the snow lies during the whole of the year.

The weather is not severely cold, except for a few days in the winter, when the mercury is sometimes as low as 32° below zero, in Faranheit's thermometer. The remainder of the season, is much milder than it is on the other side of the mountain, in the same Latitude. The summer is never very warm, in the day time; and the nights are generally cool. In every month in the year, there are frosts. Snow generally falls about the fifteenth of November, and is all dissolved by about the fifteenth of May. About McLeod's Lake the snow sometimes falls to the depth of five feet; and I imagine that it is to be attributed to the great depth of the snow, that no large animals of any kind, excepting a few solitary ones, are to be met with.

There are a few Moose; and the Natives occasionally, kill a black bear. Cariboo are also found, at some seasons. Some smaller animals are found, though they are not numerous. They consist of beavers, otters, lynxes or cats, fishers, martins, minks, wolverines, foxes of different kinds, badgers, pole-

16

cats, hares and a few wolves. The fowls are swans, bustards, geese, cranes, ducks of several kinds, partridges, &c. All the lakes and rivers are well furnished with excellent fish. They are the sturgeon, white fish, trout, sucker and many of a smaller kind. Salmon, also, visit the streams, in very considerable numbers, in Autumn. A small share of industry, therefore, would enable the Natives, at all times, to provide for themselves a sufficient supply of agreeable, wholesome and nutritious food.

The Natives of New Caledonia, we denominate Carriers; but they call themselves Tâ-cul-lies, which signifies people who go upon water. This name originated from the fact that they generally go from one village to another, in canoes. They are of the middle stature, and the men are well proportioned; but the women are generally short and thick, and their lower limbs are disproportionately large. Both sexes are remarkably negligent and slovenly, in regard to their persons; and they are filthy in their cookery. Their dispositions are lively and quiet; and they appear to be happy, or at least contented, in their wretched situation. They are indolent; but apparently more from habit than by nature; and probably this trait in their character, originates from the circumstance, that they procure a livelihood, with but little labour. Whenever we employ any of them, either to work about the fort or in voyaging, they are sufficiently laborious and active; and they appear to be pleased, when we thus furnish them with employment. They are not in the habit of stealing articles of great value; but they are the sliest pilferers, perhaps, upon the face of the earth. They will not only pilfer from us, but, when favourable opportunities offer, they are guilty of the same low vice among their friends and relations. They are remarkably fond of the white people. They seldom begin a quarrel with any of us, though they are naturally brave. When any of our people, however, treat them ill, they defend themselves with courage, and with considerable dexterity; and some of them will fight a tolerable *Canadian* battle.

Their language is very similar to that of the Chipewyans, and has a great affinity to the tongues, spoken by the Beaver Indians and the Sicannies. Between all the different villages of the Carriers, there prevails a difference of dialect, to such an extent, that they often give different names to the most common utensils. Every village has its particular name, and its inhabitants are called after the name of the village, in the same manner as people in the civilized world receive a name, from the city or country which they inhabit.

Their clothing consists of a covering made of the skins of the beaver, badger, muskrat, cat or hare. The last they cut into strips, about one inch broad, and then weave or lace them together, until they become of a sufficient size to cover their bodies, and to reach to their knees. This garment they put over their shoulders, and tie about their waists. Instead of the above named skins, when they can obtain them from us, they greatly prefer, and make use of blankets, capots, or Canadian coats, cloth or moose and red deer skin. They seldom use either leggins or shoes, in the summer. At this season the men often go naked, without any thing to cover even that part of the body which civilized, and the most, also of savage people, think it necessary to conceal. Indeed they manifest as little sense of shame in regard to this subject, as the very brute creation. The women, however, in addition to the robe of beaver or dressed moose skins, wear an apron, twelve or eighteen inches broad, which reaches nearly down to their knees. These aprons are made of a piece of deer skin, or of salmon skins, sewed together. Of the skin of this fish, they sometimes make leggins, shoes, bags, &c. but they are not durable; and therefore they prefer deer skins and cloth, which are more pliable and soft. The roughness of salmon skins, renders them particularly unpleasant for aprons.

A few of the male Carriers recently make use of the breech-cloth, made of cloth which they procure from us; but as evidence that no great sense of delicacy has induced them to wear it, you will see it one day at its proper place, the next, probably, about their heads, and the third around their necks; and so on, repeatedly shifted from one place to another.

Both sexes perforate their noses; and from them, the men often suspend an ornament, consisting of a piece of an oyster shell, or a small piece of brass or copper. The women, particularly those who are young, run a wooden pin through their noses, upon each end of which they fix a kind of shell bead, which is about an inch and an half long, and nearly the size of the stem of a common clay pipe. These beads, they obtain from their neighbours, the At-e-nâs, who purchase them from another tribe, that is said to take them on the sea shore, where they are reported to be found in plenty.

All the Indians in this part of the country, are remarkably fond of these beads; and in their dealings with each other, they constitute a kind of circulating medium, like the money of civilized countries. Twenty of these beads, they consider as equal in value to a beaver's skin. The elderly people neglect to ornament their heads, in the same manner as they do the rest of their persons, and generally wear their hair short. But the younger people of both sexes, who feel more solicitous to make themselves agreeable to each other, wash and paint their faces, and let their hair grow long. The paint which they make use

of, consists of vermilion, which they occasionally obtain from us; or more commonly, of a
red stone, pounded fine, of which there are
two kinds. The powder of one kind of these
stones, mixed with grease, and rubbed upon
their faces, gives them a glittering appearance.

The young women and girls wear a parcel
of European beads, strung together, and tied
to a lock of hair, directly behind each ear.
The men have a sort of collar of the shell
beads already mentioned, which they wind
about their heads, or throw around their
necks. In the summer season, both sexes
bathe often; and this is the only time, when
the married people wash themselves. One of
their customs is sufficient to evince their extreme filthiness, and that is, whenever they
blow their noses, they rub the mucus between
both hands, until they become dry.

Among the Carriers, it is customary for
the girls, from the age of eight to eleven
years, to wear a kind of veil or fringe over
their eyes, made either of strung beads, or of
narrow strips of deer skin, garnished with
porcupine quills. While of this age, they are
not allowed to eat any thing, excepting the
driest food; and especially they may not eat
the head of any animal. If they should, their
relations, as they imagine, would soon lan-
guish and die. The women, also, during their
pregnancy, and for some time after they are
delivered, are restricted to the same kind of
food.

The lads, as soon as they come to the age of puberty, tie cords, wound with swan's down, around each leg, a little below the knee, which they wear during one year, and then, they are considered as men.

The Carriers are unusually talkative; and when fifteen or twenty of them get into a house, they make an intolerable noise. Men, women and children, keep their tongues constantly in motion; and in controversy, he who has the strongest and clearest voice is of course heard the most easily, and, consequently, succeeds best in his argument. They take great delight, also, in singing, or humming, or whistling a dull air. In short, whether at home or abroad, they can hardly be contented with their mouths shut. It was a long time before we could keep them still, when they came to our forts. And even yet, when they visit us, which is almost every day, during the whole year, they will often, inadvertently, break out into a song. But as soon as we check them, or they recollect of themselves what they are about, they stop short; for they are desirous of pleasing. The above trait in their character, certainly evinces much contentment with their condition, and cheerfulness of spirit.

Both sexes, of almost every age, are much addicted to play, or rather gambling. They pass the greater part of their time, especially in the winter season, and both days and nights, in some kind of game; and the men

will often loose the last rag of clothes, which
they have about them. But so far from
being dejected by such ill fortune, they often
appear to be proud of having lost their all;
and will even boastingly say, that they are
as naked as a dog, having not a rag with
which to cover themselves. Should they, in
such circumstances, meet with a friend, who
should lend them something to wrap around
their bodies, it is highly probable, that they
would immediately go and play away the
borrowed garment. Or, if the borrower belonged to another village, he would be likely
to run off with it, and the owner would
never hear of him afterward; for I never
knew a Carrier to be grateful for a favour bestowed upon him. At play, they often loose
a part of a garment, as the sleeves of a coat,
which some of them now purchase from us,
a whole, or the half of a leggin, which they
will tear off, and deliver to the winner. They
have been known to cut off a foot or more
of their guns, when lost at play; for, like
more gentlemanly gamblers, they consider
such debts, as debts of honour.

The Carriers are not so ingenious as their
neighbours, the Nâte-ote-tains and At-e-nâs.
The men, however, make canoes, which are
clumsily wrought, of the aspin tree, as well as
of the bark of the spruce fir. The former,
will carry from half a ton to a ton and a
half burthen, while the latter, will carry
from one to four grown persons. The women

make excellent nets, of the inner bark of the willow tree, and of nettles, which answer better for taking small fish, than any which we obtain from Canada, made of twine or thread.

The Carriers, in common with the other Indian tribes, before their country was visited by white people, made use of stones, instead of axes, and of bones, for knives; and with these, they constructed wooden dishes, and other vessels of the rind of the birch and pine trees, &c. Some of these vessels were used to cook their victuals in, and many of these people still make use of them; for they are too poor to purchase brass or copper kettles from us. They have, also, other vessels, which are manufactured of the small roots or fibers of the cedar or pine tree, closely laced together, which serve them as buckets to put water in. I have seen one at Fraser's Lake, made of the same materials, that would hold sixty or seventy gallons, which they make use of when a feast is given to all the people of the village. All the vessels fabricated of roots, as well as the most of their bows and arrows, they obtain from their neighbours, above mentioned.

The Carriers are remarkably fond of their wives, and a few of them have three or four; but polygamy is not general among them. The men do the most of the drudgery about the house, such as cutting and drawing fire wood, and bringing water. In the winter months, they drink but little water; but to quench their thirst, they eat half melted snow, which they generally keep on the top of a stick, stuck into the ground, before the fire.

As the Carriers are fond of their wives, they are, as naturally might be supposed, very jealous of them; but to their daughters, they allow every liberty, for the purpose, as they say, of keeping the young men from intercourse with the married women. As the young women may thus bestow their favours on whom, and as often as they please, without the least censure from their parents, or reproach to their character, it might naturally be expected that they would be, as I am informed they actually are, very free with their persons.—In the following particular, the Carriers differ from all the other Indian tribes, with whom I have been acquainted. Among other tribes, the father or mother in law, will never, excepting when drunk, speak to a son or daughter in law; but the Carriers make no distinction, in this respect.

The Carriers reside a part of the year in villages, built at convenient places for taking and drying salmon, as they come up the rivers. These fish they take in abundance, with little labour; and they constitute their principal food, during the whole year. They are not very palatable when eaten alone; but with vegetables, they are pleasant food.

The Natives, however, are too slothful to raise vegetables, and use none, excepting a few which they obtain from us.

Toward the middle of April, and sometimes sooner, they leave their villages, to go and pass about two months at the small lakes, from which, at that season, they take white fish, trout, carp, &c. in considerable numbers. But when these begin to fail, they return to their villages, and subsist on the small fish, which they dried when at the lakes, or on salmon, should they have been so provident as to have kept any until that late season; or they eat herbs, the inner bark or sap of the cypress tree, berries, &c. At this season, few fish of any kind, are to be taken out of the lakes or rivers of New Caledonia. In this manner the Natives barely subsist, until about the middle of August, when salmon again begin to make their appearance, in all the rivers of any considerable magnitude; and they have them at most of their villages in plenty, until the latter end of September, or the beginning of October. For about a month, they come up in crowds; and the noses of some of them are either worn or rotten off, and the eyes of others have perished in their heads; and yet, in this maimed condition, they are surprisingly alert, in coming up the rapids. These maimed fishes are generally at the head of large bands, on account of which, the Natives call them Mi-u-ties, or Chiefs. The Indians say that they have suffered these disasters, by falling back among the stones, when coming up difficult places in the rapids which they pass.

The Carriers take salmon in the following manner. All the Indians of the village assist in making a dam across the river, in which they occasionally leave places, to insert their baskets or nets of wicker work. These baskets are generally from fifteen to eighteen feet in length, and from twelve to fifteen feet in circumference. The end at which the salmon enter, is made with twigs, in the form of the entrance of a wire mouse trap. When four or five hundred salmon have entered this basket, they either take it to the shore to empty out the fish; or they take them out at a door in the top, and transport them to the shore in their large wooden canoes, which are convenient for this purpose. When the salmon are thrown upon the beach, the women take out their entrails, and hang them by their tails on poles, in the open air. After remaining in this situation for a day or two, they take them down and cut them thinner, and then leave them to hang for about a month in the open air, when they will have become entirely dry. They are then put into their store houses, which are built on four posts, about ten feet from the ground, to prevent animals from destroying them; and provided they are preserved dry, they will remain good for several years.

The Carriers take beavers in nets, made
of thongs of cariboo skins, or in baskets
made of young cypress stadles; and sometimes they shoot them with bows and arrows,
or guns, or take them in steel traps, which
we sell to them, and of which they begin to
understand the value. Cats, martins, fishers,
foxes, minks, &c. they take in a kind of
spring trap, which consists of a large piece
of wood, which these animals, by nibbling
at the bait, cause to fall upon and crush
them. Bears, swans and hares they generally take in snares, and the cat, also, they
sometimes take in this manner. They hunt
the beaver and bear, more for the sake of
their flesh, than to obtain the skins; for
it is with the meat of these animals that
they make their feasts, in remembrance of
their deceased relatives.

At such festivals, they cut up as many
dressed moose and red deer skins as they
can well procure, into slips, about eighteen
inches long, and twelve inches broad, and
distribute them among their friends and
relatives. And they firmly believe, that
these ceremonies must be performed, before
their departed relative can be at rest, in the
place whither he has gone, which they think
to be the interiour of the earth, where they
expect that they shall all at length be
happy.

The Carriers have little that can be denominated civil government, in the regulation

of their concerns. There are some persons among them, who are called Mi-u-ties or Chiefs, and for whom they appear to have a little more respect than for the others; but these chiefs have not much authority or influence over the rest of the community. Any one is *dubbed* a Mi-u-ty, who is able and willing, occasionally, to provide a feast, for the people of his village. An Indian, however, who has killed another, or been guilty of some other bad action, finds the house or tent of the chief a safe retreat, so long as he is allowed to remain there. But as soon as he leaves it, the Chief can afford the criminal no more protection, than any other person of the village can, unless he lets him have one of his garments. This garment of the Chief, will protect a malefactor from harm, while he wears it; for no person would attack him, while clothed with this safe guard, sooner than he would attack the chief himself; and if he should, the chief would revenge the insult, in the same manner as if it were offered directly to himself. The revenge which the Chief, in this case, would take, would be to destroy the life of the offending person, or that of some of his near relations, or the life of one of the same tribe, if he should happen to be a stranger.

When two or more persons disagree at play, as is frequently the case, or contend on any other account, the chief, or some respectable and elderly man, will step in between the two wranglers, and settle the dispute, generally without their coming to blows.

The people of every village have a certain extent of country, which they consider their own, and in which they may hunt and fish; but they may not transcend these bounds, without purchasing the privilege of those who claim the land. Mountains and rivers serve them as boundaries, and they are not often broken over.

The people of one village do not often visit those of another, as there are generally mis-understandings existing between them, which are occasioned by murders, and at times by the hunting of the people of one village, in a clandestine manner, on the territories of their neighbours. By one cause or another, they are kept in a perpetual broil. They say however, that murders do not occur so frequently among them as they did before they were visited by the white people.

The Carriers are the most ignorant people among whom I have ever been. They appear to have only a very confused and limited idea of the existence of a Supreme Being, the maker and governour of the world, or of the devil or any evil spirit; and they, therefore, neither worship the former nor fear the latter. But they believe, as it has been already observed, in the immortality of the soul, and think when it leaves its present body, it goes into the bowels of the earth, where, they suppose it will be more happy than when an inhabitant of its surface. But they seem to have no idea of future rewards or punishments, in consequence of any thing which they may have done, while resident on earth. And whether the soul will be furnished with another body, when it leaves that which it animated on earth, they say they cannot tell, it being, as they add, beyond their comprehension. They firmly believe, however, that a departed soul can, if it pleases, come back to the earth, in a human shape or body, in order to see his friends, who are still alive. Therefore, as they are about to set fire to the pile of wood, on which a corpse is laid, a relation of the deceased person stands at his feet, and asks him if he will ever come back among them. Then the priest or magician, with a grave countenance, stands at the head of the corpse, and looks through both his hands on its naked breast, and then raises them toward heaven, and blows through them, as they say, the soul of the deceased, that it may go and find, and enter into a relative. Or, if any relative is present, the priest will hold his hands on the head of this person, and blow through them, that the spirit of the deceased may enter into him or her; and then, as they affirm, the first child which this person has, will possess the soul of the deceased person.

When the Carriers are severely sick, they

often think that they shall not recover, unless they divulge to a priest or magician,
every crime which they may have committed,
which has hitherto been kept secret. In such
a case, they will make a full confession, and
then they expect that their lives will be
spared, for a time longer. But should they
keep back a single crime, they as fully believe
that they shall suffer almost instant death.
The crimes which they most frequently confess, discover something of their moral character, and therefore deserve to be mentioned.
A man will often acknowledge that he has
had a criminal and incestuous connexion with
his own daughter or sister, or a criminal intercourse with a bitch! and a woman will confess, that she has had the same infamous connexion with her own relations, or with a dog!

Murder is not considered by the Carriers
as a crime of great magnitude; and, therefore, it makes no part of their acknowledg-
ments, in their confessions to the priests or
magicians. If a murder be committed on a
person belonging to a tribe with whom they
are at enmity, they regard it as a brave and
noble action. Should one Indian kill another,
belonging to the same village with himself,
the murderer is considered as a person void
of sense; and he must quit his village and
remain away, until he can pay the relations
of the deceased for the murder; and even
after this has been done, it often occasions
quarrels, between the parties.

17

The Carriers are so very credulous, and have so exalted an opinion of us, that they firmly believe, though I have often assured them of the contrary, that any of the Traders or Chiefs, as they call us, can, at pleasure, make it fair or foul weather. And even yet when they are preparing to set out on an excursion, they will come and offer to pay us, provided we will make or allow it to be fair weather, during their absence from their homes. They often inquire of us whether salmon, that year, will be in plenty in their rivers. They also think, that by merely looking into our books, we can cause a sick person to recover, let the distance which he may be from us be ever so great. In short, they look upon those who can *read* and *write*, as a kind of supernatural beings, who know all that is past, and who can see into futurity.

For a considerable time after we had been among them, they were fully of the opinion, that the white people had neither fathers nor mothers; but came into the world in a supernatural way, or were placed on the earth by the sun or moon.

As a further specimen of their limited conceptions, they now firmly believe that a watch is the heart of the sun, because it is ever in motion, as they say, like that great body of light. They add further, that unless a watch and the sun were nearly related, it would be impossible for the watch, considering the distance which there is between them, to point out so precisely the minute when the sun is to make its appearance and to leave us. In short, they say that the one must know perfectly well what the other is about, and that there must be the same connexion between them, as between the members of the human body.

The Carriers give the following account of a tradition, which they believe, respecting the formation of the earth, and the general destruction of mankind, in an early period of the world. Water at first overspread the face of the world, which is a plain surface. At the top of the water, a muskrat was swimming about, in different directions. At length he concluded to dive to the bottom, to see what he could find, on which to subsist; but he found nothing but mud, a little of which he brought in his mouth, and placed it on the surface of the water, where it remained. He then went for more mud, and placed it with that already brought up; and thus he continued his operations, until he had formed a considerable hillock. This land increased by degrees, until it overspread a large part of the world, which assumed at length its present form. The earth, in process of time, became peopled in every part, and remained in this condition for many years. Afterwards a fire run over it all, and destroyed every human being, excepting one man and one woman. They saved them-

selves by going into a deep cave, in a large
mountain, where they remained for several
days, until the fire was extinguished. They
then came forth from their hiding place; and
from these two persons, the whole earth has
been peopled.

Besides the feasts, made for their dead,
which have been described in my Journal,
the Carriers give others, merely to enter-
tain their guests, who are frequently all the
people of a village, as well as a few who
belong to a neighbouring village. The following ceremonies attend such festivals. The
person who makes the entertainment, who is
always a Chief, boils or roasts several whole
beavers; and as soon as his guests are seated
around a fire, which is in the centre of his
house, he takes up a whole beaver, and with
a raised voice, relates how and where he
killed it, that all present may know that it
came from his own land. After that necessary explanation is over, he steps forward,
and presents the tail end to the most respectable person of the house, and stands
holding the animal with both hands until
this person has eaten what he chooses. The
chief then passes on with his beaver to the
second person, who eats as the first had
done; and then to a third; and so on, until
he has presented it to the whole circle. Should
any part now remain, it is laid down near
the centre of the house; and another whole
beaver is taken up, which is served round

in the same manner as the first. And thus the chief continues to do, until his guests have tasted of every beaver, which he had prepared for the feast. The remaining fragments of the beavers, are now cut up into smaller pieces, and distributed among the women and children, or put into dishes, which the men have before them, and which they always bring with them, when they attend upon a feast. The women then come in with large dishes full of berries, and each puts a ladle full into every dish of the men. When they have eaten what they choose of the berries, (for the Indians never urge their guests to eat more than they please) both men and women join, in singing several songs. The airs of many of these songs, which have been composed and set to musick, by their poets, expressly for the occasion, greatly resemble those which I have heard sung, in Roman Catholic churches. After singing is concluded, each guest rises, with his dish and whatever it contains, and returns to his own dwelling, and thus the festival ends. At these feasts, there are frequently Indians, who will drink at least a quart of melted bear's oil, merely to show how much they can drink.

At some of their festivals, the men and women join in a dance. Their musick on these occasions, consists of the singing of one person or more, accompanied by the shaking of the she-she-qui, which is, ordinari-

ly, a covered dish, with a handle; but sometimes it is curiously made in the form of a
bird, and within it, are either gravel stones
or shot. Others beat on a drum, with but
one head; and these are all the musical instruments, if they can with propriety be so
denominated, which I have ever seen among
them. When they dance, they paint their
faces, and put swan's down on their heads,
and while they are dancing, others are almost continually blowing more through both
their hands, on the dancers. They have
not many different kinds of dancing; but
they have a great variety of songs, the airs
of which are pleasant to the ear when heard
at some distance from the singers, who generally have strong voices. All Indians have
accurate ears; and, therefore, they keep exact
time when they dance or sing.

The Carriers are almost entirely ignorant
of medicine, not having any knowledge of
the virtue which is found in roots and herbs,
when administered to the sick. When one of
them is sick, they call in the priest or doctor,
for the same person discharges the functions
of both; and he is joined by several other
persons in singing a very melancholy air,
over the sick person, which they think serves
greatly to mitigate his pain, and often re-
stores him to perfect health. Before the
doctor will afford his assistance, in doing
which he makes many jestures, and goes
through much ceremony, he must receive a'

present. But should his patient die under his care, he must restore to the relations of the deceased, the present which he had received. The Carriers are the only Indians with whom I have been acquainted, who make no use of roots and herbs, and the bark of certain trees, with the sick. They, however, place great confidence in our medicines.

During the winter months many of the Carriers make their dwellings in the earth, in the following manner. They dig a hole in the ground to the depth of about two feet, from the opposite sides of which, they erect two considerable sticks, to support a ridge-pole. They then lay poles from the margin of the hole to the ridge-pole, until they have completely enclosed the dwelling, excepting a hole which is left near the top, which serves the double purpose of a door by which they enter, and leave the hut, upon an upright post, in which, notches are cut; and an opening for the smoke to pass off. The poles are made tight, by stopping the interstices with hay, or by covering them with bark; and dirt is then thrown over them, to a considerable thickness. These huts are far from being healthy; but they are commodious for people who are clad as poorly, as are most of the Carriers.

The Indians on the west side of the Rocky Mountain, erect buildings, in which they deposit the ashes and bones of their dead.

The side posts of these structures, are about
six feet high; a roof, covered with bark, is
erected upon these posts, in the form of the
roofs of houses in the civilized part of the
world; and around their sides, are broad
boards, made by splitting trees, which they
hew, and then smooth over with a crooked
knife. On these boards, which are about an
inch thick, they paint images to represent
the sun, moon, stars and different kinds of
animals. Within these buildings, the remains
of the dead are contained in boxes, of different dimensions, which in some instances,
stand on the top of one upright post, and
in other cases, are supported by four. The
paints which they use, in describing the
figures on these buildings, consist of black
and red stones, which they grind fine, and
of a yellow and a red earth. These substances, they mix with glue, which they
obtain by boiling the feet of the buffaloe,
or from the inside of sturgeon, where these
fish are in plenty. They put on their paints
with a brush, made of the hair which they
take from the leg of the moose.

Among the Carriers, there are some con-
jurors, who whenever they please, will vomit
blood, or swallow a small toad, alive. By
doing the latter, however, they are made
sick, for three or four days; and yet they
are ever ready to do it, for a mere trifling
recompense.

Among the Indians who inhabit New

Caledonia, the Sicannies deserve to be mentioned. They are a small part of a tribe
who, but a few years since, came from the
east side of the Rocky Mountain. They now
bring the produce of their hunts to McLeod's
Lake. The winter months, however, a greater
part of them pass among their relations,
on the east side of the Mountain, where
they subsist on buffaloe, moose and red
deer. Notwithstanding they are tolerable
hunters, they would not be able to kill a
sufficiency of beavers to serve themselves
and families, during the winter, where the
snow is so deep, as it generally is in New
Caledonia.

The people who are now called Si-can-nies,
I suspect, at no distant period, belonged
to the tribe, called Beaver Indians, who
inhabit the lower part of Peace River; for
they differ but little from them in dialect,
manners, customs, &c. Some misunderstand-
ing between the Sicannies and the rest of the
tribe to which they formerly belonged, probably drove them from place to place, up
Peace River, until they were, at length,
obliged to cross the Rocky Mountain. The
Sicannies, are more brave, and better armed
than the Carriers, who have, as yet, but
few fire arms; and it is probable that the
former will make encroachments upon the
latter. The Sicannies, however, are a wretched people; for they suffer greatly for the
want of food, during nearly one fourth part

of the year, when they barely support life, by means of a few unpalatable roots. Yet they are remarkably fond of the country, where they now are; and frequently intermarry with the Carriers, and pass a part of their time with them, at their villages. They have, also, adopted many of the customs of the Carriers, one of which is, to burn their dead; whereas, while they resided on the other side of the Mountain, they were accustomed to bury them in the earth. The Sicannies are not an ingenious people; and I know of nothing which they manufacture, excepting a few ill wrought bows and arrows, wooden dishes, &c.

There is a tribe of Indians not far from the Columbia River, who are called Flat-Heads. By fixing boards upon the heads of their children, they compress them in such a manner as to cause them to assume the form of a wedge. Another tribe in New Caledonia, denominated Nâte-ote-tains, pierce a hole through the under lips of their daughters, into which they insert a piece of wood, in the shape of the wheel of a pulley; and as the girls grow up, this wheel is enlarged, so that a woman of thirty years of age, will have one nearly as large as a dollar. This they consider, adds much to their beauty; but these wheels are certainly very inconvenient, and to us, they appear very uncouth and disagreeable.

A GENERAL

ACCOUNT OF THE INDIANS

ON THE EAST SIDE OF THE

ROCKY MOUNTAIN.

ACCOUNT, &c.

I have been acquainted with fifteen different tribes of Indians, which are the Sauteux, Crees, Assiniboins, Rapid Indians, Black feet Indians, Blood Indians, Sursees, Cautonies, Muskagoes, Chipeways, Beaver Indians, Sicannies, Tâ-cullies, Atenâs and Nâte-ote-tains. The parts of the country, which they severally inhabit, have already been noticed, in my Journal.

The tribes that are the most enlightened, and that have advanced the farthest toward a state of civilization, are the Sauteux or Chipeways, the Muskagoes and the Crees, or Knisteneux, as they have been sometimes denominated. These tribes have a greater knowledge than the other Indians, of the medicinal qualities of the bark of trees, and of herbs, roots, &c. and their medical skill, enables them heavily to tax the other tribes. Indeed, their medicines, with their skill in regard to their application, form considerable articles of commerce with their neighbours. Sometimes, for a handsome compensation, they will instruct a person where to procure ingredients, and how to prepare them as medicines, to be used in particular cases. It is very probable, however, that the Indian doctors, like some apothecaries in the civilized world, sell some medicines, of little or no value. It is also well known to those acquainted with the Indians, that their physicians frequently effect cures with their roots, herbs, &c. in cases, which would baffle the skill and the drugs, of a scientifick physician.

The white people have been among the above mentioned tribes, for about one hundred and fifty years. To this circumstance it is probably to be attributed, that the knowledge of these Indians is more extensive, than that of the other tribes. But I very much question whether they have improved in their character or condition, by their acquaintance with civilized people. In their savage state, they were contented with the mere necessaries of life, which they could procure, with considerable ease; but now they have many artificial wants, created by the luxuries which we have introduced among them; and as they find it difficult to obtain these luxuries, they have become, to a degree, discontented with their condition, and practise fraud in their dealings. A half civilized Indian is more savage, than one in his original state. The latter has some sense of honour, while the former has none. I have always experienced the greatest hospitality and kindness among those Indians, who have had the least intercourse with white people. They readily discover and adopt our evil practices; but they are not as quick to discern, and as ready to follow the few good examples, which we set before them.

The Indians in general, are subject to few diseases. The venereal complaint is common to all the tribes of the north; many persons among them, die of a consumption; fevers, also, frequently attack them; and they are likewise troubled with pains in their heads, breasts and joints. Many of them, and especially the women, are subject to fits. For a relief, in nearly all of their diseases, they resort to their grand remedy, sweating.

There is no material difference in the size, features and complexion of the different tribes, with whom I have been acquainted. The Sauteux, Crees and Assiniboins, together with the other Indians who inhabit the prairies, are, however, the fairest and most cleanly. The Sauteux women differ from all others, by turning their toes very much inwards, in walking. The Assiniboins, of both sexes, are the best made, and walk the most erect, of any tribe that I have ever seen. Fools and disfigured persons, are seldom to be met with among the Indians; the reason of which, I believe to be, that their mothers put them to death as soon as they discover their unhappy condition.

All Indian children, when young, are laced in a kind of bag. This bag is made of a piece of leather, about two feet square, by drawing a string, inserted in the lower end, and lacing the two sides together. Some moss is placed in the bottom of this bag; the child is then laid into it, and moss is inserted between its legs. The bag is then laced the fore side of the child as high as its neck. This bag is laid upon a board, to which it is fastened by means of a strip of leather, passing several times round both the board and the bag. At the top of this board, a bow passes round from one side to the other, perpendicular to its surface, on which the Indians fasten small bells, which they obtain from us, or the claws of animals, by way of ornament, and which rattle, when the child is carried by its mother, suspended from her shoulders, by means of a cord or belt fastened to the board. From two points in this bow, equally distant from the board, two strips of leather, worked with porcupine quills, are suspended, at the ends of which, tassels, composed of moose hair, are fixed. This bag is commonly ornamented, in different parts, with porcupine quills. The women who are particular in keeping their children clean, shift the moss which is put into these bags, several times in a day; but others do it not more than twice. They often fix conductors so that their male children never wet the moss. The

Carrier women will nurse their children,
when thus suspended at their backs, either
by throwing their breasts over their shoulders or under their arms. Their breasts are
larger and longer than those of the other
tribes; but I am unable to assign any cause
for this peculiarity.

The dress of the Indians is simple and
convenient. They wear tight leggins, each
of which is composed of a single piece of
leather or cloth, sewed up with a single
seam, about an inch from the edge, which
projects upon the outside. These garments
reach from the ancle nearly to the hip. They
have a strip of cloth or leather, called assi-
an, about a foot wide, and five feet long,
which passes between the legs, and over a
thong tied round the waist, so that the
ends hang down, behind and before. The
body is covered with a shirt, reaching down
to the thighs, which is belted with a broad
piece of parchment, fastened together behind.
They wear a cap upon the head, composed
of a single piece of fur sewed up, or of the
skin of a small animal of a suitable size,
which is cut off at both ends, and sewed up
at the top; and at some times it is only
cut off at the end towards the head, while
the tail is left at the top, to hang down
behind, by way of ornament. They have,
also, at the proper season, the tail of a
buffaloe, fastened to one of their wrists,
which they use in keeping off flies. A sort

18

of robe or blanket is occasionally worn over the rest of their dress. They also wear shoes and mittens. The articles of their clothing by day, constitute their covering when they lie down at night. The materials of which their clothing is composed vary with the season, consisting of dressed moose skins, beaver prepared with the fur, or European woollens. The leather, they frequently paint or work with porcupine quills, with no small degree of taste. The skirts of their shirts, and the seams of their leggins, are often ornamented with fringe and tassels, composed of the hair of the moose, which is naturally white, but which they die yellow and red. Their shoes and mittens have, likewise, an appropriate decoration. At a feast or dance, they wear the feathers of the swan, eagle and other birds; and they occasionally wind a string of the teeth, horns and claws of different animals, around their head or neck. They all rub greese upon their hair, which gives it a smooth and glossy appearance.

It belongs to the women to make up the articles of clothing. In sewing leather, instead of thread, they make use of the sinews of animals. When this substance is some moistened, they separate a fibre, and by running their finger along between it and the main sinew, they part it to a sufficient length. The sinews of the cariboo may be made as fine and even, as fine thread. These

fibres, when thus separated, they twist at
one end between their fingers, which gives
them a sharp stiff point, when they are dry.
They use awls, which they obtain from us,
or an instrument of bone which they construct themselves, in sewing. The men paint
their faces and ornament their persons, with
no less care than the women; and the married women, while they neglect not their
own persons, are still more attentive to the
appearance of their husbands. The young
women often make some ornamental articles,
particularly garters, neatly worked with
porcupine quills and present them to their
favourites; and the standing of a young
male Carrier among the young females may
often be determined by the number of garters
which he wears.

The female dress is made of the same
materials as that of the men, but differently
constructed and arranged. Their shoes are
without ornament; their leggins are gartered
beneath the knee; the shirt or coat, which
is so long as to reach the middle of the leg,
is tied at the neck, is fringed around the
bottom, and fancifully painted, as high as
the knee. Being very loose, it is girded
around the waist with a stiff belt, ornamented
with tassels, and fastened behind. The
arms are covered as low as the wrists with
sleeves, which are not connected with the
body garment. These sleeves are sewed up,
as far as the bend of the arm, having the

seam the under side; and extend to the shoulders, becoming broader toward the upper end, so that the corners hang down as low as the waist. They are connected together, and kept on, by a cord, extending from one to the other, across the shoulders. The cap, when they have one, consists of a piece of cloth, about two feet square, doubled, and sewed up at one end, which forms an enclosure for the head; and it is tied under the chin. The bottom of it falls down the back, like a cape, and in the centre, is tied to the belt. This cap is fancifully garnished with ribbon, beads or porcupine quills. The upper garment, is a robe or garment, similar to that worn by the men. Their hair is parted on the top of the head, and tied behind; or, at some times, it is fastened in large knots over the ears, and covered with beads of various colours. They prefer European clothes, when they can obtain them, to the skins, furnished by their own country. For ornaments they use bracelets, composed of brass, bone or horn; and rings, and similar trinkets. Some of the women tattoo a line, which is sometimes double, from the middle of the under lip, to the center of the chin; and two other lines, extending from the corners of the mouth, somewhat diverging from the other line, down the sides of the chin.

The greater part of the Indians, who make use of European cloths for their dress, frequently cleanse them, by washing them in cold water, without soap. They do not understand the art of making soap; and if they did, the process is so laborious, that they would readily forego the use of this article, which they consider of very little value. When their clothing consists of leather, they occasionally cleanse it, by rubbing it over with a ball of white earth. This earth, which is the same which we use for white washing, they moisten, and mould into balls, and thus preserve it for use.

The Indians who subsist principally on fish, and who kill but few large animals, cover their habitations with some kind of bark, or with mats made of rushes. But those who subsist on the buffaloe, moose and red deer, dress their skins, and cover their tents with them, as described in my Journal. When they are in their tents they sit or lie down on buffaloe or bear skins, which constitute, also, their beds; and when in bed, they cover themselves with a buffaloe skin, dressed with the hair on, or with a blanket. But many of the Carriers, have nothing to lie on, excepting the branches of the spruce fir tree, with little or nothing with which to cover themselves; and their huts constitute but a poor shelter. To keep themselves from freezing, in cold winter nights, therefore, they are under the necessity of keeping up a constant fire, to which they are compelled to turn their sides, alternately;

and they are, at such times, able to procure
but little sleep. Indeed, almost any other
people, in the same condition, would freeze
to death. But as they have always been
accustomed to such a mode of living, they
seem not at all aware of the misery of their
condition.

The Sauteux, Muscagoes, many of the
Chipewyans and some of the Crees, in short
all the Indians who live about large lakes,
subsist principally on fish, which they take
with hooks and lines, or in nets. Their
hooks they frequently obtain from us; and
when this is impracticable, they make them,
by inserting a piece of bone obliquely into
a piece of wood, and reducing the upper
end of the bone to a point. Their lines are
either single thongs of leather, tied together,
or they are braided of the bark of the willow.
The Assiniboins, Rapid Indians, Black feet
Indians and those Crees who remain in the
strong thick woods, or on the large plains,
live upon the flesh of the buffaloe, moose,
red deer, antelope, bear, &c. which they
either boil or roast. Those of them who
can obtain brass or copper or tin kettles
from us, use them for boiling their food;
and hang them over the fire. Those who
cannot obtain such kettles, use those which
are made of bark. Although water might
be made to boil in these bark kettles over
the fire, yet they would not be durable;
and therefore, this operation is more com-

monly performed, by throwing into them, heated stones. Those Indians, however, who have only bark kettles, generally roast their meat. This they do, by fixing one end of a stick, that is sharpened at both ends, into the ground, at a little distance from the fire, with its top, on which the meat is fixed, inclining towards the fire. On this stick, the meat is occasionally turned, when one part becomes sufficiently roasted.

The Indians, in general, like to have their food, whether boiled or roasted, thoroughly done; but those who inhabit the plains, frequently make their meals without the aid of fire, of particular parts of the entrails of the buffaloe, which I have, also, eaten raw, and have found to be very palatable. When there is no water to be found, they at times kill a buffaloe, and drink his blood, or the water which they find in his paunch. The paunch of a male buffaloe, when well cooked, is very delicious food. The Natives scarcely ever wash it; but boil it with much of its dung, adhering to it; and even then, the broth has an excellent taste, to those who can forget, or from habit pay no regard to the filth, which settles, to the thickness of two fingers, at the bottom of the kettle. Many consider a broth, made by means of the dung of the cariboo and the hare to be a dainty dish.

The Chipewyans can never patiently see a fish without gouging out its eyes, and eating them in a raw state; and they say, that they are delicious. They, also, often make their meals upon raw fish or meat, that is frozen; and appear to relish it fully as well, as when cooked.—The Carriers, when they take fish that have roes in them, squeeze them, with their thumb and finger, through their natural outlet, into their mouths, and swallow them down, with avidity. They also bury in the earth large boxes, filled with the roes of salmon, where they are suffered to remain, until they are a little putrified, when they take them out, and eat them, either cooked or raw; and they appear to relish them well, though they fill the air with a terrible stench, for a considerable distance round. A person who eats this food, and rubs salmon oil on his hands, can be smelt in warm weather, to the distance of nearly a quarter of a mile.

The natives in a part of the country called *Nipigon*, as well as in some other parts of the country, are frequently obliged, by necessity, to subsist on a kind of moss, which they find adhering to the rocks, and which they denominate As-se-ne Wa-quon-uck, that is, eggs of the rock. This moss when boiled with pimican, &c. dissolves into a glutinous substance, and is very palatable; but when cooked in water only, it is far otherwise, as it then has an unpleasant, bitter taste. There is some nourishment in it; and it has saved the life of many of the Indians, as well as of some of our voyagers.

On the Columbia River, there is a people who subsist, during the greater part of the summer, on nothing but roots, and a kind of bread, if it may be so called, made of the mossy stuff, which grows on the spruce fir tree, and which resembles the cobwebs, spun by spiders. This substance contains a little nourishment. They gather it from the trees, and lay it in a heap, on which they sprinkle a little water, and then leave it, for some time, to ferment. After that, they roll it up into balls, as large as a man's head, and bake them in ovens, well heated, which are constructed in the earth. After having been baked about an hour, they are taken out for use. This substance is not very palatable; and it contains but little nourishment. It will, however, barely support life, for a considerable time.

The Indians frequently eat the flesh of the dog; and our Canadian voyagers are as fond of it, as of any other meat. I have frequently eaten of them myself; and have found them as palatable as a young pig, and much of the same flavour. These dogs are small; and in shape, very much resemble the wolf. The large dogs are of a different breed, and their flesh always has a rank taste; but this is never the case with the small kind.

Perhaps I cannot more properly, than

in this connexion, state, that all the Indians, when they look in each other's heads, and find lice, of which they have a plenty, both there and on their bodies, crush them between their teeth, and frequently swallow them. The reason which they give for this nauseous custom is, that, as the lice have first bitten them, they are only retaliating the injury upon them.

As the Indians use no salt in the preservation of their meat, the lean part is cut into thin slices, and hung up in their tents, and dried in the smoke, and the fat is melted down; and in this situation, it will keep for years. They make marrow fat, by cutting the joints of the bones, which they boil for a considerable time, and then skim off the top, which is excellent to eat with their dried meat. They find a root in the plains, that is nearly a foot long, and two or three inches in circumference, which is shaped like a carrot, and tastes like a turnip, which they pound fine, and then dry it in the sun. This, when boiled in fat broth, is one of their most dainty dishes, at their feasts. The ordinary drink of the Indians is the broth of flesh or fish, or only water.

The Indians on the east side of the Rocky Mountain, pound choke cherries fine, and dry them in the sun, which are palatable, either eaten alone, or boiled in broth. They have also a small berry, about the size of

a common currant, shaped like an egg, which
I have called, in my Journal, shad berries,
as I have heard them so denominated in New
England, which they dry in the sun, and
either boil them in broth, or mix them with
pounded meat and fat, in making pimican.
But the Carriers prepare these berries in a
different manner, in order to preserve them.
They make a kind of tub, which will contain twenty or thirty gallons, of the bark
of the spruce fir tree. Into the bottom of
this tub they put about a peck of these
berries, and upon the top of them stones,
that are nearly red hot; they then put another layer of berries, and upon these, a
layer of stones, and so on until the tub is
full. They then cover it up, and let it remain in that situation for about five or
six hours, when they will have become perfectly cooked. They are then taken out,
and crushed between the hands, and spread
on splinters of wood, tied together for the
purpose, over a slow fire; and, while they
are drying, the juice which ran out while
they were cooking in the tub, is rubbed
over them. After two or three days drying,
they will be in a condition to be kept for
several years. They are very palatable,
especially when a few whortleberries are
mixed with them. The above described
method of cooking berries, is far better than
doing them in brass or copper kettles, as I
have proved by repeated experiment.

The Carriers cut off the heads of salmon, and throw them into the lake, where they permit them to remain a month, or at least until they become putrified. They then take them out, and put them into a trough, made of bark, filled with water. Into this trough they put a sufficiency of heated stones, to make the water boil for a time, which will cause the oil to come out of the heads of the salmon, and rise to the top of the water. This they skim off, and put into bottles made of salmon skins; and they eat it with their berries. Its smell however is very disagreeable; and no people would think of eating it excepting the Carriers.

The Indians are not regular in their meals; and they will eat a little, half a dozen times in a day, if they have food at hand. But they are not great eaters; and they often subsist for a great length of time, upon a very little food. When they choose, however, and in a particular manner, sometimes at feasts, they will gorge down an incredible quantity. They do not drink largely, excepting the Carriers, who live upon dry fish. They will sometimes swallow, at one draught, three pints, or two quarts. When they can procure food that is palatable, they will eat in the same proportion. No favour which can be bestowed upon them is so gratefully received, as the means of making a good meal.

From the month of June, until the latter

end of September, all animals have but little
fur; and therefore, at this season, the Indians
do not hunt them much. The greater part
of the Indians, on the east side of the Rocky
Mountain, now take the beaver in steel traps,
which we sell them; frequently they shoot
them, with fire arms; and sometimes they
make holes through their lodges or huts,
and then spear them. Otters they take in
the same manner as beavers. The lynx or
cat, they take in snares. Foxes, fishers,
martins, minks, &c. they take in a spring
trap.—The large animals are hunted chiefly
for their flesh; and are therefore killed,
principally when they are the fattest, which
most of them are in the fall, and some of
them in the winter. Buffaloes, moose, red
deers, bears, &c. are generally killed with fire
arms. The Indians, however, in the plains,
have other methods of killing the buffaloe.

Sometimes the young men mount their
horses, and pursue them and bring them
down with their bows and arrows, which
they find more convenient for this purpose
than fire arms, as they can more easily
take an arrow from the quiver, than load
a musket, in such a situation. The following,
is another method of taking the buffaloe.
The Natives look out for a small grove of
trees, surrounded by a plain. In this grove
they make a yard, by falling small trees,
and interweaving them with brush; and they
leave an opening into it about twenty feet

broad. They select, for this purpose, a rising piece of ground, that the yard may not be seen at a distance. From each side of this opening, they fix two ranges of stakes, at about an angle of ninety degrees from each other, extending about two miles into the plains. These stakes rise about four feet above the ground, and are about forty feet apart. On the top of each stake, they put buffaloe dung, or tie a wisp of hay. After this preparation, when a herd of buffaloes is seen at no great distance off, thirty or forty or more young men mount their racers, which are well trained to this business, and surround them; and little difficulty is found in bringing them, within the range of the stakes. Indians are stationed by the side of some of these stakes, to keep them in motion, so that the buffaloes suppose them all to be human beings. The horsemen press forward by the sides of the herd and behind them, until, at length, with their tongues lolling from their mouths, they are brought to the entrance of the yard; and through it they rush without perceiving their danger, until they are shut in, to the number, often-times, of two or three hundred. When they find themselves enclosed, the Indians say, and I have frequently seen myself, that they begin to walk around the outside of the yard, in the direction of the apparent rev-olution of the sun, from east to west. Be-fore any of them are killed, the Indians go into the tent of the chief to smoke, which they denominate making the buffaloe smoke. They then go out to the yard, and kill the buffaloes with bows and arrows; and there are Indians, who will send an arrow, entirely through one buffaloe, and kill, at the same time, a second. When the buffaloes are all killed and cut up, the tongues of all of them are taken to the tent of the chief; and with a part of them he makes a feast, and the remainder he allows his neighbours to keep. The meat and skins are then distributed among the people of the whole camp; and whether equally or not, no one will complain. Should any be displeased with their share, they will decamp, and go and join another party.

The Natives generally cut up the body of an animal into eleven pieces, to prepare it for transportation to their tents, or to our forts. These pieces are the four limbs, the two sides of ribs, the two sinews on each side of the back bone, the brisket, the croup, and the back bone. Besides these, they save and use the tongue, heart, liver, paunch, and some part of the entrails. The head, they carry home, the meat which is on it they eat; and the brains they rub over the skin, in dressing it.—After they have taken all the meat off from the skin, they stretch it on a frame, and suffer it to dry. They next scrape off all the hair, and rub the brains of the animal over the skin, and

then smoke it; after which they soak it in
water, for about a day. They then take it
out and wring it as dry as possible; and a
woman takes hold of each end, and they
hold it over a fire, frequently pulling it and
changing its sides, until it is perfectly dry.
After this it is smoked with rotten wood,
and it becomes fit for use. This last part
of the process, is to prevent it from becoming hard after it has been wet.

The Sauteux, who remain about the Lake
of the Woods, now begin to plant Indian
corn and potatoes, which grow well. The
Mândans, also, along the Missouri River,
cultivate the soil, and produce Indian corn,
beans, pumpkins, tobacco, &c. As they do
not understand curing their tobacco, it is of
little use to them. The Sauteux, who live
back from Mackana, raise large quantities of
Indian corn, beans, &c. And also make
much sugar, from the maple tree, which they
dispose of to the North West Company, for
cloth and other articles. As soon as the
animals become scarce, that are hunted for
their furs, the Natives must till the ground
for subsistence, or live upon fish. This state
of things already exists, in many places;
and must, in all probability, be extended.

The Indians sometimes take the largest
fish, such as sturgeon, trout, and some
white fish, with spears. At other times, they
take their fish in drag-nets or scoop-nets.
But the more general way of taking them

is the following. They have nets, of from twenty to sixty fathoms, in length, which contain from twelve to forty meshes, of from two to seven inches in depth. Upon lines, which are fixed upon each side of the net, for the purpose of strengthening it, they fasten, opposite to each other, a small stone and a wooden buoy, once in about the distance of two fathoms. The net is carefully thrown into the water, and by means of the stones on the one side, and the buoys on the other, it becomes extended, to its full breadth. The ends of the net, which forms a semicircle, are secured by stones; and it is visited every day, and taken out of the water every second day, to be cleaned and dried. This is a very easy operation, when the water is not frozen. But the ice which, at some places, acquires the thickness of five feet, renders the setting and taking out of the nets, a work of greater difficulty. They then cut holes, at the distance of thirty feet from each other, to the whole length of the net, one of which, is larger than the rest, being generally about four feet square, and is called the basin. Through these holes, by means of poles of a suitable length, the net is placed in and drawn out of the water.

The Indians, throughout the whole country that I have visited, have no other animals domesticated, excepting the horse and the dog. Of the latter, they have several different species. Some of them are very large

19

and strong, and are employed in carrying burdens; while others, which are small, assist their masters in the chace.—All Indians are very fond of their hunting dogs. The people on the west side of the Rocky Mountain, appear to have the same affection for them, that they have for their children; and they will discourse with them, as if they were rational beings. They frequently call them their sons or daughters; and when describing an Indian, they will speak of him as father of a particular dog which belongs to him. When these dogs die, it is not unusual to see their masters or mistresses place them on a pile of wood, and burn them in the same manner as they do the dead bodies of their relations; and they appear to lament their deaths, by crying and howling, fully as much as if they were their kindred. Notwithstanding this affection, however, when they have nothing else with which to purchase articles which they want, they will sell their dogs.

Those Indians, who live in a woody country, make no use of horses, but employ their large dogs, to assist in carrying their baggage from place to place. The load is placed near their shoulders, and some of these dogs, which are accustomed to it, will carry sixty or seventy pounds weight, the distance of twenty five or thirty miles in a day.

The Assiniboins, Rapid Indians, Black feet and Mândans, together with all the other

Indians who inhabit a plain country, always perform their journies on horse back. Indeed they seldom go even a short distance from their tents, in any other manner. They have some excellent horses, which will carry them a great distance in a day. They sometimes go seventy miles, in twelve hours; but forty or forty five miles is a common day's ride. They do not often use bridles, but guide their horses with halters, made of ropes, which are manufactured from the hair of the buffaloe, which are very strong and durable. On the back of the horse, they put a dressed buffaloe skin, on the top of which, they place a pad, from which are suspended stirrups, made of wood, and covered with the skin of the testicles of the buffaloe.

Some of these Indians have forty or fifty horses; and they attach a great value to those, that are distinguished for their speed. Whenever an Assiniboin sells a racer, he separates from him, in a most affectionate manner. Immediately before delivering him to the purchaser, he steps up to the favourite animal, and whispers in his ear, telling him not to be cast down or angry with his master for disposing of him to another, for, he adds, "you shall not remain long where you are. I sold you to obtain certain articles, that I stood in great need of; but before many nights have passed, I will come and steal you away." And, unless great vigilance on

the part of the purchaser prevent, he generally fulfils his promise; for they are the greatest horse thieves, perhaps upon the face of
the earth. As there never falls much snow
on the large plains, the horses have not much
difficulty in finding a sufficiency of grass, on
which to subsist, during the whole year; and
they are generally in good order.

The Indians who reside about large lakes
and rivers, voyage about in the summer
season, in canoes, made of the bark of the
birch or spruce fir tree; and two persons in
one of them, will easily go fifty miles in a
day. The paddles, with which the canoe is
moved, are about five feet long, half of which
length, is a blade, four inches wide.

The Indians are good walkers; and will
at sometimes, travel forty miles in a day,
with a pretty heavy load upon their backs.

In the winter season, the Indians use snow
shoes; and it would be impossible to travel
without them. They are constructed in several different shapes; but the following is the
most common form. They take a piece of
wood, and with a crooked knife, work it
down, until it is about two inches wide, and
an inch thick. These sticks are fastened together at one end, which constitutes the hind
part; they are then bent so as to be about
a foot asunder in the middle, and to come
nearly together forward. The space between
these sticks, they fill up with a lace work of
thongs of deer skin. Other snow shoes come

quite to a point before, where they are turned up; the side pieces are from eighteen to twenty four inches apart, and, in the fall of the year, when the snow is light, they are seven feet in length. The inner side piece is nearly straight, and the outside is arching, and the extremities behind, come together in a point. The space between them, is worked as above mentioned. It is a little surprising that the Indians, who are accustomed to them, will walk farther in a day on good snow shoes, than they could do on bare ground. But it is very fatiguing for those to walk on them, who are not accustomed to do it. The Indians are trained to this exercise from the age of four years. Even at that early age, they will go five or six miles in a day upon them, through the whole winter, as often as the Indians decamp, which, at sometimes, is every day, and at other times, once in eight or ten days. Indians, who live upon the chace, in a country where animals are scarce, cannot remain long in a place; and those who hunt the beaver and some other animals, must continually shift their residence.

Few of the Indians live in a state of celibacy. They generally marry when they are between eighteen and twenty five years of age. Polygamy is allowed among all the tribes; but only a few persons among them, have more than one wife, each. I knew, however, a chief, among the Beaver Indians, who had eleven wives, and more than forty children.

Their courtship and marriage are conducted in the following manner. A young man who is desirous of taking a wife, looks around among the young women of his acquaintance, to find one that pleases his fancy. Having thus singled out one, to her he makes known his intentions; and if his addresses are favourably received, he visits her, in the night season, by crawling softly into the tent where she lodges, and where she is expecting him, after the other inhabitants of the lodge are asleep. Here they pass the night, by conversing in a whisper, lest they should be heard by the rest of the family, who all occupy the same apartment. As the morning light approaches, he withdraws in the same silent manner, in which he came. These nocturnal visits are kept up for several months; or, until the young couple think that they should be happy, in passing their days together. The girl then proposes the subject to her mother, and she converses with the father in regard to the intended match. If he give his consent, and the mother agree with him in opinion, she will direct her daughter to invite her suitor to come and remain with them. It is now only, that they cohabit; and whatever the young man kills, he brings home and presents it to the father of his wife. In this way he lives, during a year or more, without having any property

that he can call his own. After his wife has
a child, she calls her husband by no other
name but the father of her son or daughter.
And now he is at liberty to leave the tent
of his wife's father, if he pleases. All the
Indians on the east side of the rocky mountain, think it very indecent for a father or
mother in law, to speak to, or look in the
face of a son or daughter in law; and they
never do either unless they are very much
intoxicated. The reason which they give for
this custom, when questioned on the subject
is, the peculiar intercourse which this person
has had with their child.

When two young persons of different sexes,
have an affection for each other, and wish
to be connected in marriage, to which the
father of the girl will not consent, they frequently leave the tents of their parents, and
go and join some distant band of Indians.
They are, however, often pursued, by the
father of the young woman; and should he
overtake them, he will bring his daughter
back, and keep a strict watch over her conduct, to prevent all intercourse between her
and her suitor. All neighbouring tribes frequently intermarry.

Chastity in young women, is considered as
a virtue, by the Indians, generally, on the
east side of the Rocky Mountain; and many
mothers, among some tribes are so particular, that they never allow their daughters,
who have arrived at a certain age, to go

from home alone, but always send some person with them, as a protector. Chastity in married persons is universally regarded as a virtue; and the want of it in a woman, is frequently the cause of her being rejected by her husband. A separation, also, at some times, takes place, on account of the slothfulness of the woman. When such an event does occur, all the children, if small, remain with their mother, but should they have sons, advanced beyond the period of childhood, they remain with their father. Their separations, however, are seldom lasting; and after a few days absence, the parties generally have an inclination to return to each other. These separations commonly take place in obedience to the will of the husband, only because, possessing greater physical strength, he has more power to drive his wife from him, or to retain her with him, against her choice, than she has to treat him in a similar manner.

The Indian women sit down in a decent attitude, placing their knees close to each other. They are very particular, also, in regard to their behaviour, during their periodical illness. They then leave the tents where their families reside, and go and put up temporary ones, at a little distance from them, where they remain during the continuance of their illness. While they are there, the men will not deign to hold any conversation with them; nor will they suffer

them to make use of any article, which they
expect to want the use of afterwards. This
custom prevails among all the tribes, with
whom I have been acquainted. The first
time that the young women, among the
Sauteux, Crees and some other tribes, experience this illness, they run into the woods,
and remain there for several days. They
then return to their tents, and immediately
proceed to cut and pile up a cord of wood,
as high as their heads; after which all the
women of the camp come and scramble for
it, and carry it away, saying, that the person who cut the wood, is now a woman like
themselves, and that they hope she will prove
to be industrious.

The men among the Indians, are very subject to be jealous of their wives. In their fits
of jealousy, they often cut off all the hair
from the heads of their wives, and, not unfrequently, cut off their noses, also; and
should they not in the moment of passion
have a knife at hand, they will snap it off
at one bite, with their teeth. But such a
circumstance does not ordinarily produce a
separation between them. The man is satisfied in thus revenging a supposed injury;
and having destroyed the beauty of his wife,
he concludes that he has secured her against
all future solicitations to offend.

All the Indians consider women as far inferiour in every respect, to men; and, among
many tribes, they treat their wives much as

they do their dogs. The men chastise their wives, frequently, with an axe, or with a large club; and in the presence of their husbands, the women dare not look a person in the face. When they decamp, the women transport the baggage; and when they stop, while the men are quietly smoking their pipes, the women are required to pitch the tents, and to set the encampment in order. Among the Sauteux, Crees, Muscagoes and Assiniboins, however, the women are treated with more gentleness and respect. The husband shares the labour with his wife; and the women govern every thing in their tents, so that the husband presumes not to dispose of the most trifling article, without the consent of his wife. Among them the husband kills animals and generally brings the meat to his tent, where his wife prepares it for drying, and melts down the fat. She, also generally does the cooking; not, however, without the occasional assistance of her husband. He assists her, likewise, in taking care of the children; and, if his wife is too much loaded, in marching from one place of encampment to another, he will take one óf the small children in addition to the load already on his own back. But the Indians, who inhabit the plains, never carry any thing on their backs, as they are well supplied with horses.

The following ceremonies attend the birth of children. When the time of a woman approaches, she erects a small hut, at a little distance from the tent in which she usually lives; and at the time of labour, she sends an invitation to several neighbouring women, to come to her assistance. As soon as the child is born, it is washed in water, that had been previously prepared, by boiling in it a sweet scented root. The mother then orders a feast to be prepared. As soon as it is ready, the most aged woman of the company, takes a little out of the dish, and throws it into the fire, and then helps the whole company; not passing by the mother of the child, who is generally able to join them in the repast. The old lady of ceremonies, now offers up a short prayer to the Creator, or the Master of life, as they denominate him, in behalf of the new born babe, the substance of which is, that its life may be spared, and that it may grow; and if a son, become a handsome young lad.

A woman after child birth, remains in the separate dwelling which she had erected, for the space of about thirty days, during which time, no man would, on any account, enter the place of her residence. At the close of this period, she returns to her tent, and the father of the child prepares a feast to which all their neighbours are invited, the object of which as they say, is, to welcome the arrival of the little stranger, from a far country.

Should a male child live, the parents dry the meat of the first animal that he kills, and carefully keep it, until they can collect a sufficiency of something to make a feast. They then invite their friends, of both sexes, to come and partake of the fruits of the hunt of their son; for, they so call it, because the animal which he killed, they mix with what his parents have procured. Before any taste of the feast, one of the most respectable men present, takes a little out of the dish, and throws it into the fire; and then beseeches the Great Spirit, to be kind to the lad, and to allow him to grow up, and to become a skilful hunter; and to cause that when he goes to war, he may not behave like an old woman, but may return with the scalps of his enemies.

Indian women appear to suffer less pain in child birth, than women in civilized countries. They rarely ever take any medicine, at the time of delivery, though they do, at times, drink water, in which the rattle of a rattlesnake has been boiled. In the season of labour, they place their knees upon the floor or ground, and lean forward over something, raised about two feet high. It is seldom more than a quarter or a half an hour, before the child is born; and, in a few days the mother is as active and vigorous as ever. The Indian women rarely ever die, at this critical period.

Among the natives, those persons who are in any way deformed, or have any blemish about them, receive their name from this circumstance; while the others are named, after some beast or bird. No Indian will inform another, even if requested, what his own name is; though he will, if asked, give the name of other Indians. Of the reason of this reserve I am ignorant.

It is not often that an Indian chastises his children; and, indeed, it is not necessary, for they appear, in general, to have much affection and respect for their parents, and are therefore ready to obey them. A father never interferes in the bringing up of his daughter; but leaves her wholly to the care of her mother. When a son becomes of a suitable age, his father takes him with him in hunting, and learns him the different modes of taking animals. A son until he is married, considers himself as under his father's controul; and even after that, he will generally listen to any advice, which his father may give to him. The aged are commonly treated with much respect, which they consider themselves as entitled to claim. Should a young man behave disrespectfully toward an old man, the aged will refer him to his hoary head, and demand of him, if he be not ashamed to insult his grey hairs. In short, the aged of both sexes are generally treated with kindness; and are not suffered to want any thing which they need, and which it is in the power of their relations to procure for them.

The superior influence of the white people,

where they have, for a considerable time, resided among the Indians, has very much diminished their respect for their own chiefs; though there are some among them, who bear this title. The feasts are commonly made by the chiefs; and they, also, generally make the harangues, in behalf of their bands, when they visit our forts. Their war chiefs have considerable influence over the young men, who accompany them, in their war parties.

Murder and theft are considered as crimes; and the former is always punished with death, unless the murderer makes his escape, which is generally the case. Theft, also, is frequently punished in a similar manner. Sometimes, the party offended will be appeased, by the restoration of the stolen property, or of an equivalent.

Generosity is among the Indian virtues. They are more ready, in proportion to their means, to assist a neighbour who may be in want, than the inhabitants, generally, of civilized countries. An Indian rarely kills an animal, without sending a part of it to a neighbour, if he has one near him.

The private property of the Indians, consists of horses, dogs, tents, guns, and the utensils that belong to their tents. Some of these things, a little before their death, they bequeath to some of their friends; but all of their clothing, guns, powder horns, &c. are buried with them. Indeed, the Indians suffer nothing to remain in or about the tent of a person who has died, which he was accustomed to make use of while he was alive. They consider it a kind of sacrilege to mention the name of a person after he is dead; and they never speak of him as dead, but as miserable, because, they say, he has taken a long journey alone, to the country, to which his deceased relations had gone before him.

Whenever any one is very sick, the whole of his family, and frequently all of his relations, will give some part of their clothing in sacrifice to the devil or evil spirit, who, they suppose, is the cause of his illness. They, however, pray to the Good Spirit, or Master of life, for his recovery, as they believe that he has the power, if he choose to exercise it, of restoring him to health, notwithstanding the design which the evil spirit has, of taking his life from him.

All the Indians on the east side of the Rocky Mountain, *bury* their dead. After a person is dead, some of his deceased relatives cut off a lock of his hair, which they carefully lay up; and they sometimes preserve such relicks, for a great number of years. Preparatory to its interment, they dress the corpse in as gay a manner as possible; and then wrap a blanket, over the whole. But they never sew or pin this blanket together, lest he should be unable to shake it off with ease, when he arrives in the other world. If it were fastened, they say, he might lie in it for several days, after his arrival in the land of his departed relations, before any one would meet with, and release him. The bottom and sides of the grave, which is two or three feet deep, are lined with the branches of trees. The corpse is then deposited in it; and along with it, a pipe and tobacco, a dish or small kettle, an awl and sinews to repair his shoes, and a sufficiency of provisions, to support him for a few days, until he shall arrive in the land of plenty. They then cover the body with branches, and fill up the grave with earth; and on the top of it, they place bark, to protect it from the rain or snow. They then clear off the bushes and grass, for eight or ten feet around the grave; and every spring, the ground is thus renewedly cleared, for several years after. About the grave, they set up a few stakes on which they hang strips of cloth, tobacco, &c. While the ceremonies of interment are performing, the relatives and friends of the deceased, make the most dismal moans and cries; and, to convince others of their grief, and, as they say, to ease their wounded hearts, some of them cut the hair of their heads short, or make incisions in their faces and arms, while others, to whom the deceased was more dear, will seize an arrow, in an agony of grief, and run it through the fleshy part of their thighs.

The Indians generally appear to be more

afflicted with the loss of an infant, helpless child, than of a person that has arrived to mature age; for the latter, they say, can provide for himself, in the country whither he has gone, while the former, is too young to depend upon himself.

The men appear to be ashamed to manifest their grief at the loss of any one, however dear he might have been to them; but the women give full vent to the feelings of nature. The fond mother, when she looses a young child, will pull out all the hair of her head; cut her face, arms and legs, in a shocking manner; burn all her clothes, excepting a few rags, which she has upon her; and, to render herself as wretched, as she expresses it, as her child, when the weather is stormy, she will stand for hours at a time, in the open air, and pitifully moan, in such language as this. "How wretched are you, my child, to be torn from your friends while so young and helpless; and to be sent alone, into a strange country! Who will now give you bread when you are hungry, and water, when you are thirsty, and make a covering for you to lie under when it rains or snows! O that I could once more press you, my dear child, to my troubled breast! Of what use to me are all my medicines, since they could not save your life, and keep you a little longer with us!" Then, in a rage of passion and of grief, she will rush into her tent, and seize her medicine bag, and throw it into the fire.

All the Indian tribes are frequently at war with each other; and at some times, two tribes will league together, against one tribe or more. Those who reside in a woody country, do not as frequently wage war against their neighbours, as those who live in the large plains. The latter, generally engage in war, either offensive or defensive, at the opening of every spring. The summer is the only season of military operations, among the Indians; though they frequently employ much time in the winter, in providing bows, arrows, guns and ammunition, with reference to a campaign, the ensuing season. Preparatory to hostilities, the chiefs, toward the close of winter, send young men with presents of tobacco, to the whole tribe, who are scattered over their territory, inviting them to meet, at a specified place, early in the spring, in general council. At this meeting, chiefs are appointed to conduct the war. The war pipe is then lighted up, and those who are willing to become soldiers in the campaign, smoke the pipe. None are compelled to enlist; but, to excite in the young men a martial spirit, and to stimulate them to become his followers, the war chief makes a long harangue, in which he relates the injuries, that they have received from their enemies. By a strong appeal to their savage feelings, he labours to convince them, that it will be sweet and manly, to revenge these insults; and to return from the war, with the scalps of their enemies, and with their wives, and children, and horses, &c.

A feast is then made, of which all partake, after which, the young men dance, and sing war songs. After these ceremonies are ended, the chief or chiefs set out on the war expedition, with as many as choose to follow them; and as they leave the camp, the war party join in a war song. After their departure, the old men and women and children pursue their usual occupations, to obtain a subsistence. Frequently, after the war party has been gone several days, some of the young men return, to join their relations or lovers. All the punishment to which they subject themselves is, to be called old women, by which is meant, cowards; a charge which touches an Indian to the quick.

War parties frequently travel four or five hundred miles, before they reach the territory of their enemies. On their way, they subsist upon animals which they kill, and fish which they take, from the lakes and rivers. These supplies are often very inadequate, and they suffer greatly by hunger.

Having arrived near the place where they expect to find their enemies, the chiefs send out scouting parties, in order to ascertain their position, numbers and any other circumstances which it may be necessary for them to know, in order to form a plan for taking them by surprise. The Indians never attack their enemies in the open day; but fall upon them when asleep, near the approach of the light of the morning.

If they succeed in conquering their enemies, as is generally the case, since those who make the attack have greatly the advantage, they make terrible havoc among the men; but they labour to take as many of their women and children alive, as they possibly can, in order to carry them home as slaves. They never torture these captives; but keep them to perform the menial service about their tents, or dispose of them to others. Sometimes they are adopted into the families of their enemies, in the place of children that they have lost; and then they are treated with all the tenderness and affection, which would be exercised toward a near relation.

On their return from the expedition, the war party approach the tents of their band, with their faces blackened, and singing the war song. Their relations immediately make a feast, at which the warriours dance, with the scalps of their enemies which they have taken, in their hands; and recount the history of the expedition, particularly relating the manner in which they fell upon their enemies, the number of men that they killed, and of slaves, horses, &c. which they have taken. They then distribute a part of the booty, among the aged chiefs, and most respectable men of the tribe, who remained at home. The young men, who deserted the party, are treated with contempt; and the

young women, whose charms may have at-
tracted them back, frequently compose songs
of derision, in regard to their behaviour.

The occasions of war among the Indians
are various. Sometimes a person in one
tribe has been murdered by a person belonging to another tribe; sometimes the
members of one tribe have hunted on the
lands of another; and sometimes horses
have been stolen. The Indians, who inhabit
the large plains, who always go to war on
horseback, frequently attack their neighbours
merely to obtain, by this means, horses and
slaves. It is not uncommon, also, for the
Natives, when they lose a respected chief,
or any other person generally beloved, either
by an ordinary or a violent death, to form
a war party, for the purpose of killing one
person or more, of a neighbouring tribe; and
the case is the same, whether this tribe be
at peace with them, or not. This slaughter,
they say, enables them to calm their grief,
and sets their hearts at rest, as blood has
thus been offered to the manes of their departed friend.

A person appointed to head a war party,
is called a chief, or O-ke-maw. He must
have given distinguished proof of his bravery,
prudence and cunning, in former war expeditions, in order that he should be considered as qualified to fill this post. Great
skill, in coming upon an enemy by surprise,
as on this circumstance the success of an

attack depends, is considered as the first requisite in a military leader. It is considered necessary, also, that he should be well acquainted with the situation of the territories of the enemy, and with the course leading to them, in which provisions can most easily be obtained. A war party sometimes consists of several hundreds; but frequently it does not amount to more than twenty. The war chief has no authority over his followers, but his advice is generally respected and followed.

It is not often that two tribes, who have been in the habit of carrying on war against each other, formally enter into terms of peace. When such an event does take place, the following circumstances attend it. One chief or more, and several young men of his tribe, go with their pipe of peace, to find their enemies; and on their arrival among them, they express a desire to hold a council with them. Upon this, all the elders of the tribe visited are called together; and the chief, who is an ambassadour for peace, makes known his business, and strives to convince his enemies, that it will be for their advantage to live on amicable terms with his tribe.

Should the terms of peace be agreed on, the parties smoke in each other's pipes, after which a feast is prepared; and when that is concluded, the remainder of the night is spent in singing and dancing.—But should the

embassy be unsuccessful, the chief, with his
attendants, will return, and make report of
his proceedings to his own tribe; and those
of them who are able and willing to bear
arms, will immediately, though as secretly as
possible, commence making preparations for
a campaign, the ensuing spring. The points
of the arrows, which the Indians use in attacking their enemies, are sometimes dipped
in a poisonous liquid which they extract
from certain roots.

All the Indians spend much of their time
in some kind of amusement. The inhabitants of the plains, generally, and of New
Caledonia, live in large bands; and are much
more addicted to a usements, than the inhabitants of woody countries who are more
scattered. Every tribe has amusements peculiar to itself; but some plays are common to all, who reside on the east side of
the Rocky Mountain. The Assiniboins, as
well as all the other Indians in the plains,
spend much of their time about their horses,
and are fond of trying their speed. Their
youth, from the age of four or five to that
of eighteen or twenty years, pass nearly
half of their time in shooting arrows at a
mark; and to render this employment more
interesting, they always have something at
stake, which is generally nothing more than
an arrow, or something of small value. From
so early and constant a practice, they become,
at length, the best marksmen, perhaps, in

the world. Many of them, at the distance
of eight or ten rods, will throw an arrow
with such precision, as twice out of three
times, to hit a mark of the size of a dollar.
The young men often amuse themselves, in
the summer season, by a game of ball.

What is denominated by the Indians, the
dish game, is played with peculiar interest,
by all the tribes with whom I have been
acquainted. Eight or ten little pieces of
bones, or so many buttons, or some similar
things, have a certain number of marks upon
their different sides, so that they bear
some resemblance to dice. These are put into
a dish, which two persons shake alternately,
and turn its contents on the ground. The
marks on the sides of the bones, &c. which
are uppermost, are then counted; and, in a
given number of throws, he who can count
the greatest number of marks, wins whatever
is at stake; for they never play, without
something.

The Sauteux and Crees are very fond of
playing at draughts; and they are considerably skilful, at this game. They have, also,
many other plays and diversions, which
enable them to pass away the greater part
of their leisure time, gaily. The Indians,
generally, appear cheerful and contented,
when oppressed by no present difficulty or
danger; for they take little thought for the
things of the morrow.

The Indians do not often dance, in the

day time; but they frequently spend their long winter evenings, in this amusement, accompanied by singing; and they appear to enjoy themselves fully as well, on such occasions, as civilized people do, at their more refined assemblies.

All the Natives are accustomed to make feasts, on various occasions, and particularly when any uncommon or important business is to be transacted. When a band of from thirty to fifty tents is collected, scarcely a day passes without an entertainment, made by some one of the number.

When a chief proposes to make a feast, he invites such guests as he pleases, by sending to them quills, or small pieces of wood. Every person, who attends, brings with him a dish and a knife. The chief generally receives his guests, standing, but oftentimes, sitting; and a person who assists him, seats them, according to their ages or respectability, the most honourable place being next to the chief. After having made a division of what had been provided, into a number of parts, equal to the number of persons present, the chief lights his pipe, and smokes a few whiffs himself; and he then presents the stem toward the sun, as if offering it to that luminary, and to the earth, and then to his deceased relations, pointing it toward the fire. These ceremonies being over, he presents it successively to each person present, who smokes a few whiffs in his turn.

A small quantity of meat or drink is then sacrificed, by throwing it into the fire, or on the earth, and the provisions are served round. While the company are partaking of them, the chief sings, and accompanies his song, by the che-che-quy or tambourin. The person who devours his portion the soonest, is considered as deserving applause. If any cannot eat all that is set before him, as custom does not allow him to leave any thing, he endeavours, by the promise of a reward of tobacco or ammunition, to prevail upon his friends to assist him. These substitutes, it is frequently difficult to procure, as the food provided on these occasions, is generally much more than is necessary to satisfy the calls of nature. At some of their feasts, a more rational custom prevails, of permitting the guests to carry away what they do not wish to eat, of their portions. The meat which is generally eaten on these occasions, is that of the beaver; and the bones of this animal, which are extremely hard, that remain after the feast, are burned, lest the dogs, by attempting to break them, should injure their teeth.

The public feasts are conducted in the same manner, but with additional ceremony. Several chiefs unite in preparing a suitable place, and in collecting sufficient provisions, for the accommodation of a numerous assemblage. To provide a place, poles are fixed obliquely into the ground, enclosing a suf-

ficient space to hold several hundred, and at
times, nearly a thousand people. On these
posle, skins are laid, at the height of twelve
or fifteen feet, thus forming a spacious court,
or tent. The provisions consist both of dried
and of fresh meat, as it would not be practicable to prepare a sufficient quantity of
fresh meat, for such a multitude, which,
however, consists only of men. At these
feasts, the guests converse only on elevated
topics, such as the public interests of the
tribe, and the noble exploits of their pro-
genitors, that they may infuse a publick and
an heroic spirit, into their young men. Dancing always forms the concluding ceremony,
at these festivals; and the women, who are
not permitted to enter the place where they
are celebrated, dance and sing around them,
often keeping time with the music within.

All the different tribes of Indians, on the
east side of the Rocky Mountain, believe in
the existence of one Supreme Being, the
creator and governour of the world, whom
they call Kitch-e-mon-e-too, or the Great
Spirit; and to him they ascribe every perfection. They consider him as the authour
of all good, and as too benevolent to inflict
any evil upon his creatures. They render him
little worship; but occasionally supplicate of
him success in their important undertak-
ings, and very rarely, render him some sacrifices, consisting of some part of their property.

They, also, believe in the existence of a
bad spirit, whom they call Much-e-mon-e-too,
to whom they ascribe great power, and who,
they believe is the authour of all evils, by
which mankind are afflicted. To him, therefore, in order to obtain deliverance from
evils which they either experience or fear,
they offer many, and sometimes expensive,
sacrifices. They consider him as ever employed, in plotting against their peace and
safety; and they hope, by such means, to
appease his anger.

They, also, believe that there are good
and bad spirits, of an inferiour order, who
are superiour to men in the scale of existence,
and who have allotted spheres of action, in
which they are contributing to the happiness
or misery of mankind. These beings they
suppose preside over all the extraordinary
productions of nature, such as large lakes,
rivers and mountains, and spacious caverns,
&c. and likewise over the beasts, birds, fishes,
vegetables, and stones, that exceed the rest
of their species in size, or in any other remarkable quality. On this account, they pay
to all these objects, some kind of adoration.

They, also, believe in a future state of
existence. Those who, while in the present
world, have, according to their ideas of right
and wrong, led a good life, will, at death,
immediately enter on another and a better
state of existence, where they will meet their
departed relatives and friends, who will

welcome them in the most affectionate manner,
to their happy abode.   In the future world,
they believe that they shall possess bodies
more beautiful and healthy and vigourous,
than those which they animated on earth;
and that they shall be much more happy,
than they were in the present life, since the
country in which they will reside, abounds
with all kinds of game, which they will be
able to take, with little or no trouble, and
supplies every gratification, in which they
now delight, in perfection and without end.

But those who lead wicked lives on earth,
they suppose will, at death, be conveyed
into the middle of an extensive swamp or
marsh, where they will, for a considerable
length of time, be doomed to wander about
alone, in search of their deceased friends.
After having suffered greatly, from hunger
and cold, they suppose that they will, at
length, arrive at the pleasant habitation of
their departed relatives, and participate with
them, in all its delights forever.

The religious observances of the Indians,
consist of prayers, of feasts, and of a sacrifice
of some part of their property.—Their prayers, which are offered only on special occasions, are always, addressed to the Supreme
Being, or Master of Life. Their religious
festivals are attended with much serious ceremony. They commence with opening the
medicine bag, and displaying its contents,
and with smoking out of the sacred stem.

Almost every male Indian has a medicine bag,
which is commonly made of leather, and is
about two feet long, and a foot broad. The
following articles are generally contained in
this bag. The principal in importance is
a small image, carved to resemble a bird,
beast or human being, which they seem to
consider as the peculiar residence of their tutelary spirit. This image, they carefully wrap
in down, around which a piece of birch bark
is tied, and the whole is enclosed in several
folds of red and blue cloth. Every Indian
appears to have a reverence for the Image
in his own medicine bag; but will often
speak disrespectfully of one, belonging to
another person. The next article in the
bag, is the war cap of its owner, which is
decorated with the plumes of scarce birds,
and with the claws of the beaver, eagle, &c.
It has also a quill or feather, suspended from
it, for every enemy, whom its owner has slain
in battle. The other contents of the bag are
a piece of tobacco, and some roots and other
substances, which are supposed to possess
valuable medicinal qualities. To the outside
of the bag, the sacred stem is tied, which is
generally about six feet long. This stem is
used only for smoking on sacred occasions.
This medicine bag is generally hung, in fair
weather, on the limb of a tree, or on a stake,
at a little distance from the tent; and an
Indian would severely beat his wife, if she
should presume to touch it. This is the

only article which the men invariably carry
themselves, when they are decamping. Many
of them pretend, that by examining it, they
can foretel future events.—The women, also,
have their own medicine bag; but they are
not considered as of a sacred character, and
merely contain their own articles of medicine.
—Smoking out of the sacred stem, is performed with numerous ceremonies, many of
which are probably unmeaning.

Some Indians make a promise to the
Master of Life, that they will make a feast
every spring during a certain number of successive years, if their lives are spared; and
they religiously fulfil such vows.

Some of their feasts are designed to propitiate the evil spirit, as are nearly all the
sacrifices which they make of their property.
Sometimes in an open enclosure, on the bank
of a river or lake, they make large sacrifices
of their property. They choose a conspicuous
situation, that those who pass by, may
be induced to make their offering. If any
of the tribe that makes these offerings, or
even a stranger who is passing these places,
should be in urgent want of anything
which has been deposited as an offering, he
is allowed to take it, by replacing it with
another article which he can spare, though
of inferiour value; but to take wantonly any
of those devoted articles, is considered as
sacrilege.

There are also certain large rocks and

caves, which they never pass without leaving
at them some trifling article; for they suppose that they are the habitations of
some good or evil spirits. Indeed they
think that almost every lake, river and
mountain has its tutelary spirit, whom they
attempt to propitiate, by some offering.

All the Natives suppose the earth to be
an extensive plain, and that it is always at
rest; and that the sun and moon and many
of the stars continually revolve around it.
The sun, they believe to be a large body
of fire. To many of the stars they have
given names, such as the morning star, the
evening star, and the seven stars; and
by their position in the heavens, they are
able to determine the time of night. They,
also, direct their course by them in travelling, in the night season. The stars which
they have named, they perceive change their
position continually in the heavens; and they
believe that, like the sun and the moon, they
revolve around the earth. Of the motion of
the other stars, they take no notice and consider them as stationary. The following is
the manner in which they divide a day and
night, or twenty four hours: from the first
appearance of day light to sunrise, from this
time till noon, from noon to sunset, from
this to midnight, and from midnight to day
break. They are ignorant of the number of
days, which there are in a year; but reckon
thirteen moons, to complete the four seasons.

The following are the names of the four seasons, in the Cree tongue. Winter, A-pe-pook or Pepoon; Spring, Me-is-ka-mick or Se-gum-uck; Summer, Nic-pin; Autumn, Tuck-wâ-gin.

The names, which they give to the moons that compose the year, are descriptive of the several seasons, and in Cree, are the following:

May, I-ich-e Pes-im, Frog Moon.

June, O-pin-â-wâ we Pes-im, the Moon in which birds begin to lay their eggs.

July, O-pus-ko we Pes-im, The Moon when birds cast their feathers.

August, O-pâ-ko we Pes-im, The Moon when the young birds begin to fly.

September, Wâ-wâs-kis o Pes-im, The Moon when the moose cast their horns; or A-pin-nâs-ko o Pes-im, The Moon when the leaves fall off from the trees.

October, O-no-chi-hit-to-wa o Pes-im, The rutting Moon; or O-ke-wa-ow o Pes-im, The Moon when the fowls go to the south.

November, Ay-e-coop-ay o Pes-im, Hoar frost Moon. Kus-kut-te-no o Pes-im, Ice Moon.

December, Pa-watch-e-can-a-nas o Pes-im, Whirlwind Moon.

January, Kush-a-pa-was-ti-ca-num o Pes-im, Extreme cold Moon.

February, Kee-chay o Pes-im, The Moon when small birds begin to chirp or sing; or Kich-ee o Pes-im, Big, or old Moon.

March, Me-ke-su o Pes-im, Eagle Moon.

April, Nis-ka o Pes-im, Goose Moon, as at this season, these animals return from the south.

The Indians compute the distance from one place to another, by the number of nights which they have passed, in performing a journey from one to the other.

All the Natives employ hieroglyphicks, for the purpose of conveying information to those who are distant from them; and this mode of communication, is often of great service to them, as the following circumstances will evince. Portions of each tribe, generally assemble at certain places, every year. When they separate, they proceed in different directions; and at every place where they severally encamp, they fix a number of sticks in the ground, leaning towards the place where they next intend to pitch their tents. If they have been successful in the chace, they paint or draw on a piece of bark, the number and kinds of animals which they may have killed, and hang the bark upon a stake. When Indians who have been unsuccessful in regard to killing animals, fall upon these notices, they derive important advantages from them, as they are thus guided to the place, where they may probably obtain a supply of food. Indeed, without some such regulation, the Natives would often be in great danger of perishing with hunger. On the piece of bark, containing information respecting their past success, and their future course, they leave, also, the date of their encampment, by painting the animal, or whatever else it is that gives name to the then present Moon, or month, and by describing the figure of the Moon at that particular time. And so correct is this mode of conveying intelligence, that a person accustomed to it, will generally ascertain, within from twelve to twenty four hours, the time designed to be specified.

The Indians possess a quick perception, and strong curiosity, and a very retentive memory; and every circumstance which occurs, and the various objects which present themselves to their view, are noticed and recollected. And, therefore, at the expiration of twenty years after they have passed only once through a country, to the distance of several hundred miles, they will return by the same way in which they came. Mountains, hills, prairies, lakes, valleys, remarkable rocks, &c. are the objects which they especially notice, and the situation of which, they treasure up in their memories; and by these they are enabled to follow a former track. Almost any Indian, who has passed once through a country, is able to draw so correct a chart of it, with a piece of charcoal, on bark, that an entire stranger, by its assistance, would be able to direct his course to a particular place, several hundred miles distant, without varying a league from his object.—The Natives are never at a loss in regard to the different points of the compass, particularly in a woody country, as they well know, that on the north side of the trees, more moss is found, than on the other sides.

The priest among the Indians, is also a physician and a conjurer or magician.—When he acts as priest, he presides at feasts and funerals.—In the capacity of physician, when sent for, he visits the sick and wounded, and prescribes medicines for their healing, and directs in their application, in doing which he goes through with many ceremonies, with great gravity. If the patient is very ill, he attends him at least every morning, and sings and shakes his che-che-quy, for an hour or two, over his head, making an unpleasant noise, which, it would seem, must do injury to the sick person. These Indian physicians do at times, however, perform distinguished cures. Their medicines consist of the bark of particular trees, of roots and of herbs, used at some times in their simple state, and at others in a compounded form. For wounds and sores, they use, chiefly, decoctions of roots. The doctor is always well paid for his services, and his profession is the most lucrative of any among the Indians.—When he acts as conjurer, he shuts himself up in a small cabin, where he is completely concealed from the view, and where he remains silent, during ten or fifteen minutes. He then begins to sing, and to beat his drum, and continues to do so, for about half an hour. And then, if any one has a question to propose respecting futurity, he is ready to answer it, which, however, he will not do, without a trifling recompense. It is not uncommon for events to take place, much as these conjurers predict; but whether this is to be attributed to their natural sagacity, or to accident, or to other circumstances, I pretend not to determine.

A person who is desirous of becoming a physician or conjurer, is publickly initiated, with much mysterious ceremony. Among these ceremonies are the following. The old physicians prepare an entertainment for a certain number of people; and for the young candidate, they have a peculiar mess, which consists of a bitch, boiled with her young in her. A part of this animal, he must eat; and they suppose that it possesses the magical power, of inspiring him with a knowledge of the medicinal qualities of all kinds of barks, herbs, roots, &c.—A woman, who wishes to become a midwife, must not only eat a part of the bitch, but must, also, partake of her puppies, and drink of the broth in which they were boiled; and by this means, she gains, as is supposed, all the knowledge requisite to the practice of this difficult art.

The Indian physicians never fail of leaving in the place where they collect the roots, herbs, &c. which they use as medicines,

some trifling article, as a recompense to the
guardian spirits, that preside over these
substances, for what they have taken. An
omission of this would, in their apprehension,
destroy most, if not all the efficacy of their
medicines.

The Natives, in general, are very credulous and superstitious. They believe that
many of their own medicines, when properly
applied, will effect almost any thing. They
think, however, that we possess some, which,
for certain purposes, are much more effica-
cious than their own. All Indians are very
desirous of having a numerous offspring; and,
therefore, those, whose wives are barren, will
frequently apply to us for such a medicine
as will cause them to become the mothers of
children.—The young women, also, make use
of a certain powder, of their own composition, for the purpose of engaging or increasing the affections of their favourites, for
them. By throwing this even upon a stranger, who is passing, they believe, it will cause
him to be in love with them. In a word,
they ascribe a power to this medicine, like
that, which more refined imaginations have
attributed to the arrows of Cupid. The
young women, also, employ many other
magical arts, to accomplish the same object.
—A woman who is fond of her husband, and
who supposes that he has little affection for
her, will rub a certain medicine in the palm
of her hand, as she is going to bed; and

after he falls asleep, she will lay her hand on his heart; and the medicine, she thinks, possesses the power of uniting their hearts together, and of causing their affection, ever afterward, to be reciprocal.

The Indians have no professional mechanicks among them. Every man is his own artificer, and is able to construct the few domestick manufactured articles, which he uses. Some persons among them, more ingenious than the rest, are frequently applied to, to execute some things which require considerable skill, such as putting a stock to a gun; but they take no compensation, for such a service. Their bows and arrows are neatly constructed. In order to make their arrows round and straight and smooth, after they have been reduced nearly to their proper size with a knife, they use the following method. They take two pieces of wood, of suitable thickness, which are several inches long, and cut in each of them a straight channel, of the same size, and of such a shape, that, when both are placed together, they form a circular hole. Over this channel, they spread glue, and upon that they sprinkle sand; and they repeat the operation, until a complete file is formed. The arrow is then placed in the channel, between the two pieces of wood, and is briskly passed backward and forward, until it is reduced to its proper size. Their pipes are made of a soft stone. The bowl, into

which the tobacco is put, is circular, and
at the bottom it is flat, and much broader.
These pipes are frequently carved, in a curious manner. The pipe is connected with its
stem by a chain, generally made of brass
wire, which the Indians obtain from us, and
which hangs loosely from one to the other.
The stem is of wood, such as has a small
pith; and as their sacred stems are about
six feet in length, the manner in which they
extract this pith, deserves to be mentioned.
They use, for this purpose, a piece of sea-
soned hard wood. It is sharpened to a
point, at one end; and at a little distance
from this, it is reduced to a smaller size,
by a perpendicular cut around it, by which
a kind of head or barb is formed. By
pushing this in and drawing it out, the
pith is gradually extracted. The wood which
forms the handle to this barb, is reduced to
a very small size, as fast only as is required
by the length of the hole. Wooden dishes,
they construct, with crooked knives. The
women manifest much ingenuity and taste,
in the work which they execute, with porcupine quills. The colour of these quills is
various, beautiful and durable; and the art
of dying them, is practised only by females.
To colour black, they make use of a chocolate coloured stone, which they burn, and
pound fine, and put into a vessel, with the
bark of the hazel-nut tree. The vessel is
then filled with water, and into it the quills

are put, and the vessel is placed over a small fire, where the liquor in it is permitted to simmer, for two or three hours. The quills are then taken out, and put on a board, to dry, before a gentle fire. After they have been dried and rubbed over with bear's oil, they become of a beautiful shining black, and are fit for use. To dye red or yellow, they make use of certain roots, and the moss which they find, on a species of the fir tree. These are put, together with the quills, into a vessel, filled with water, made acid, by boiling currants or gooseberries, &c. in it. The vessel is then covered tight, and the liquid is made to simmer over the fire, for three or four hours, after which the quills are taken out and dried, and are fit for use. Feathers, they also dye in a similar manner, and these colours never fade.

Many of the Indians, particularly those on the west side of the Rocky Mountain, who have not procured steels from us, for the purpose of striking fire, produce it, by placing one end of a small dry stick against another piece of dry wood; and by rolling it briskly between their two hands, the friction, in a short time communicates fire to dry hay or touchwood, placed around it.

Among the Indians, there are poets, who are also musicians. The person who composes a song, does it by singing it over alone, in the air which he designs shall accompany it; and he repeats this exercise, until he has committed both sufficiently to memory. After that, he frequently teaches it to others. Songs are frequently composed for particular occasions, such as feasts, &c. Among the Carriers, there are often several competitors for this honour; and he who composes the best song, is rewarded, while the unsuccessful poets are treated with derision. The subjects of their songs are generally love and war, though they have some which are ludicrous and obscene. They have a great variety of songs; and I have known an Indian who could sing at least two hundred, and each song had its peculiar air. Female poets are not common among them. Some of the women, however, are excellent singers.

No two, of the fifteen tribes of Indians, with whom I have been acquainted, speak precisely the same language; but the languages of nine of them only, seem to be radically different. There is only a variation of dialect among the Crees, Sauteux and Muscagoes. The same is true of the Chipewyans, Beaver Indians, Sicannies, Tacullies and Nateotetains. The language spoken by the Sauteux, Crees and Muscagoes is by far the most copious and manly; but that used by the Assiniboins, is the most harmonious and elegant.

Every tribe has its particular tract of country; and this is divided again, among the several families, which compose the tribe.

Rivers, lakes and mountains, serve them *e*
boundaries; and the limits of the territor
which belongs to each family are as wei
known by the tribe, as the lines which sep-
rate farms are, by the farmers, in the civilized world. The Indians who reside in the
large plains, make no subdivisions of their
territory; for the wealth of their country
consists of buffaloes and wolves, which exist
in plenty, everywhere among them. But the
case is otherwise, with the inhabitants of the
woody countries. These people have nothing
with which to purchase their necessaries, excepting the skins of animals, which are valuable for their fur; and should they destroy
all these animals in one season, they would
cut off their means of subsistence. A prudent Indian, whose lands are not well stocked
with animals, kills only what are absolutely
necessary to procure such articles as he cannot well dispense with.

The foregoing account of the Natives, having a principal reference to the tribes on the
east side of the Rocky Mountain, it may be
proper, in concluding it, to make a few general remarks on the country which they
inhabit.

That part of it which lies between the
44th and the 52d degrees of north latitude,
is a plain or prairie country, almost wholly
destitute of timber, of any kind. It is, in
general, sufficiently dry for any kind of cultivation; and is covered with grass, which

commonly grows to the height of from six inches to a foot, though in some marshy places it is much higher. This grass furnishes food for innumerable herds of buffaloes, which are constantly roving about, from place to place, followed by thousands of wolves, and many grey and black bears, that are always on the watch, for favourable opportunities to fall upon and devour them. The grey bear, on account of his strength and ferocity, may well be denominated the monarch of the forest; and should he at any time find an hundred wolves or more, feeding on the carcase of the buffaloe, the sight of him would cause them all to retire, with all the humility and submission of conscious weakness, and he would be permitted to make his meal, at his leisure and in quietness.

The country lying between the 52d and the 70th degree of north latitude, may be denominated mountainous. Between its elevated parts, however, there are valleys and plains, of considerable extent, and which are covered with timber, of a small growth, more than one fourth part of which is the spruce fir. The other kinds of timber are aspin, poplar, birch, hemlock, spruce, cedar, willow, and a little pine. Much of this country, in its less elevated parts, is covered with large rocks and stones, with so thin a coat of earth upon them, that it could not be cultivated. I am of opinion, however,

that one fourth, if not one third part, of
the whole of this great extent of country,
might be cultivated to advantage. The soil,
in general, is tolerably good; and, in many
places, is not exceeded in richness, by any
part of North America. I think it probable,
that as much as one sixth part of the whole
of this country, is covered with water. The
great number of large lakes, which are scattered over it, and of noble streams, which
pass through it, afford a water communication, in almost every direction.

As this country is so extensive, it is natural to suppose, that the climate is various.
In all parts it is considerably cold. In
latitude 54° or 55° the mercury, for
several successive days, in the month of
January, is as low as 30 or 32 degrees below zero. There are not, however, more
than ten or twelve days, during a winter,
that are so severely cold. The summers are
sufficiently warm and long, to bring most
kinds of grain and vegetables to perfection.
Indian corn will never ripen farther north,
than about latitude 53°.

The following fact may be interesting to
some persons, as perhaps no similar discovery has been made, equally far north.
In the summer of 1816 there was found, on
the margin of a small stream that falls into
Peace River, in about the 56th degree of
north latitude, and the 118th of west longitude, a part of the thigh bone of a Mam-

moth, which was about eighteen inches in length, and which weighed twenty eight pounds. During that summer, the waters rose very high, in all the streams in that region; and when they subsided, the banks in many places, fell in. It was in such a place, that this bone was found. It was sent to Canada, and I believe, thence to England.

A SPECIMEN

OF THE

CREE OR KNISTENEUX TONGUE,

WHICH IS SPOKEN, BY AT LEAST THREE FOURTHS
OF THE INDIANS OF THE NORTH WEST
COUNTRY, ON THE EAST SIDE OF THE

ROCKY MOUNTAIN.

———

Good Spirit	Kitch-e-mon-e-too
Evil Spirit	Mutch-e-mon-e-too
Man	A-ye-nu
Woman	Es-qui
Young man	Os-kin-e-gew
Young woman	Os-kin-e-gis-qui
Infant	A-wâ-sis
Head	Is-te-gwen
Forehead	Mis-kaw-tick
Cheek	Mon-o-wy
Chin	Tâ-lis-kun
Hair	Mis-te-ky-ah
Eye	Mis-kee-sick
Nose	Mis-kee-won

Nostril	O-tay-e-cum
Mouth	Mee-toon
Tooth	Mee-pit
Tongue	O-tay-e-nee
Beard	May-ist-won
Brains	We-it-tip
Ear	Me-tâ-wâ-ki
Neck	Me-qui-yow
Throat	Me-koo-tâ-gun
Arms	Mis-pe-toon
Hands or fingers	Me-chee-chee
Thumb	Me-se-chee-chon
Nail	Mis-cus-see
Side	Ose-pe-ki
Back	Mis-pis-quon
Belly	Mot-ti
Thigh	Me-pwâm
Body	Me-yow
Knee	Mitch-e-quon
Leg	Mis-kâte
Foot	Me-sit
Heart	Me-tay
Spirit or soul	Me-châ-châke
Father	O-tâ-we
Mother	E-ka-we
Son	E-qus-sis
Daughter	E-ta-nis
Brother (elder)	E-stays
Sister (elder)	E-miss
Brother (younger) } Sister (younger) }	E-shim
Grand Father	E-mo-shome
Grand Mother	O-kome

Uncle	O-ko-mis
Aunt	E-to-sis
Nephew	E-to-sim
Niece	E-to-sim-es-qui
Father in law	E-sis
Mother in law	E-se-goose
Brother in law	Ish-taw
Sister in law	E-tim
Friend	E-wich-i-wâ-gun
Husband	Ne-nâ-bem
Wife	E-che-mâ-gun
Old man	Kis-a-ye-new
Old woman	No-to-ca-ow
Chief	O-ke-mow
Thief	Ke-mo-tisk
Coat	Pis-is-cow-e-gun
Shirt	Pe-puck-e-wy-un
Breech cloth	As-si-an
Leggin	Me-tâss
Garter	Sis-ca-pis-soon
Shoe	Mos-ca-sin
Hat or cap	As-to-tin
Handkerchief	Tâ-bis-kâ-gun
Mittens (a pair)	Us-tis-uck
Petticoat	Kis-ke-sâ-ki
Bracelet	Us-ton
Ring	Us-ton-is
Ear knobs	Tâ-be-ta-soon
Comb	Se-ca-hoon
Needle	Sâ-bo-ne-gun
Pin (headed needle)	Is-te-goine Sâ-bo-ne-gun
Scissors	Pus-co-ma-to-in
Blanket	Wa-bo-e-un

22

Gown	Pa-to-nis
Horse	Mish-ta-tim
Buffaloe	Moos-toosh
Ferret	Se-goose
Skunk	Se-hawk
Elk	A-wâs-kis
Moose	Moose-wâ
Carriboo	At-tick
Beaver	A-misk
Wolverine	Ke-quâ-a-kisk
Squirrel	An-nick-o-chass
Mink	At-châ-kass
Otter	Ne-kick
Wolf	My-e-gun
Hare	Wâ-poos
Martin	Wâ-pis-ton
Bear	Musk-quaw
Fisher	O-chake
Lynx	Pe-su
Hog	Ko-koosh
Porcupine	Kâ-quaw
Fox	Muck-ca-sis
Musk rat	Wâ-chesk
Cat	Kâ-sha-kess
Mouse	A-pe-co-sik
Meat	Wee-as
Dog	At-tim
Bitch	Kis-ke-sis
Eagle	Me-ke-su
Duck	See-sip
Crow	Kâ-kâ-ku
Swan	Wa-pis-see
Pheasant	O-kis-kew

Bird	Pe-a-sis
Outard	Nis-kâ
White goose	Why-why
Grey goose	Kitch-a-ca-pi-sis
Partridge	Pe-yew
Water hen	Se-kip
Pigeon	O-ma-mee
Egg	Wâ-wâ
Pike	I-e-ne-ke-no-see
Carp	Na-ma-be
White fish	At-tick cum-mick
Pickerel	O-cow
Fish (in general)	Ke-no-see
Fish roes	Wâ-quock
Fish scales	Wâ-wâ-ki
Trout	Na-ma-goose
Frog	I-ick
Wasp	A-mo
Turtle	Mis-ca-nâck
Snake	Ke-na-bick
Rattle snake	Si-si-qua ke-na-bick
Toad	Pe-pe-quot-ta-tu
Lizzard	O-sick-ke-ask
Owl	Oh-ho
Fire steel	Pe-wâ-bisk Ap-pit
Fire wood	Mis-tick
Cradle	Wa-wa-bis-soon
Dagger	Tâ-cuch-e-gun
Lance	Se-mâ-gun
Bow	A-châ-pee
Arrow	At-toos
Fish hook	Quâs-qui-pitch-e-gun
Axe	Chee-ki-e-gun

Hoe	Pe-mich-e chee-ki-e-gun
Net	I-ap-pee
Tree (wood standing upright)	Mis-tick A-che-mus-so
Paddle	A-buy
Canoe	O-see
Birch bark	Wâs-qui
Bark	Wy-a-kisk
Touch wood	Poos-sa-gun
Gun Flint	Chak-is-say-e-gun
Grass	Mos-ko-se-ah
Leaf (of a tree)	Ne-pee-ah
Raspberries	I-os-cun-nuck
Strawberries	O-ta-me-nah
Whortleberries	I-e-ne-me-nah
Choke berries	Tuck-quy-me-ne-nâ-nah
Gooseberries	Sâ-sa-bo-min-uck
Grapes	Sho-min-is-uck
Ashes	Pe-co
Fire	Es-quit-tu
Current	Kis-se-che-win
Rapid	Pow-is-tick
Winter	Pe-poon
Spring	Me-os-kum-ick
Summer	Ne-pin
Autumn	Tuck-wa-gin
Island	Me-nis-tick
Lake	Sâ-ki-e-gun
River	Se-pee
Sun	Pe-sim
Moon (night sun)	Tip-is-co pe-sim
Stars	At-tâck
Sky	Kee-sick

Clouds	Mâ-ma-musk-wow
Thunder	Pe-is-su
Lightning	Wâ-wâs-sis-quit-a-pi-u
Rain	Ke-me-won
Snow	Mis-poon
Hail	Sa-sa-gun
Calm	I-wâs-tin
Day light	Wâ-bun
Morning	Ke-ke-jape
Day	Ke-se-cow
Night	Tip-is-cow
Noon (half the day)	A-be-tow Ke-se-cow
Sun setting	Pung-kis-se-mo
Midnight	A-be-tow Tip-is-cow
Snow	Ko-nah
Drift	Pe-won
Ice	Mis-co-mi
Frost	Ya-ya-co-tin
Dew	A-co-sa-pa-ow
Water	Ne-pee
World	Mis-si-wa-as-kee
Mountain	Wâ-chee
Sea	Kitch-e-gâ-ming
Portage	O-ne-gâpe
Rivulet	Se-pe-sis
Sand	Ya-cow
Earth	As-kee
Heat	Ke-se-ta-ow, or Ke-jas-ta-ow
Tomorrow	Wâ-bunk
Yesterday	O-tâ-ca-sin
To day	A-nouch ke-se-cow
Bone	Ose-kun

Broth	Mich-e-ma-boi
Provision	Me-chim
Feast	We-ko-ka-ow
Grease or oil	Pe-me
Marrow fat	Ose-kun-e-pe-me
Marrow	We-ne
Sinew	As-tis
Lodge or tent	Me-ke-wâpe
Bed	Ne-pa-win
Door	Es-quâ-tem
Dish	We-â-gun
Spoon or ladle	A-me quen
Plate	Na-puck-e-â-gun
Knife	Mo-cum-mon
Fork	Chis-ti-e-gun
Kettle	As-kick
Tea kettle	Se-sip as-kick
Sack or bag	Mus-ca-moote
Trunk	Mis-tick-o-wis
Table	Mit-te-sou-win-â-tic
Chair	Ta-e-tup-pe-win
Fort or house	Wâs-ky-e-gun
Floor	A-nâs-cun
Window	Wâs-sa-e-mon
Chimney	Cou-tâ-nâ-bisk
Cupboard	A-cou-cha-gun
Keg	Muck-kuck
Sledge	Tâ-bin-ask
Cincture or belt	Pâ-quâ-ta-hoon
Socks	As-se-gun
Cloth	Mon-ne-too-wa-gen
Thread	As-se-bâpe
Smoking bag	Ap-pit

Portage sling	Ap-pe-can
Powder	Kus-ke-ta
Balls	Mo-sus-se-nu
Shot	Nis-cus-se-ne-uck
Powder horn	Pa-che-pa-quon
Shot bag	Pa-tus-se-non
Gun	Pâw-skis-se-gun
Ramrod	Se-se-quit-is-ca-we-â-gun-a-tick
Gun case	As-pick-e-nâ-gun
Pistol	Pâw-skis-se-gun-is
Steel trap	Pe-wâ-bisk-won-a-e-gun
Grave	Ni-e-now
Grave yard	A-quâ-os-cun
Spirits	Squit-te-wâ-bo
Wine	Sho-min-â-bo
Milk	To-toos-â-bo
Breasts	To-toos
Butter	To-toos-â-bo pe-me
Flour or bread	Pâ-qui-se-gun
Indian corn	Mun-dâ-nin-uck
Potato	Aske-pwow-wâ
Turnip	O-te-se-kân
Onion	We-cha-kus-ka-se
Carrot	Os-kate-ask
Tea or medicine water	Mus-ca-kee-wâ-bo
Sugar	Se-se-bas-quit
Wild rice	Mus-co-se-me-nah
Glass or mirror	Wâ-bim-oon
General or great chief	Kitch-e-o-ki-mow
Soldier	Se-mâ-gun-is

Home	E-ke-nâke
Iron	Pe-wâ-bisk
Money	So-ne-ah
Book or letter	Mish-e-my-e-gun
Medicine	Mus-ca-kee
Lover	Jim-is-sim
Pipe	Os-poâ-gun
Tobacco	Chis-ta-mow
Weed for smoking	A-châ-câ-che-puck-wow
Part (of a thing)	Puck-ee
Slave	A-wâ-kun
Orphan	Ke-wâtch-e-wâ-sis
Peninsula	Kis-is-tig-guy-ow
Relation	E-to-tame
Ship	Na-pe-quon
Sword	She-maw-gun
Stone	As-se-ne
Store	Tut-tow-o-way-gum-mick
White earth	Wâ-but-toon-isk
Tatler	O-zom-e-toon-ew
Liar	Kâ-ke-as-ku
Bad man	Much-e-pe-mâ-tis-su
Good man	Me-u-pe-mâ-tis-su
Earthquake	An-ne-mus-kum-ke-py-you
Track (of the feet)	I-a-sa-se-ta-you
Road or path	Mays-ke-now
Whirlwind	Cus-tin
Good weather	Me-u-ke-si-cow
Bad weather	Mut-cha-ke-si-cow
Male	Nâ-bew
Female	O-ne-châ-nee

Cloudy	A-quos-quon
Windy	E-o-tin
North	Ke-wa-tin
South	Sâ-win-oke
East	Cos-kow-kos-take
West	Ke-wa-noke
Straight	Qui-esk
Crooked	Wâ-kow
Red	Me-quow
Blue	Che-ba-tock-wow
Yellow	O-saw-wow
Green	As-ke-tuck-wow
Black	Kus-ke-ta-wow
Ugly	My-â-te-su
Handsome	Cut-e-wâ-se-su
Beautiful	Me-u-nog-won
Deaf	Nâ-mo-tâ-wâ-cow
Good natured	Me-wâ-tick-e-su
Pregnant	Pwow-wew
Fat or fleshy	We-in-no
Large	Me-chus-ca-wâ-ke-su
Small	Up-pe-se-se-su
Short	Che-mis-se-su
Tall	Me-sick-e-tu
Merry	Me-wa-tick-won
Melancholy	Pe-kis-câ-tum
Long	Keen-wow
Strong	Mus-ca-wow
Weak	Nâ-mâ mus-ca-wow
Cowardly	Sa-koo-ta-ow
Brave	So-ca-te-ow
Lean	Se-kut-chu
Foolish	Ke-squiow

Sensible	I-e-ne-su
Stiff	Se-tâ-wow
Sick	A-quis-su
Dead	Ne-poo
Alive	Pe-mâ-tis-su
Miserable	Kit-te-mâ-ga-su
Upper	Is-pe-mink
Lower	Tup-pa-sis
All	Kuck-e-ow
Half	A-be-tow
Drunken	Ke-squi-ba-ow
English	A-qui-as-se-wock
French	Wa-mis-to-go-she-wock
Equal or alike	Tâ-bis-kootch
Far off	Wy-yow
Nigh	Kis-se-wâke
Few or little	Up-pa-sis
Fatigued	Ty-is-co-sin
Good	Me-wâ-shin
Bad	My-â-ton
Avaricious	Sâ-sâ-kis-su
Generous	May-ye-kis-ku
Greedy	Ka-shock-ca-ow
Hidden	Kâs-so
Lazy	Kit-te-mew
Lame	Mus-kip-pi-you
Much	Me-chet
Flat	Nah-puck-ow
Round	Wâ-way-ye-you
Quick	Kâ-ke-e-pe
That	A-o-co
This	Muck-o-mâo
Too little	O-som-up-pe-sis

Too much	O-som-me-chet
Deep	Tee-mew
Shallow	Pâke-wow
Frightful	Sa-sis-ke-nâ-guon
Wicked	My-â-che-ta-ow
Difficult	I-ye-mon
First	Ne-kân
Behind	O-tâke
Last	Squi-atch
More	Me-nah
Better	Kâ-me-wâ-shin
Good scented	We-cum-â-gun
Each	Pâ-pa-uck
Other	Pa-toosh
My own	Nene-ty-un
Your own	Kene-ty-un
His or her own	We-ah-one-ty-un
Their own	We-ah-wow-one-ty-un
Our own	Nene-ty-un-e-non
We?	Ne-on
Who?	A-way-nah
What?	Ka-qui
I am angry	Ne-kis-se-wâ-sin
I fear	Ne-koos-tâ-chin
To rejoice	Me-wâ-tum
To hear	Pa-tum
To see	Wâ-ba-tum
To smell	Me-â-tum
To taste	Goo-chis-tum
To feel	Goo-te-num
To come in	Pe-to-ca
To sing	Ne-cum-moon
To halloo	Ta-boi

To whistle	Ques-qui-su
To weep	Mâ-too
To laugh	Pâ-pee
To sigh	Mâ-ca-tâ-tum
To arrive	Tuck-a-shin
To depart	Che-boi-ta-ow
Assist me	Ne-sho-cum-a-win
To beat	O-tom-me-wow
To believe	Tâ-boi-tum
To rattle	Se-se-quin
To suck	No-nu
To puke	Pâ-cum-moon
To carry	Ni-och-e-ga-ow
I am cold	Ne-cow-â-chin
To take courage	Ye-ag-wâ-me-se
To dance	Ne-me-too
To jump	Quâs-quit-ta
To slide	So-squotch-e-wew
To run	Pe-me-pâ-tow
To walk	Pe-mo-ta-ow
To ride (horseback)	Tay-tup-pew
To finish	Po-ne-ton
To starve	Kâ-wâ-cut-tis-so-wock
To fall	Punk-a-sin
To strike fire	Se-kâ-ta-ow
To find	Mis-cum
To loose	Won-e-ton
To paddle	Pim-is-cow
To give	Me-yow
To take	O-te-nah
To hate	Much-a-ye-mow
To keep	Kun-ne-wa-e-ten
To know	Kis-ka-e-ta-gwun

To leave	Nuck-â-tum
To love	Sâ-ke-how
To go to bed	Kâ-wish-e-mo
To arise from bed	O-nis-caw
To sit down	Ap-pee
To get up	Pus-se-co
To marry	Wee-ke-mow
To play	Ma-te-way
To make peace	We-tus-ke-to-wuck
To make war	Nâ-to-py-e-wuck
To pray	I-ye-me-how
To take notice	Cun-ne-wâ-bum
To respect	Ke-tay-e-mow
To sail	A-cus-tim-moon
To steal	Ke-mo-tu
To sleep	Ne-pow
To talk	A-che-moon
To lie	Ke-as-ku
To go	Ke-to-tain
To lend	Ow-we-hin
To groan	Mâ-mâ-pin-ow
To beat	O-tom-me-wew
To cut	Kis-ke-sah
To cover	A-quoon-e-hah
To dispute	Ke-ka-to-wuck
To give	May-gu
To do	Oo-she-hah
To tie	Tuck-oop-e-tah
To unite	Ap-pu-co-nah
To sew	Kus-ke-quâ-so
To sit down	Up-pu
To fall	Pun-ga-sin
To work	O-se-che-ga-ow

To kill	Ne-pâ-how
To sell	Ut-tâ-wa-ow
To come	Us-tom-e-tay
Always	Kâ-ke-ca
Because	A-o-co-chee
By and bye	Pitch-is-quâ
Doubtless	Mos-kootch
Formerly	Gy-ass
Here	O-tâw
How	Tâ-ne-say
How many	Tâ-ne-tut-to
Immediately	Kâ-qui-ah-ho
Lately	Gy-ass-an-e-watch
Never	Nâ-mow-we-kâtch
No	Nâ-maw
Yes	Ah-hah
Not yet	Nâ-mas-quâ
Not at all	Nâ-mâw-wâw-wâtch
Good for nothing	Nâ-mâw-ca-qui-me-wâ-sin
There	A-quo-tah
Truly	Tâ-boi
Together	Tâ-bis-cootch
Where	Tâ-ne-tay
Yet	Ka-â-bitch
Oh	Ah !
Now and then } Sometimes } Seldom }	I-os-cow
Thank you	We-nâ-cum-mâ
What is that?	Ka-qui-o-ko
What now?	Tâ-ne-me-ne-kick
Who is there?	A-way-nâ-nah

Get out of the way	A-wis-se-tay
What is your name?	Tâ-ne-tick-o-way-on
Where are you going?	Tâ-ne-ta ke-we-to-tain
I wish to depart	Ne-we-ke-won
What do I hear?	Ka-qui-kâ-pa-tum-mon
Will you trade?	Ke-we-ut-tâ-won-chee

NUMERICAL TERMS

OF THE CREES OR KNISTENEUX.

One	Pa-uck
Two	Ne-sho
Three	Nish-to
Four	Nay-o
Five	Nay-ah-nun
Six	Ni-co-twâ-sick
Seven	Ta-boo-coop
Eight	I-a-nâ-na-on
Nine	Ka-gâte me-tâ-tut
Ten	Me-tâ-tut
Eleven (and one more)	Me-tâ-tut pa-uck o sawp
Twelve	Me-tâ-tut ne-sho sawp
Thirteen	Me-tâ-tut nish-to sawp
Fourteen	Me-tâ-tut nay-o sawp
Fifteen	Me-tâ-tut nay-ah-nun o sawp
Sixteen	Me-tâ-tut ne-co-twâ-sick o sawp
Seventeen	Me-tâ-tut ta-boo-coop tah-to sawp
Eighteen	Me-tâ-tut i-a-nâ-na-ow tah-to sawp

Nineteen	Ka-gâte me-ta-tut tah-to sawp
Twenty	Ne-sit-te-no
Twenty one	Ne-sit-te-no pu-uck o sawp
Twenty two &c.	Ne-sit-te-no ne-sho sawp
Thirty	Nish-to mit-te-no
Forty	Nay-o mit-te-no
Fifty	Nay-ah-nun o mit-te-no
Sixty	Ne-co-twâ-sick o tut-to mit-te-no
Seventy	Ta-boo-coop o tut-to mit-te-no
Eighty	I-a-nâ-na-ow o tut-to mit-te-no
Ninety	Ka-gâte me-tâ-tut o mit-te-no
Hundred	Me-ta-tut-to mit-te-no
One thousand	Me-ta-tut o tut-to mit-te-no

A SPECIMEN OF

THE TACULLY OR CARRIER TONGUE.

Man	Ten-nee
Woman	Cha-ca
Young man	Chilk
Infant	Chu-tun
Head	Pit-sa
Eyes	O-now

23

Hair	Ote-zega
Nose	Pa-nin-chis
Teeth	Oh-goo
Tongue	Tsoo-lâ
Ears	O-cho
Hands	O-lâ
Belly	O-put
Legs	O-ca-chin
Knees	O-kate
Feet	O-ca
Nails	E-lâ-ki
Grand father	Ut-che-yan
Grand mother	Ut-soo
Father	Ap-pâ
Mother	Un-nung-cool
Son	E-yaze
Daughter	E-â-cha
Brother	E-chill
Sister	E-taze
Nephew	Quâze
Grand child	E-chi
Husband	E-ki
Wife	Ay-eye
Aunt	A-ki
Old man	O-yun
Blood	Sko
Path or road	Tee
Chief	Me-u-tee
Excrement	Chou
Urine	Al-luze
Coat	Chute
Breech cloth	Chon
Leggins	Ca-chy

Shoes	Kis-coot
Hat or cap	Tchâ
Handkerchief	Za-zo
Mittens	Pat
Petticoat	Cha-ca-chute
Bracelet	Nal-ton
Comb	Chil-cho
Ring	Ne-lâ-ta-ah
Needle	A-a-bâte-so
Scissors	Clay-yee
Blanket	A-â-pi
Frock or robe	Nal-tay
Goat or sheep	Spye
Ferret	Nah-pye
Moose	Ten-nee
Cariboo	O-chee
Beaver	Châ
Otter	A-bay
Hare	Kah
Martin	Chin-nee
Bear	Suss
Lynx	Wâs-say
Porcupine	Cho
Musk rat	Cha-kate
Fisher	Chin-ne-cho
Mouse	Ten-ne-tay
Meat or flesh	Ut-son
Dog	Cling
Bitch	Clee-chay
Crow	Tâte-sun
Swan	Chin-cho
Outard	Hok
Partridge	Teel

Water hen	Chel
Eggs	O-gaze
Loon	Tâd-joy
Sturgeon	Clay-cho
White fish	Clo
Fish (in general)	Cloo-lay
Fish roes	O-koon
Trout	Pilt
Salmon	Tâl-loo
Fire steel	Kone
Wood or tree	Tuch-in
Dagger	Pa-she-al
Bow	Al-tung
Arrow	Kâ
Axe	Cha-chill
Net	Clim-pelt
Paddle	Chell
Canoe (bark)	Al-lâ-chee
Canoe (wooden)	Tuch-in-chee
Touch wood	Kel-cha
Gun flint	Sâ-zo-en
Grass or hay	Clo
Whortleberries	Chil-cho
Ashes	Clees
Fire	Kone
Winter	Yas-ca
Autumn	Tâ-ca-ta
Summer	Ole-ol-tâ
Sun	Sâ
Moon (night sun)	Châ-ol-cus sâ
Stars	Clum
Thunder	Date-nee
Day	Ja-ness

Rain	Nâ-ol-ton
Snow	Nâ-châze
Night	Al-cheese
Morning	Pun-e-tâ
Sun setting	Nâ-ah
Ice	Clum or Ton
Water	Too
World	Ton-ate-suck
Mountain	Chell
Sea	E-â-pâck
Earth	Ote-luss
Heat	O-zell
Tomorrow	Pun-tay
Yesterday	Hul-tâ
To day	Un-tit
Broth	Tâ-zell
Grease	Kane-loo
Sinews	Tsay
Tent or lodge	Yâh
Bed	Kus-tee
Door	Tâ-tee
Dish	Tsi
Kettle	O-sâ
Spoon or ladle	Chin-ne-sko
Knife	Cles-tay
Sack or bag	Aze-lâ
Trunk or box	Chin-kale
Chimney	Pa-kone-tas-kone
Fort or house	Yock
Sledge	Sclu-sa
Cincture or belt	Say
Socks	Ca-tell
Cloth	Tell-kuz-za

Thread	A-â-bâte-say
Garters	Chal-chase
Medicine	You
Portage sling	Ka-nal-ta
Powder	Al-la-cha
Balls	Câ-tee
Shot	No-do-tone
Powder horn	Da-kâ
Shot bag	No-do-to-bost-lâ
Gun	Al-tee
Gun case	Al-tee-zus
Steel trap	Châ-co
Stench	Ill-chun
Skin	O-zuss
Melancholy	Cho-let-nee
Spirits	Kone-too
Breasts	Tsoo
Flour or bread	Clays
Vegetables	Hon-elt-ya
Heart	O-gee
Entrails	At-zee
Home	E-yok
Iron	Cles-tay
Letter or book	Dush-lush
Lover	Nâ-ho-hul-ya
Pipe	Da-kâte-say
Tobacco	Da-kâ
Orphan	Till-in-yaze
Ship	Chee-cho
Stone	Tsay
Gooseberries	Ton-gueese
Strawberries	In-gee
White earth	Clis-paw

Windy	Days-chee
White	Yell
Red	Ten-il-cun
Black	Tel-kuz-zay
Yellow	Dat-leese
Ugly	Ne-chay
Handsome	Ne-zo
Deaf	Ot-so-hoo-lah
Pregnant	El-chon
Short	En-took
Long	En-yeaze
Strong	Nâ-chet
Weak	At-too-nâ-cnet
Heavy	Nâ-kull
Foolish	Wos-se-nay
Sensible	Ho-na
Sick	Tut-tay
Dead	Tâs-si
Alive	An-nâ
Miserable	Til-len
All	Tche-ow
Drunken	Too-nis-to
French	Ned-do
Distant	Nee-zolt
Nigh	Nill-toor
Few or little	En-soole
Shameful	Clou-châ
Full	Dees-pun
Good	Oo-choh
Bad	Ni-ka-tel
Avaricious	Kane-chee
Much	Clyne
Quick	Ut-cho-in-tin

Deep	Tâ-kull
Shallow	Too-hoos-kâ
I am angry	Son-e-chee
To hear	At-tade-zuck
To see	Nee-tlen
To smell	In-chis
To feel	Oan-ton
To eat	A-al
To drink	Ate-ni
To sing	Ut-chin
To halloo	Câ-an-ni
To whistle	Yool
To weep	A-chuck
To laugh	At-lo
To arrive	Nâ-tell
To depart	Ni-ne-tell
Assist me	Sly-en-e-lay
To beat	Chil-tul-tâ
To suck	El-took
To be cold	Nâ-zes-lay
To dance	Nâte-tah
To walk	Ni-yah
It is done	A-chel-ist-la
To starve	Ne-cho-al-hoo-lah
To fall	Nal-chet
I will go	O-che-to-se-ah
Come with me	An-nee
To give	Won-nel-lay
To take	Ill-shute
To hate	O-cha-dus-se-ne
I do not know	Tuch-a-hoo-ny
To keep	Hone-lay
To know	At-dy-e-tay

To love	Qui-see or Kane-chee
To lie down	Sin-tee
To arise from bed	Tâ-deen-yal
To sit down	Sin-taw
To be merry	Ous-tâ
To paddle	At-to
To steal	Way-to
To sleep	Nâ-mis-tee
Go away	Us-se
To talk	Yal-tuck
To lie	On-chit
That	In-tee
My own	Se-ilt sun
Your own	Ne-ne-ilt sun
Our own	Wa-ne-ilt sun
I or me	Se
Thou or thee	Ne or Ye
We	Wa-ne
Above	Ya-took
Because	A-doo-aw
Bye and bye	Kud-dah
Enough	Coo-lâ or Ate-sel
Formerly	Ul-tâ
Here	Ne-chan
How	Tuch-ah
How many	Tâ-nil-suck
Immediately	An-tit
No	Own-too
Yes	Ah-âh or A-mâ
Not yet	Katch-ah-own-too
There	En-chan
Truly	Al-lâte-ne
Too little	Stân-soel

Too muck	Stân-clyne
Where	En-chay
Yet	Kâ-châ
I thank you	Se-nâ-chal-le-ah
What is that?	Tee
What is the matter?	Tâ-how-châ
Who is there?	Te-ween-tal
What is your name?	Ba-zee
Where are you going?	Ne-cha-en-e-gal
Let us depart	Nâ-zo-tell
Will you trade?	Ba-che-o-kate
Whence are you?	Ne-cha-si-il-tal

NUMERICAL TERMS

OF THE TACULLIES.

One	Clot-tay
Two	Nong-ki
Three	Toy
Four	Ting-kay
Five	Skoon-e-ly
Six	Al-ke-tâte
Seven	Te-kal-ti
Eight	Al-ke-tin-ga
Nine	Clo-hoo-ly
Ten	Lân-ne-zy
Eleven	O-un-na Clot-tay
Twelve	O-un-na Nong-ki
&c. to	
Twenty	Not-won-ne-zy
Twenty one	Not-won-ne-zy O-ât Clo
Twenty two	Not-won-ne-zy O-ât Nong-ki
&c. to	
Thirty	Tât-won-ne-zy-ah
Forty	Tit-won-ne-zy-ah
Fifty	Skoo-nee-lot-won-ne-zy
Sixty	Al-ke-tâte-won-ne-zy

Seventy	Tee-kal-ty-o-tâte-won-ne-zy
Eighty	Al-ke-ting-o-tâte-won-ne-zy
Ninety	Clo-hoo-ly-o-tâte-won-ne-zy
Hundred	Nâ-ne-zy-o-ne-ze-ah
Thousand	Lân-ne-zy-o-lân-ne-zy-o-lân-e-zy

A CONCISE ACCOUNT

OF

THE PRINCIPAL ANIMALS

WHICH ARE FOUND IN THE NORTH WESTERN
PART OF

NORTH AMERICA.

———

BUFFALOES are found in great numbers, in
all of the plain or prairie countries, on both
sides of the Rocky Mountain, as far north
as about latitude fifty six or seven. The
bull is larger than an ox, has short black
horns, and a beard under his chin; and his
head is filled with a long, fine hair, which
falls over his eyes, and gives him a frightful
aspect. On his back is a bunch or excres-
cence, commencing a little forward of his
haunches, the highest part of which, is over
his shoulders, and which terminates at the
neck. His whole body is covered with a long
hair or wool, of a dark brown colour, the
whole of which, and particularly that which
is on the fore part of the body, would answer well for manufacturing coarse cloths

and blankets. The head of the buffaloe is larger than that of the bull, his neck is short, his breast is broad; and his body decreases towards the buttocks. He will generally flee, at the approach of a man, excepting the male, at the rutting season, when he becomes ferocious.

The flesh of the buffaloe is excellent food; the hide is applied to many important uses; and the long soft hair, the natives put into their shoes, about their feet, which supplies the place of socks; and it is fully as warm. The speed of the buffaloe, is much the same as that of an ox; and when he runs he inclines his fore feet considerably on one side of his body, for a short distance, and then shifts them upon the other, and continues thus, alternately to change them.

Those that remain in the country between the Sisiscatchwin and Peace rivers, are called the wood buffaloes, because they inhabit a woody country; and they are considerably smaller than those, which inhabit the plains. They are, also, more wild and difficult to approach.

The horses, which the Indians possess, came originally from Mexico, and are of the Spanish breed. They are in general stout, and well built; and many of them are of great speed. They are very serviceable to the Natives in the plain countries, are used to transport their property from place to place; and on them they run down and kill their game. These animals will subsist, during the winter months, on the grass which they find under the snow, which is seldom more than six inches deep, on the plains. There are but few horses to be found, farther north than latitude fifty four or five.

There are three kinds of bears, the grey, the brown or chocolate coloured, and those which are perfectly black. The grey bear, which are by far the largest, are about the size of a common cow; and are remarkably strong built, and very ferocious. They attack human beings, as well as all kinds of beasts, that fall in their way; and in their terrible paws, the resistance, even of the male buffalo, weighing fourteen or fifteen hundred pounds, is utterly vain. Three or four of the Natives join together whenever they attempt to hunt them, and each man is well armed, with a musket and a long spear.

The grey bear differs but little in shape, from those of a smaller kind and of a different colour. Their heads are rather shorter, in proportion to their bodies, their noses are less pointed; and they are more stoutly built. Their colour is a beautiful lively silver grey. Their flesh has not so good a flavour as that of the black bear, it being more rank. The Natives, formerly, made use of their skins for beds; but now, they always exchange them with us, for blankets, &c.

The grey, in common with the other kinds of bears, pass the winter months, without taking any kind of nourishment. Their retreats are by the sides of the roots of large trees, that have fallen down, or in the caverns of rocks; and in some instances they dig holes, in the sides of hills. These habitations are enclosed on every side, with the branches of trees, filled in with moss, &c. so as completely to surround the animal, excepting his nose, where a small hole is left, to enable him to breathe fresh air. They leave these retreats, as soon as the warm weather comes on in the spring, when they are apparently as fat, as they were when they entered them, in the preceding autumn.

This flesh has less substance, probably, as they loose most of it, soon after their egress; though they then devour, with an appetite rendered strong by a winter's abstinence, whatever comes in their way. Their food, however, at this season, is not so abundant as it is afterwards, as they generally live upon roots, and the different kinds of fruit. They eat, likewise, ants and honey, whenever they meet with that which is made by bees and wasps. They rarely eat animal food.

The brown and black bear differ little, excepting in their colour. The hair of the former, is much finer than that of the latter. They usually flee from a human being. One, however, that has been wounded, or a female that has cubs, will attack a pursuer. The brown and the black bear, climb trees, which the grey, never does. Their flesh is not considered so pleasant food as that of the moose, buffaloe or deer; but their oil is highly valued by the Natives, as it constitutes an article at their feasts, and serves, also, to oil their bodies, and other things. Occasionally, a bear is found, the colour of which is like that of a white sheep, and the hair is much longer than that of the other kinds which have been mentioned; though, in other respects, it differs not at all from the black bears.

There are two kinds of wolves, one of which is rather larger than a stout dog, and the other is not more than half as large. Their legs are long, in proportion to their slender bodies. Their heads, also, are long; and their noses are sharply pointed. Their tails are long and bushy. The colour of the larger kind, is generally a light grey; but some of them, are nearly white. The smaller kind are commonly a silver grey; but some of them are nearly black. They are all very voracious; but they never attack a human being, unless when suffering greatly from hunger. They display great ingenuity and cunning; generally, herd together, especially in the winter season; and make a hideous noise, particularly when thirty or forty of them are employed in surrounding a herd of the buffaloe or deer,

24

in order to drive them down a precipice.
They frequently take this method to make
these animals their prey; and, in order to
carry a project of this kind into execution
they form lines, by separating to a certain
distance from each other, and frequently
make noises, resembling the human voice;
and they appear to act in concert, as regularly as the Indians themselves do, when they
drive the buffaloes into their yards.

The wolves know the effects of a discharge
of a musket; and when a hunter fires his gun
at a buffaloe or deer, in a few minutes, from
ten to twenty of them will rush to the spot
whence the report proceeded; and, at some
times, they are so pinched with hunger, that
while standing beside his game, it is with
difficulty that the hunter preserves it from
being devoured by them.

There are three sorts of foxes, which,
however, differ only in their colour. The
most common are of a yellowish red, some
are of a beautiful silver grey, and some in the
more northern latitudes, are almost black.
The last, are by far the most valuable.

The Indians have several kinds of dogs.
Those which they make use of in hunting,
are small, their ears stand erect; and they
are remarkable for their fidelity to their
masters.—They now have a large breed
among them, which were brought into their
country from Newfoundland, by the English,
when they first established themselves on

Hudson's Bay; and from that place they have been spread into every part of the country, east of the Rocky Mountain. They are used only as beasts of burthen. In the summer season, they carry loads upon their backs; and in the winter when there is snow, they draw them upon sledges. These sledges are made of two thin boards, turned up at the fore end, and joined closely together, so that this vehicle is twelve or fourteen inches broad, and seven or eight feet in length. The collar, by which the dogs draw, is much like that with which a horse is usually harnessed, in the civilized parts of the country. Their weight is, generally, from sixty to one hundred pounds

The cat or lynx, in its shape and nature resembles the domestic cat; but is much larger. It has long legs and a long body; but a very short tail. Its hair is exceedingly fine, considerably long, and of a lively and beautiful, silver grey colour. When full grown, the cat will weigh thirty five or forty pounds; and when fat they are excellent food. They generally live on mice, the dead fish which they find along the rivers and lakes, and partridges and hares. In taking their prey, they manifest all the adroitness and activity of the domestic cat. In some years, these animals are very numerous; and, frequently, the following year, very few can be found.

There are two species of the deer. One of

these, denominated the jumping deer, is like
those which are found in the northern parts
of the United States; and none of them are
found farther north than about latitude
48° or 50°. The other kind is sometimes
called the red deer or the elk. They are
about the size of a horse; and their bodies,
are shaped like those of the jumping deer.
Their tails are remarkably short, being not
more than three inches long. Their hair,
which is three inches in length, is of a light
grey colour, and is as coarse as that of the
horse. The horns of these animals grow to
a prodigious size, their extreme points are
about six feet asunder; and they branch
out before and behind, like those of the
common deer. Their bodies are well proportioned, their air is noble; and, on the
whole, they are the most majestick animal,
that I have ever seen. They shed their horns,
in the month of February or March; and by
August, the new ones are nearly at their
full growth. Notwithstanding the size and
strength of these animals, and the means
of defence with which they are furnished,
they are as timorous as a hare. Their skins
are very useful, and will dress as well as
that of a buck. They feed on grass and
buds, and the twigs of trees. Their flesh
is tender, and of a fine flavour.

The moose is, in size, next to the buffaloe,
among the animals of the North West. The
body is in shape, somewhat like that of

an ox, raw boned, with high haunches;
but its neck and head resemble those of a
horse. The ears are large, like those of an
ass. The horns are flat, and branched out
only behind; and are shed every year. The
feet resemble those of the deer, excepting
that they are much longer and broader; and
when it puts them on the ground, the hoofs
separate, two or three inches. The head is
about two feet long. The upper is much
longer than the under lip of this animal;
and the nostrils are so wide, that a man
might thrust his hand into them, to a considerable distance. The colour of the moose
is a light grey, mixed with a deep red, and
the hair is so elastic, that its shape cannot
be altered by beating. The flesh of this
animal is exceedingly good food, it being
easy of digestion, and very nourishing, as
well as very palatable. The nose and the
upper lip, which is large, and loose from the
gums, are esteemed a great delicacy; it is
of a consistence between marrow and gristle,
and when properly dressed, it is a rich and
luxurious dish. The hide of this animal
makes excellent leather, as it is thick and
strong; and when dressed it is soft and pliable. The pace of the moose, is a walk or
trot; and it is exceeded in swiftness, by few
of its fellow tenants of the forest. It will,
with ease, trot over a fallen tree, of five
feet in diameter. This animal is commonly
found in low grounds, where it feeds on

moss, and the buds of trees. The moose, generally, remains alone; though at some-times five or six of them are found together. Their senses of hearing and smelling are uncommonly acute; and, therefore the least noise made by a hunter, such as the rustling of dry leaves, or the breaking of a small branch, will be heard by this animal, at a great distance, and will alarm its fears. When put to flight, the moose does not like the deer and most other animals, run a little distance, and then stop, until a new appearance of danger; but, oftentimes, he will not make the least halt, until he has run ten or fifteen miles. No other animal that runs in the woods, is so difficult of approach.

There are two kinds of the cariboo. The only difference between them is, that the one is about twice as large as the other, and the hair of the smaller, is of a much lighter colour. The larger, will weigh nearly as much as the elk; but, in shape and the colour of the hair, it more nearly resembles the moose; and like this animal it feeds only on moss, and the buds of trees. The horns are round, like those of the elk; but they approach nearer to each other, at the extremities, and bend more over the face, than those of either the moose or the elk. The gait of this animal is much the same as that of the moose, and it is almost as difficult of approach.

The flesh is equally good for food; and the tongue, particularly, the Natives consider as one of the greatest dainties, which their country affords. The skin, being smooth and free from veins, makes the finest of leather; and of it, excellent leggins and shirts are made. The Indians attach great value also to the dung of the cariboo, of which they make, what they consider, a delicious broth. They make use of the lower bone of the leg of this animal, in the place of a tanner's scraping knife, to separate the hair from skins.

There are two kinds of antelope, which differ only in size, and in the colour of their tails, which are about two inches long. The colour of these animals is a light grey or mouse colour, with here and there a spot of white. The tail of the larger, is of the same colour as the body, while that of the smaller, is white. The larger, is about the size of the jumping deer, which animal it, also, very much resembles, in shape. The smaller, will weigh about as much as a sheep; and the flesh resembles mutton, in its taste. These animals herd together, like the deer, and always remain in an open country; and their speed is little inferiour to that of the horse. They are very timorous, and as soon as they perceive a human being, they run off to a considerable distance, but soon make a halt; and, if the person hides himself, they will soon return, near to the spot

where they had seen the object which alarmed
them. It is thus that the Natives manage,
in hunting them. Their skin is thin, and will
dress equally well with that of the chamois;
and the leather is very suitable for leggins
and shirts for the Natives, during the summer
months. The males have horns, resembling
those of the deer, excepting that they are
smaller.

The carcajou or wolverine, in shape and
the colour of the hair, greatly resembles
the skunk: but it is nearly twice as large.
The hair of the carcajou is about the same
length as that of a bear: and its colour
is black, excepting a narrow strip of white,
on the rump. The tail is about six inches
long, and is very bushy. This animal is
remarkably strong built, for its size: and is
extremely voracious. He feeds on dead fish,
which he finds along the shores of the rivers
and lakes: and on mice, hares, &c. He is
often found about the places where human
beings have been interred; and, if they have
not been buried deep in the earth, he will
take them up, and feed on their carcases.
On this account, the Natives never feed on
the flesh of this animal, though it has an
excellent flavour. When he falls upon a large
animal, that has been killed and cut up and
left by the hunter, he will, within a very short
time, remove the whole of it to a considerable distance, and strive to hide it under the
grass, or the branches of trees.

The skunk differs not at all from the same
animal, as it is found in most parts of the
United States: and it is too well known to
need a description.

The porcupine, in shape, and size, differs
but little from the skunk. Its tail is much
shorter, and has little hair on it. The body
is covered with hair of a dark brown colour,
about four inches in length. This hair is
interspersed with quills, about the size of a
straw, that are white, with black ends, sharply pointed: and for about half an inch from
the end, they are covered with a kind of
beard, which renders it very difficult to extract them from any soft substance which
they have entered. These quills are merely
defensive weapons: for it is not true, though
it has by some been asserted, that they can,
at pleasure, eject them from their bodies.
They are an inoffensive animal, move very
slowly; and when overtaken by man or
beast, they place their heads and their legs
under their bodies, and place all their reliance on their quills, for protection. The
Indian women highly value these quills,
which they die of different colours, and use
for garnishing their shoes, leggins, &c. They
also hold their flesh in high estimation, as
an article of food.

There is a small animal, found only on
the Rocky Mountain, denominated, by the
Natives, Quis-qui-su, or whistlers, from the
noise which they frequently make, and always

when surprised, strongly resembling the noise
made by a person in whistling. They are
about the size of a badger, are covered with
a beautiful long silver grey hair, and have
long bushy tails. They burrow in the sides
of the mountain, and feed on roots and
herbs. Their flesh is very delicious food.
They generally produce two young at a
time; and sit upon their hind feet when they
give them suck. The skins of these animals
are very useful to the Natives, for clothing.
They dress them, with the hair on; and sew
a sufficient number of them together, to make
a garment, as large as a blanket, which they
wrap around their bodies.

The racoon is an animal never found
farther north, than about latitude forty
eight. It is considerably smaller than a
beaver, with legs and feet resembling this
animal. The legs are short in proportion
to the body, which is like that of a badger.
It has a head like that of a fox; but with
ears shorter, rounder, and more naked. The
hair is thick, long, soft and black at the
ends, like that of a fox. On the face there
is a broad stripe, that runs across it, which
includes the eyes, which are large. The tail
is long and round, with annular stripes
upon it, like those of a cat. The feet have
five slender toes, armed with sharp claws,
by which it is enabled to climb trees. It
feeds itself with its fore feet, as with hands.
The flesh of this animal is very good, in the

months of September and October, when
fruit and nuts, on which it likes to feed,
are found in plenty.

The martin is some larger than a squirrel,
which it resembles in shape, excepting that
its legs and claws are considerably shorter.
In the darkness of the night, the eyes have
a shining appearance, like those of a cat.
It has short ears, which are of a roundish
shape. The whole body is covered with a
thick fur, which in a mild climate, is of a
yellowish colour; but in the colder regions
of the north, it becomes of a dark brown,
and, in some instances, is nearly black. The
skins, which have this dark coloured fur,
are much more valuable than the others.
The tail is covered with long hair; and under
the neck, even of those of the darkest colour,
there is a small spot, of a yellowish cast.
The flesh of this animal has a rank, disagreeable taste; and is, therefore seldom
eaten.

The muskrat, which receives its name
from the musk that it affords, resembles
the beaver, in every respect excepting its
size, which is little larger than the badger.
It builds for itself a cabin in marshy places,
at no great distance from some water : and
feeds on roots, herbs, mice and fish, which
it finds dead, on the margin of lakes and
streams. In the spring, these animals leave
their huts, as they are built in places so
low, that they are generally, at that season,

overflowed by water. During the summer months, they have no fixed residence: but are found in different places, among the grass. As the winter approaches, they erect new huts, in which they pass the winter. Carver is surely mistaken when he states, that they winter in hollow trees, without any sustenance, and that, in the summer, they feed on raspberries, strawberries and other kinds of fruit.

In the North West country, there are only three kinds of squirrels, which are the red, the striped and the flying. The black and grey squirrel, seldom go farther north, than latitude forty five or six.

The beaver has been so frequently and so minutely described, and his sagacity, ingenuity and industry are so well known, that a very particular account of this animal, in this place, would be superfluous. As some other animals, in the foregoing description, have been compared with the beaver, it may be necessary to state, that his weight is usually about sixty pounds: that his body is about four feet in length, and that his legs are short, particularly his fore-legs, which are not more than four or five inches in length. His fore feet are armed with claws, and his hind feet are furnished with a web or membrane between the toes, for the convenience of swimming, as he is an amphibious animal. His fore-teeth stand obliquely, projecting forward out of his mouth, and are broad, crooked and sharp. His incisors, or side teeth, are firmly set and sharp, and his grinders are very strong. By means of these teeth, he is able to cut down considerable trees, and to break the hardest substances. The ordinary colour of the beaver is brown, which becomes darker in the northern, and lighter in the more southern latitudes. The number of beavers in the North West country, is continually diminishing. The skins of this animal constitute, with the Natives, the principal article of trade; and the price of other things is computed, by comparing them with a beaver skin.

The otter is an amphibious animal, bearing some resemblance to the beaver, and yet in many respects, differing from it. His body is, in every part, less than that of the beaver, though it is nearly as long. His teeth are different, being in shape like those of a dog or wolf. The hair of the otter is not more than half the length of the beaver; and in some parts particularly under the neck, stomach and belly, is more greyish. This animal, when closely pursued, will not only defend himself; but he will attack dogs and even men. His food consists of roots and fish; and his flesh tastes and smells of the latter, and is not very palatable food.

The mink is of the otter kind, and subsists on similar food, and resembles this animal in its colour. In shape and size,

it bears a strong resemblance to the martin;
but its hair is much shorter. A musky scent
proceeds from this animal. It is generally
found along small rivers.

The following catalogue of animals, will
exhibit the comparative value of the furs,
which are annually purchased and exported
to the civilized parts of the world, by the
North West Company. The animal is first
mentioned, the skins of which will amount
to the greatest sum; and so on, in order,
to the last, the skins of which, will amount
to the smallest sum.—Beaver, otter, muskrat, martin, bear, fox, lynx, fisher, mink,
wolf, buffaloe.

The following catalogue will exhibit the
comparative weight of the skins, of the different animals, which are annually purchased
and exported, as above mentioned.—Beaver,
martin, muskrat, bear, otter, wolf, buffaloe,
lynx, &c.

END.